Questions & Answers
Wills, Trusts, and Estates

CAROLINA ACADEMIC PRESS
Questions & Answers Series

Questions & Answers

Wills, Trusts, and Estates

Multiple-Choice and Short-Answer
Questions and Answers

FOURTH EDITION

Thomas M. Featherston, Jr.
MILLS COX PROFESSOR OF LAW
BAYLOR UNIVERSITY SCHOOL OF LAW

Victoria J. Haneman
FRANK J. KELLEGHER PROFESSOR OF TRUSTS & ESTATES
CREIGHTON UNIVERSITY SCHOOL OF LAW

CAROLINA ACADEMIC PRESS
Durham, North Carolina

LIBRARY OF CONGRESS CATALOGING-IN-PUBLICATION DATA

Names: Featherston, Thomas M., author. | Haneman, Victoria J., author.
Title: Questions & answers. Wills, trusts & estates / Thomas M. Featherston, Jr.,
    Victoria J. Haneman.
Other titles: Wills, trusts & estates
Description: Fourth edition. | Durham, North Carolina : Carolina Academic Press, 2023. |
    Series: Questions & answers | Includes bibliographicalreferences and index.
Identifiers: LCCN 2023033723 | ISBN 9781531024239 (paperback) |
    ISBN 9781531024246 (ebook)
Subjects: LCSH: Wills--United States--Examinations, questions, etc. | Trusts and trustees--
    United States--Examinations, questions, etc. | Estate planning--United States--
    Examinations, questions, etc.
Classification: LCC KF753 .F43 2023 | DDC 346.7305/076--dc22
LC record available at https://lccn.loc.gov/2023033723

Carolina Academic Press
700 Kent Street
Durham, North Carolina 27701
(919) 489-7486
www.cap-press.com

Printed in the United States of America

Contents

Preface to the Fourth Edition

The law governing wills, trusts, and estates in the United States finds its origins primarily in the common law of England. Today, it is increasingly based on statutory law. It is also largely "state law" oriented. Each state has its own set of rules, procedures, statutes, and case law. While there are many common denominators, the law can, and frequently will, differ from state to state. Some of these differences are significant.

To address this reality, most of the problems in this book are to be solved using the law of the hypothetical state of X. It is assumed that X has adopted both the Uniform Probate Code (1990, with amendments through 2011) and the Uniform Trust Code (2000, with amendments through 2011). Throughout the book, the Uniform Probate Code and the Uniform Trust Code are abbreviated "UPC" and "UTC," respectively. Occasionally, some questions will instruct the student to assume that a particular provision of one of the uniform acts is not part of the law of X or that another relevant statute is to be interpreted a certain way.

If neither the Uniform Probate Code nor the Uniform Trust Code provides the "answer," it is assumed that X's courts have adopted a generally accepted principle of the law of wills, trusts and estates. These generally-accepted principles may be the positions taken in a relevant Restatement of the Law published by the American Law Institute or explained in a recognized hornbook or treatise, such as ROGER W. ANDERSEN, UNDERSTANDING TRUSTS AND ESTATES (6th ed. 2020), or WILLIAM M. MCGOVERN, SHELDON F. KURTZ & DAVID M. ENGLISH, PRINCIPLES OF WILLS, TRUSTS & ESTATES (2d ed. 2012). At times, reference will be made to the "old reliables" like GEORGE T. BOGERT, TRUSTS (6th ed. 1987), THOMAS E. ATKINSON, HANDBOOK OF THE LAW OF WILLS, § 138 (2d ed. 1953), and JESSE DUKEMINIER & ROBERT H. SITKOFF, WILLS, TRUSTS AND ESTATES (9th ed. 2013). Also, in recognition of the differences in states' laws, most answers will also attempt to explain how the result may differ in a state that does not follow the position taken by the Uniform Probate Code, the Uniform Trust Code, or the "majority" case law rule. Regardless of the state law that the student has learned in class, the key issues are identified, and it is hoped that the relevant answer is discussed for each question.

Further, the practical application of this area of the law continues to evolve. Today, fewer assets pass through probate administration than in the not too distant past. Increasingly, wealth transfers take the form a nonprobate or nontestamentary disposition. The revocable trust has become a popular "will substitute" in many states. Lawyers practicing in this area of law spend increasing amounts of time coordinating the disposition of the client's life insurance, retirement benefits and bank accounts with the client's key planning document — either the client's will or revocable trust. Consequently, many of the questions in this edition reflect this growing trend.

Accordingly, a primary purpose of this book is to test the student's practice-oriented understanding of this area of the law. This book supplements the student's casebook and includes questions and answers in fourteen units by subject area (plus a practice final exam) that correspond to basic topics covered in a typical wills, trusts, and estates course. Unfortunately, space does not allow for the coverage of every topic. For example, issues related to future interests and the administration of trusts are integrated into some questions but not addressed as their own topics.

When answering most questions, it is suggested that the student (i) identify the type of disposition in question (testamentary, inter vivos, nonprobate, etc.); (ii) identify the parties involved (transferor, transferees, creditors, assignees, etc.); (iii) determine the effective date of the disposition (date of delivery, date of death, date of possession, etc.); (iv) understand the issue presented (who gets what, when, and how); and (v) apply to the facts the appropriate substantive principle (the relevant statute or case law precedent).

In order to focus questions on specific issues, unless otherwise instructed, or the question itself suggests the contrary, the student should assume as follows:

- There are no administration expenses or creditors' claims that affect the proper conclusion. For example, if a question asks about the proper distribution of an intestate's estate, simply divide the assets described assuming there are no estate administration expenses or debts of the decedent.

- There are no individuals relevant to determining the proper distributees other than those specifically identified.

- That none of the property is community property unless the question directs your attention to a potential problem. Also, ignore homestead, exempt property, and family allowance rights. Assume relevant state law has abolished the common law doctrines of dower and curtesy.

- That a decedent's will was valid and duly admitted to probate. If the question recites that an individual died testate, assume there are no problems with the will, unless the question directs your attention to a potential problem.

- That all trusts are valid, irrevocable express trusts. If the question describes a trust that a settlor has established, assume the trust is valid and enforceable, unless the question directs your attention to the trust's validity, enforceability, or revocability.

- That individuals are not married and/or are alive at all relevant times. For example, if the question states that an individual died, assume he or she was single unless the question directs your attention to a potential problem. If the question states an individual was survived by a child, assume that the child is living at all times relevant to any legal analysis involved in the question.

Attention has been paid to using inclusive names and pronouns as a pedagogical choice. The structure of the modern family is shifting and evolving. Estate planning involves clients, and the families of clients, with diverse identities and perspectives. Some clients will choose to arrange their families (and distribute wealth) in ways that are not historically normative. Also, it is not the intent of the authors to raise questions concerning whether a couple (opposite sex or same sex) is validly married. Terms such as "spouse" and "marriage" are used to refer to individuals who have that status and the relationship resulting from that status, regardless of whether the characters in the question appear to be opposite sex or same sex. This edition assumes the couple in question has the status of being married under applicable law.

Finally, for any questions involving federal transfer taxes, the law is in a state of flux as this edition is published. At the end of 2017, Congress enacted the Tax Cuts and Jobs Act ("TCJA," effective January 1, 2018). TCJA increased the lifetime exemption amount to $10 million as adjusted for inflation by the chained CPI for years 2018 to 2025. In 2023, the unified estate and gift tax lifetime exemption is $12,920,000, and the annual exclusion for gift tax purposes is $17,000. Absent further action by Congress, this amount halves in 2026 to its former $5 million inflation adjusted amount. Also, students should assume that State of X has neither a state-level estate nor inheritance tax.

Professor Tom Featherston
Professor Victoria J. Haneman
September 2023

About the Authors

Thomas M. Featherston, Jr., is the Mills Cox Professor of Law at Baylor University's School of Law in Waco, Texas. He earned his J.D. with highest honors from Baylor in 1972. After graduation, he entered private practice in Houston, Texas from 1973 through 1982. He joined the Baylor Law School faculty in 1982, and in 1990, he was appointed to the Mills Cox Chair.

Professor Featherston was elected as an Academic Fellow of the American College of Trust and Estate Counsel in 1991 and a Fellow of the American Bar Foundation in 1993. He is active in both the State Bar of Texas and the American Bar Association. He is a past chair of the Real Estate, Probate and Trust Law Section of the State Bar of Texas and has served on the governing council of the Real Estate, Trust and Estate Law Section of the American Bar Association. He is a frequent author and lecturer in the areas of trusts, estates, marital property, fiduciary administration and other related topics, the subjects that he teaches at Baylor Law School. In 2009, he was honored as the Distinguished Texas Probate and Trust Attorney by the Real Property, Probate and Trust Law Section of the State Bar of Texas. In 2018, he received the Terry Lee Grantham Award by the Texas Bar Foundation for his service to the practicing bar.

Victoria J. Haneman is the Frank J. Kellegher Professor of Trusts and Estates at Creighton University School of Law in Omaha, Nebraska. She is a BARBRI lecturer for wills and trusts and was elected as an Academic Fellow of the American College of Trust and Estate Counsel in 2022. Professor Haneman has authored four books, including the practice guide Planning for Large Estates (Matthew Bender, forthcoming 2023 ed.), the casebook Federal Taxes of Gratuitous Transfers: Law & Planning, 2d. ed. (Aspen, 2023) with Joseph M. Dodge, Wendy C. Gerzog, Bridget J. Crawford & Jennifer Bird-Pollan, and the casebook Making Tax Law (Carolina Academic Press, 2014) with Daniel M. Berman. She has also published more than twenty law review articles and essays in journals that include Harvard Journal on Legislation, North Carolina Law Review, Virginia Tax Review, Wake Forest Law Review, University of Richmond Law Review, and Columbia Journal of Gender and the Law. Professor Haneman is the 2023 chair of the Association of American Law School's Women in Legal Education Section, and the incoming chair of the Trusts and Estates Section.

Professor Haneman is a regularly engaged expert by media including PBS NewsHour, National Public Radio, The New York Times, The Wall Street Journal, Wired, Forbes, and Fox Business. She has a particular interest in tax policy, innovative death technology, and women and the law. She may be found on Twitter, Threads, BlueSky, and Instagram at TaxLawProf.

Questions

Intestacy

1. Basilio died partially intestate in a state that has adopted the Uniform Probate Code. His validly executed attested will contains a provision that reads, "My sister Alba should not receive any of my property." Basilio is survived by Alba and her two children, Danita and Edgar. He is also survived by Fermina, the surviving child of his predeceased brother. Basilio's exotic widget collection, with more than 100 rare and exotic widgets valued at $10,000 each, will be distributed under the intestacy statute. How will the widget collection be distributed?

    A. Alba takes 50 widgets; Fermina takes 50 widgets.

    B. Danita, Edgar, and Fermina each take 33 1/3 widgets.

    C. Fermina takes 50 widgets; Danita and Edgar each take 25 widgets.

    D. Fermina takes 100 widgets.

2. Gisela and Petra were married. Neither had children. Petra died one year ago, intestate. She was survived by her father (Father) and mother (Mother). Gisela has now died intestate, survived by her brother (Finn) and mother (Lena). How is Gisela's estate to be distributed?

    A. Lena will take 100% of the estate.

    B. Lena and Finn will each take 50%.

    C. Lena, Finn, Father, and Mother will each take 25%.

    D. Finn will take 100% of the estate.

3. Gisela and Petra are legally separated but not yet divorced. Gisela and Petra have one child, Elias. Both of Petra's parents are living. Petra dies intestate. How is Petra's estate to be distributed?

    A. Elias takes the estate.

    B. Gisela takes the estate.

    C. Elias takes half of the estate, and Petra's parents take the other half of the estate.

    D. Petra's parents take the estate.

4. Yindi died recently. Yindi was not married and did not have any children. Yindi was survived by her parents, Kirra and Coen, and all four of her grandparents. Yindi was also survived by four siblings: Siblings 1 and 2 (who share parents Kirra and Coen); Sibling 3 (Coen's child from a prior marriage); and Sibling 4 (Kirra's child from a prior marriage).

   Yindi executed a will that leaves all of her property to Waru, a friend. Yindi had not had any contact with the members of her family for years due to the family's disapproval of her relationship with Waru. Waru has filed the will for probate. Which answer best describes the members of Yindi's family who have standing to contest the will?

   A. Kirra and Coen.

   B. Siblings 1, 2, 3, and 4, as well as Kirra and Coen.

   C. Siblings 1 and 2, as well as Kirra and Coen.

   D. Proof of Yindi's strained relationship with her family revokes the family's standing to contest the will.

5. Yindi died recently. She was unmarried and did not have any children. Yindi was survived by her divorced parents, Kirra and Coen. Coen is currently married to Jedda, and Kirra is currently married to Alinta. During her lifetime, she maintained a close relationship with her parents and their new spouses.

   Yindi executed a will prior to death leaving all property to her friend. The friend has filed the will for probate. Which answer best describes the members of Yindi's family who have standing to contest the will?

   A. Kirra and Coen, and their new spouses Jedda and Alinta.

   B. Kirra and Coen, and any living ancestors or descendants of Kirra and Coen.

   C. Kirra and Coen, and the friend named in Yindi's will.

   D. Kirra and Coen.

6. Assume the same facts as Question 5 except that following the divorce of Yindi's parents, Yindi had been adopted by Kirra's new spouse Alinta. The adoption was done solely to allow Yindi to be covered by Alinta's medical and dental insurance coverage at work. Which answer best describes the members of Yindi's extended family who have standing to contest the will?

   A. Kirra and Coen.

   B. Only Kirra would have standing.

   C. Kirra and Alinta—and likely Coen—would have standing.

   D. Kirra and Alinta—and never Coen—would have standing.

7. Assume the same facts as Question 6 except that Coen died intestate after Yindi was adopted by Alinta but before Yindi died. Which answer best describes the identity of Coen's heirs?

   A. Yindi.

   B. Yindi and Coen's parents.

   C. Coen's parents.

   D. Coen's parents and siblings.

8. Refer to the facts of Question 6, which provide that Yindi was adopted by Alinta. Assume that shortly thereafter, Kirra died intestate, survived by Yindi, Alinta, and Alinta's two children from a prior marriage, S1 and S2. Discuss the likely distribution of Kirra's estate.

   Answer:

9. Assume the same facts as Question 8 except that Alinta did not adopt Yindi. What is the likely distribution of Kirra's estate?

   A. Yindi inherits the entire estate.

   B. Alinta inherits the entire estate.

   C. Alinta inherits the first $300,000, and Alinta and Yindi share the excess.

   D. Alinta inherits the first $150,000, and Alinta and Yindi share the excess.

10. Is it possible that the property of a decedent may pass by intestate succession to the decedent's heirs even though the decedent had a validly executed, unrevoked will at the time of death?

    Answer:

11. Aoife died recently. Aoife's divorced parents, Father and Mother, did not survive Aoife. Aoife was survived by three siblings: S1 (born to Father and Mother); S2 (Father's child from a prior marriage); and S3 (Mother's child from a subsequent marriage). Mother's second husband, Sean, had a child from a prior marriage, S4. Aoife was raised in the home of Mother and Sean with S1 and S4. Identify Aoife's heirs.

    A. S1, S2, S3, and S4.

    B. S1, S2, and S3.

    C. S1 and S2.

    D. S1.

12. Aaron died intestate recently. Aaron was survived by a parent, Batsheva. Additionally, a twice-divorced Aaron was also survived by a child from Aaron's first marriage, C1; another child born to Aaron during Aaron's second marriage, C2; and a child born to Aaron's second spouse during a prior marriage of that spouse, C3, who lived with Aaron during the second marriage. C1, C2, and C3 are still minors and still in the custody of their respective surviving parents. Which answer best describes Aaron's heirs?

A. Batsheva, C1, C2, and C3.

B. Batsheva, C1, and C2.

C. C1, C2, and C3.

D. C1 and C2.

13. Assume the same facts as Question 12 except that, in addition to C1 and C2, it was rumored that Aaron had fathered a non-marital child born prior to meeting his first wife; this child is C4, who is now an adult. Aaron never even met C4 and had not had any contact with C4's mother for years. Discuss the individual(s) who will take as Aaron's heir(s).

Answer:

14. Aart died recently without a will. Aart had four children born during Aart's two marriages, both of which ended in divorce over twenty years ago while all four children were minors. Aart's first spouse was awarded custody of the two older children. Aart's second spouse was awarded custody of the two younger children. The children were C1, C2, C3, and C4. C1 died one day prior to Aart; C2 died the same day as Aart; C3 died one day after Aart; and C4 died one week after Aart. The children never married and did not have any children of their own. Which answer best describes the identity of Aart's heirs?

A. C1, C2, C3, and C4.

B. C2, C3, and C4.

C. C3 and C4.

D. C4.

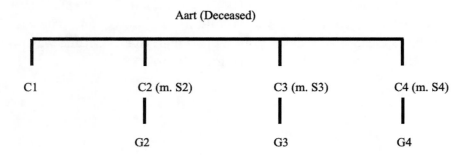

15. Refer to Question 14 and the diagram. Also, assume that C2 was married to S2, and they had one child, G2; C3 was married to S3, and they had one child, G3; and C4 was married to S4, and they had one child, G4. C1 died one day prior to Aart; C2 died the same day as Aart; C3 died one day after Aart; and C4 died one week after Aart. Each of C2, C3, and C4 had a valid, probated will leaving their property to their spouse. Following the payment of all debts and taxes, which answer best describes those who will actually take possession of Aart's estate?

A. S2, S3, and S4, equally.

B. G2, S3, and S4, equally.

C. G2, G3, and S4, equally.

D. G2, G3, and G4, equally.

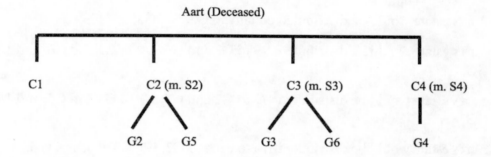

16. Refer to Question 15 and the diagram. How would your answer differ if C2's wife was pregnant at the time of the deaths of both Aart and C2; this child, G5, was born six months later. In addition, before Aart's death, C3 had adopted G6, a child of S3 by a prior marriage.

A. G5 would share equally with G2 one-third of the estate, but G6 is excluded.

B. G6 would share equally with G3 one-third of the estate, but G5 is excluded.

C. G5 would share equally with G2 one-third of the estate, and G6 would share equally with G3 one-third of the estate.

D. G5 would share equally with G2 one-third of the estate, and G6 would share with G3 one-third of the estate, but G3 would receive twice as much of that one-third as G6.

17. Assume the same facts as Question 16 except that C1, C2, C3, and C4 all died before Aart. Who will take possession of Aart's estate following formal administration?

Answer:

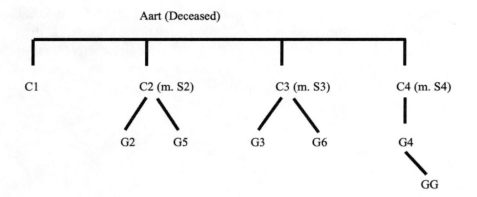

18. Refer to Question 17 and the diagram, but assume that G4 also died before Aart, and G4 was survived by G4's child, GG. Which answer best describes who will take possession of Aart's estate following formal administration?

A. Aart's estate would be distributed equally to G2, G5, G3, and G6.

B. Aart's estate would be distributed 4/9 to G2 and G5; 4/9 to G3 and G6; and 1/9 to GG.

C. Aart's estate would be distributed 1/3 to G2 and G5; 1/3 to G3 and G6; and 1/3 to GG.

D. Aart's estate would be distributed 1/5 to each of G2, G5, G3, G6, and GG.

19. Camille died recently. Camille's closest living relatives at the time of her death were A, the first cousin of Camille's mother, and B, a child of a great uncle of Camille's father. Which answer best describes the identity of Camille's heirs at law?

A. A and B.

B. A.

C. B.

D. The state where Camille resided.

20. Assume the same facts as Question 19 except that, in addition to A and B, Camille was survived by C, the child of Camille's deceased first cousin. Which answer best describes who succeeds to Camille's probate estate?

A. The state where Camille resided.

B. The state and C.

C. C.

D. The first cousin's estate.

21. Refer to Question 20. How would your answer differ, if at all, if C were a citizen of a foreign country residing in that country?

Answer:

22. Diego died recently without a will. Diego never married but had two non-marital children. The children are A and B, and they both survived Diego. The children have never married and do not have any children. Prior to Diego's death, he conveyed Blackacre to B. There is no evidence that B paid any consideration for Blackacre. Discuss the effect, if any, the conveyance has on the distribution of Diego's probate estate.

Answer:

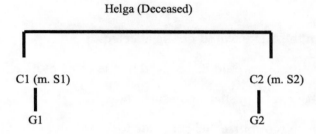

23. Helga died recently without a will. Helga had two children born of Helga's only marriage, which ended when her spouse died years ago. The children were C1 and C2. C1 died one month before Helga, and C2 died one month after Helga. C1 was married to S1, and they had one child, G1. C2 was married to S2, and they had one child, G2. Each child had a valid, probated will leaving his or her property to his or her spouse. Identify Helga's heirs.

A. C2.

B. C2 and S1.

C. C2 and G1.

D. C2 and C1's estate.

24. Refer to Question 23. Following the payment of all debts and taxes by the personal representative of Helga's estate one year later, which answer best describes those who will actually be entitled to the distribution of Helga's estate?

A. S2 and S1, equally.

B. S2 and C1, equally.

C. S2 and G1, equally.

D. G2 and G1, equally.

25. Assume the same facts as Question 23 except that one year prior to Helga's death, she had conveyed Blackacre to C2. Which answer best describes the effect the conveyance would have on C2's share in Helga's probate estate?

   A. C2's share of the estate would not be affected.

   B. C2's share of the estate would be reduced by the value of Blackacre.

   C. C2 would be barred from sharing in the estate.

   D. C2's estate would have to reimburse Helga's estate for one-half of the value of Blackacre.

26. Assume the same facts as Question 25 except that Blackacre had been conveyed to C1, not C2. Which answer best describes the effect the conveyance will have on G1's share of the estate?

   A. G1's interest in the estate would not be affected.

   B. G1's share of the estate would be reduced by the value of Blackacre.

   C. G1 would be barred from sharing in the estate.

   D. G1 would have to reimburse Helga's estate for one-half of the value of Blackacre.

27. Refer to Question 25 and assume that, prior to the death of Helga, she had conveyed Blackacre to G2, not C2. Which answer best describes who succeeds to Helga's estate after the completion of formal administration?

   A. S2's interest in the estate would not be affected.

   B. S2's share of the estate would be reduced by the value of Blackacre.

   C. S2 would be barred from sharing in the estate.

   D. S2 would have to reimburse Helga's estate for one-half of the value of Blackacre.

28. Assume the same facts as Question 27 except that C2 also died one month before Helga and that Helga conveyed Blackacre to G2 two months before she died. What effect does the conveyance have on G2's share of the estate?

Answer:

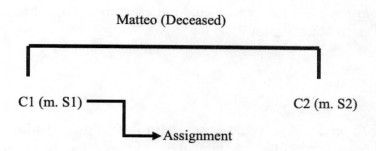

Matteo (Deceased)

C1 (m. S1) ——— ┐   C2 (m. S2)
                 └──→ Assignment

29. Matteo died intestate recently. Matteo had two children born of Matteo's only marriage, which ended in divorce years ago. The children were C1 and C2. C1 died one month before Matteo, and C2 died one month after Matteo. Both children's valid wills left their estates to their respective spouses. There were no grandchildren. Prior to Matteo's death, C1 assigned C1's "interest in Matteo's estate" to an unrelated third party. Explain the proper disposition of Matteo's estate.

   A. The assignment has no legal effect on the distribution of Matteo's estate. C2 is the only heir.

   B. The interest in Matteo's estate that would have passed to C1's spouse had it not been for the assignment passes to the third-party assignee.

   C. The interest in Matteo's estate that would have passed to C1's spouse had it not been for the assignment passes to the third-party assignee if the third-party assignee paid good and valuable consideration for the assignment.

   D. The third party has a claim against Matteo's estate as a creditor if the third-party assignee paid good and valuable consideration for the assignment.

30. Refer to Question 29. How would your answer differ if, following Matteo's death, but prior to C2's death, C2, not C1, would have assigned C2's "interest in Matteo's estate" to an unrelated third party.

   A. My answer would not change; the assignment has no legal effect on the distribution of Matteo's estate.

   B. The interest in Matteo's estate that would have been distributed to C2's spouse had it not been for the assignment should be distributed to the third-party assignee.

   C. The interest in Matteo's estate that would have been distributed to C2's spouse had it not been for the assignment passes to the third-party assignee if the third-party assignee paid good and valuable consideration for the assignment.

   D. The third-party assignee has a claim against Matteo's estate as a creditor if the

31. Refer to Question 30. What effect would the assignment have if C2's assignment had occurred prior to Matteo's death?

Answer:

32. Refer to Question 29. How would your answer differ if there had not been an assignment, but a creditor of C1 had a judgment lien against C1 at the time of C1's death?

   A. My answer would not change; the lien cannot attach to any part of Matteo's estate.

   B. The creditor can attach the one-half interest that would have passed to C1's spouse.

   C. The creditor can attach the one-half interest that would have passed to C1's spouse if the original debt was tortious in nature.

   D. The creditor has a claim against Matteo's estate.

33. Refer to Question 32. How would your answer differ if C1 would not have died until one day after Matteo?

   A. The lien cannot attach to any part of Matteo's estate.

   B. The creditor can attach C1's one-half interest.

   C. The creditor can attach C1's one-half interest, if the original debt was tortious in nature.

   D. The creditor has only an unsecured claim against Matteo's estate.

34. Refer to Question 33. What would your answer be if C1 would have survived Matteo by one week?

   A. The lien cannot attach to any part of Matteo's estate.

   B. The creditor can attach the one-half interest that would be distributed to C1's spouse.

   C. The creditor can attach the one-half interest that would be distributed to C1's spouse if the original debt was tortious in nature.

   D. The creditor has only an unsecured claim against Matteo's estate.

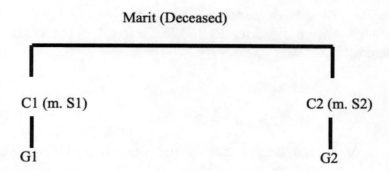

Marit (Deceased)

C1 (m. S1)

G1

C2 (m. S2)

G2

35. Marit died recently without a will. Marit had two children born of Marit's only marriage, which ended when Marit's spouse died years ago. The children were C1 and C2. C1 survived Marit, and C2 died one month after Marit. C1 has a child, G1. C2 was survived by a child, G2. Following Marit's death, a qualified disclaimer of C2's interest in Marit's estate was properly filed in the probate proceedings of Marit's estate by C2's personal representative because a creditor of C2 had filed a large judgment lien against C2 prior to Marit's death. What is the legal effect of the disclaimer on C2's interest in Marit's probate estate?

Answer:

36. Refer to Question 35 but assume that (i) the judgment lien did not exist and (ii) the disclaimer was filed in order for C2's one-half interest in Marit's estate to pass to G2 for "transfer tax" purposes. Which answer best describes the federal transfer consequences, if any, of the disclaimer?

A. There are no transfer tax consequences.

B. If C2 filed the disclaimer, it would be considered a gift to G2 of C2's interest in Marit's estate. If the executor filed the disclaimer, C2's one-half interest in Marit's estate would be included in C2's gross estate for federal transfer tax purposes.

C. If C2 filed the disclaimer, there would be no transfer tax consequences. If the executor filed the disclaimer, C2's one-half interest in Marit's estate would be included in C2's gross estate for federal transfer tax purposes.

D. If C2 filed the disclaimer, it would be considered a gift to G2 of C2's one-half interest in Marit's estate. If the executor filed the disclaimer, there would be no transfer tax consequences.

37. Refer to Question 35 and assume that C1 had borrowed $12,000 from Marit and had not repaid the debt prior to Marit's death. What effect does the $12,000 debt have on C1's interest in Marit's estate?

Answer:

38. Refer to Question 35 and assume that C1 and a family friend discovered Marit had died when C1 and the friend took breakfast to Marit as they had done every day for several months. C1 and the friend entered Marit's house through the back door directly into Marit's kitchen using a key Marit had given to C1. Upon entering the kitchen, C1 and the friend found an envelope with C1's name on it; they opened the envelope and discovered $10,000 in cash and an unrecorded deed signed by Marit whereby Marit conveyed her house to C1. After opening the envelope, C1 and the friend discovered Marit had died the night before. Which answer best explains the likely disposition of the house and the $10,000?

   A. Both the house and the $10,000 pass as part of Marit's probate estate.

   B. Because Marit made a gift to C1 of the house and the $10,000, the house and the $10,000 belong to C1 and are not part of the probate estate.

   C. Since Marit made a gift to C1 of the $10,000, but not the house, the $10,000 is not part of the probate estate, but the house is part of Marit's probate estate.

   D. Since Marit made a gift to C1 of the house, but not the $10,000, the house is not part of the probate estate, but the $10,000 is part of Marit's probate estate.

39. Refer to Question 35 but assume that C1 murdered Marit. Which answer best describes the effect of C1's crime on the disposition of Marit's estate?

   A. The fact that C1 murdered Marit disqualifies C1 as an heir, and the half of the estate to which C1 would have been entitled is forfeited to the state where Marit resided.

   B. The fact that C1 murdered Marit disqualifies C1 as an heir, and the half of the estate to which C1 would have been entitled passes to G1.

   C. The fact that C1 murdered Marit disqualifies C1 as an heir, and the half of the estate to which C1 would have been entitled passes to C2.

   D. The only legal remedy of C2 is to impose a constructive trust on C1 to avoid unjust enrichment.

Probate and Nonprobate Assets

Facts for Questions 1 through 6

Daisy died recently. Immediately prior to Daisy's death, she owned:

- Fee simple title to certain real and personal property.
- A life estate in Blackacre (Avery owns the remainder interest).
- A remainder interest in Whiteacre (Brooklyn owns the life estate interest).
- A savings account with the following designation: "payable on Daisy's death to Chester."
- An insurance policy on Daisy's life payable on her death to Ellis.

Avery, Brooklyn, Chester, and Ellis survive and are not related to Daisy.

1. Daisy dies intestate. Her sole heir, Huxton, inherits the entire probate estate. What interest, if any, is Huxton likely to acquire in Blackacre, Whiteacre, the savings account, and the life insurance policy?

   Answer:

2. How would your answer differ if Daisy had died with a valid will that had been admitted to probate leaving "all my property" to Daisy's friend Grady?

   A. My answer would not change.

   B. Grady acquires the remainder interest in Whiteacre but acquires no interest in Blackacre, the account, or the policy.

   C. Grady acquires the account but acquires no interest in Blackacre, Whiteacre, or the policy.

   D. Grady acquires the proceeds of the policy but acquires no interest in Whiteacre, Blackacre, or the account.

3. Assume that Daisy dies with a valid will that has been admitted to probate leaving "all my property" to Daisy's friend Grady. How does your answer differ if Avery, Brooklyn, Chester, and Ellis had died before Daisy?

   A. My answer would not change.

   B. Grady acquires Whiteacre—but no interest in Blackacre, the account or the policy.

   C. Grady acquires the account and the policy—but no interest in Whiteacre or Blackacre.

   D. Grady acquires Whiteacre, the account, and the policy—but no interest in Blackacre.

4. Assume that Daisy dies with a valid will that has been admitted to probate leaving "all my property" to Daisy's friend Grady. Assume that Avery and Brooklyn die before Daisy, but Chester and Ellis survive Daisy by only two days.

   Which answer best describes the interest, if any, Grady is most likely to acquire in the savings account and the life insurance policy?

   A. Grady acquires ownership of the account and the policy proceeds.

   B. Grady acquires ownership of the account but no interest in the policy or its proceeds.

   C. Grady acquires ownership of the policy and its proceeds but no interest in the account.

   D. Grady acquires no interest in the policy, its proceeds, or the account.

5. Assume that Daisy dies with a valid will that has been admitted to probate leaving "all my property" to Daisy's friend Grady. Avery, Brooklyn, Chester, and Ellis do not survive Daisy, but Chester and Ellis are each survived by a child.

   Which answer best describes the interest, if any, Grady is most likely to acquire in the savings account and the life insurance policy?

   A. Grady acquires ownership of the account and the policy proceeds.

   B. Grady acquires ownership of the account but no interest in the policy or its proceeds.

   C. Grady acquires ownership of the policy and its proceeds but no interest in the account.

   D. Grady acquires no interest in the policy, its proceeds, or the account.

6. Daisy dies with a valid will that has been admitted to probate leaving "all my property" to Daisy's friend Grady. Avery, Brooklyn, Chester, and Ellis do not survive Daisy, but Chester and Ellis are each survived by a child. Assume that Chester and Ellis are Daisy's grandchildren.

Which answer best describes the interest, if any, Grady is most likely to acquire in the savings account and the life insurance policy?

A. Grady acquires ownership of the account and the policy proceeds.

B. Grady acquires ownership of the account but no interest in the policy or its proceeds.

C. Grady acquires ownership of the policy and its proceeds but no interest in the account.

D. Grady acquires no interest in the policy, its proceeds, or the account.

7. Imani, a single non-binary individual, took out a life insurance policy on themself. The policy named B1 as the beneficiary to receive the proceeds on Imani's death. Several years later, Imani signed and delivered the appropriate beneficiary designation form to the insurance company, naming B2 rather than B1 as the beneficiary. Neither of the beneficiary designation forms was witnessed or otherwise executed in compliance with the statutory formalities for a will. Imani died intestate, survived by both B1 and B2. Neither B1 nor B2 is an intestate heir of Imani.

Which of the following best describes the proper disposition of the insurance proceeds?

A. The policy proceeds are probate assets to be distributed to Imani's heirs.

B. The policy proceeds are payable to B2.

C. The policy proceeds are payable to B1.

D. B1 owned the policy and is entitled to the proceeds.

8. How would the results differ if Imani had validly executed a will that specifically devised the policy and its proceeds to their alma mater, UC Sunnydale. Would Imani dying testate affect the result?

Answer:

Facts for Questions 9 and 10

Jojo owned and lived on Blackacre, the family farm. Jojo's grandson, GS, operated the farming activities. Jojo wanted GS to have Blackacre after she died because she believed he would continue to operate the family farm. To encourage GS, she conveyed Blackacre to GS in a deed reserving a life estate for herself but conveying the remainder to GS. GS died before Jojo. Under the terms of his will, he left his entire estate to his spouse, Spouse. After GS died, Jojo executed a will leaving the farm to her granddaughter, GD.

9. Assuming both Spouse and GD survived Jojo, who gets the farm?

   A. GD because GS did not survive Jojo.

   B. GD because Jojo's will revoked the earlier gift to GS.

   C. Spouse because she inherited GS's remainder interest in the farm.

   D. GD, unless the deed was executed in compliance with the statutory formalities for wills, in which case, Spouse.

10. Assume that Jojo, rather than conveying GS the remainder interest, executed and recorded a valid deed conveying the farm to Jojo and GS, as joint tenants with rights of survivorship. Explain who gets the farm under those circumstances.

    Answer:

Facts for Questions 11 and 12

Hector and Winnie were married. They had two sons, C1 and C2. Hector purchased an insurance policy on his life. The beneficiary designation is "to Winnie, if Winnie survives the insured, otherwise, to the insured's children." Hector has died. Hector's will devised "all of my property" to Faber College. Winnie and C2 predeceased Hector. However, C2 was survived by his daughter, Grandchild.

11. Which of the following best describes the proper disposition of the proceeds at Hector's death?

    A. C1 is entitled to receive the proceeds under the terms of the beneficiary designation.

    B. C1 and Grandchild are entitled to receive the proceeds equally.

    C. C1 and Grandchild are entitled to receive the proceeds, 2/3 and 1/3 respectively.

    D. The proceeds will be paid to Hector's probate estate and distributed to Faber College.

12. Assume that Hector also had a retirement account with a payable on death provision naming C2 as the beneficiary. Who would be entitled to the account at Hector's death?

    A. C1.

    B. Grandchild.

    C. Faber College.

    D. The bank.

Facts for Questions 13 through 18

Two friends, Quill and Xavier, have a joint savings account at a local bank. Quill has contributed $1,000 to the account. Xavier has contributed $500. There has been $100 in interest paid. The current balance in the account is $1,600. There have not been any withdrawals from the account.

13. Which of the following is the best statement as to the ownership of the account?

    A. They each own $800 of the account.

    B. Quill owns $1,066.66 and Xavier owns $533.33 of the account.

    C. Quill owns $1,050 and Xavier owns $550.

    D. Quill owns the account and owes Xavier $500.

14. If Quill dies intestate, who owns the account?

Answer:

15. Assume that Quill, Xavier, and Quill's wife Yolanda had been parties to the account. Yolanda had made no contributions or withdrawals. Would your answer change if Quill died, survived by Yolanda and Xavier?

Answer:

16. If Quill and Yolanda were unmarried partners, how would the account have been owned after Quill's death?

Answer:

17. Refer to Question 16. What would Yolanda own when Xavier later dies?

Answer:

18. When Xavier dies in Question 17, assume that Xavier's probate estate is insufficient to pay Xavier's estate's debts. Is this account subject to those claims?

Answer:

19. Mary opens a bank account and designates that it should pay on Mary's death to Nasir. Mary has deposited $5,000, and the account has earned $200 in interest. The total balance is $5,200. What are Nasir's rights to the account before and after Mary's death?

Answer:

Facts for Questions 20 and 21

Pablo had deposited $10,000 into a savings account in his name "payable on Pablo's death to Ruby" and another $10,000 into a checking account in the names of Pablo and Stella "with rights of survivorship." Pablo has recently died, survived by Ruby and Stella.

20. Which answer best explains whether these accounts would be included in Pablo's gross estate for federal transfer tax purposes?

   A. The checking account and the savings account would be included in Pablo's gross estate.

   B. Neither the checking account nor the savings account would be included in Pablo's gross estate.

   C. The checking account, but not the savings account, would be included in Pablo's gross estate.

   D. The checking account and half of the savings account would be included in Pablo's gross estate.

21. Assume that, at Pablo's death, he also owned two life insurance policies: one is a term policy made payable at Pablo's death to his estate, and the other is a whole life policy made payable to Ruby. Which answer best explains whether the policies would be included in Pablo's gross estate for federal transfer tax purposes?

    A. Both policies would be included in Pablo's gross estate.

    B. Neither policy would be included in Pablo's gross estate.

    C. The whole life policy, but not the term policy, would be included in Pablo's gross estate.

    D. The term policy, but not the whole life policy, would be included in Pablo's gross estate.

22. Zelda died recently. Immediately prior to Zelda's death, she had been participating in a 401(k) plan created and funded by her employer; at the time of her death, the value of the 401(k) plan was $1,000,000. In addition, Zelda had been voluntarily contributing to another 401(k) plan, which had a value at the time of her death of $500,000. During her lifetime, Zelda designated a child, C, as the beneficiary of both 401(k) plans. Which answer best explains whether the 401(k) plans would be included in Zelda's gross estate for federal transfer tax purposes?

    A. Both plans would be included in Zelda's gross estate.

    B. Neither plan would be included in Zelda's gross estate.

    C. The employer's plan, but not the voluntary plan, would be included in Zelda's gross estate.

    D. The voluntary plan, but not the employer's plan, would be included in Zelda's gross estate.

Testamentary Capacity & Will Contests

1. Undue influence and fraud are "fellow travelers" in examination fact patterns, meaning, it is not uncommon to spot both of these issues arising from the same set of facts. Explain the difference between undue influence and fraud. What effect does each have on the execution of a will by the testator?

   Answer:

2. Daisy is a wealthy entrepreneur. She went to her attorney's office to discuss estate planning matters. During an initial meeting, Daisy discussed her property and outlined the friends and family she would like to take many of her assets. After the meeting, Daisy provided the attorney with a more detailed spreadsheet setting forth each of her assets, with valuations totaling $12.3 million. The market for several of Daisy's assets had surged. Because Daisy did not follow the market regularly, she was unaware that her assets were actually worth $22.1 million at the time of will execution. Because Daisy was unaware of the nature and extent of her property, did Daisy have the capacity to execute the will?

   A. No. A testator must know the nature and extent of his property in order to have the requisite mental capacity to execute a will, and understanding the valuation of each item of property is an important part of property ownership.

   B. No. While a testator need not know the exact nature and extent of his property in order to have the requisite mental capacity to execute a will, the magnitude of Daisy's mistake is such that she clearly lacks capacity.

   C. Yes. The test for mental capacity does not refer to a testator's property since a testator's property has nothing to do with his or her mental state when the will is being executed.

   D. Yes. A testator must only be capable of knowing and understanding in a general way the nature and extent of his or her property in order to have the requisite mental capacity. Clearly, Daisy had the capability to know her assets' value and understood what her assets were in a general way.

3.   Malee is receiving palliative care because of an illness that renders her physically weak. She is mentally alert but is living in tremendous pain. The palliative care provider is doing their best to manage Malee's pain and discomfort, but no medical treatment is being administered to prolong her life, and she is not expected to live for much longer. Malee is aware that death is imminent, and she has contacted her attorney to request that a will be prepared. Malee's son and daughter-in-law are killed in an automobile accident. Her other relatives have decided not to tell her about the tragic accident for fear that it would weaken her resolve to live and ruin the little time that she has remaining. One day after the accident, she executes her will. The will makes gifts to her son and daughter-in-law. Does her ignorance of the deaths affect her capacity to execute the will?

   A.   Yes. Malee did not have actual knowledge as to her family members.

   B.   Yes. Malee was acting under a substantial mistake with respect to her family members, and such a mistake may have affected her testamentary plans.

   C.   No. The test for mental capacity does not refer to a testator's family members since they have nothing to do with his, her, or their mental state when the will is being executed.

   D.   No. A testator must only be capable of knowing about his, her, or their family members to have the requisite mental capacity.

4.   In Questions 2 and 3, how would the result change, if at all, if the testators had been executing a revocable inter vivos trust and will substitutes?

Answer:

5.   In Questions 2 and 3, assuming the wills were executed in compliance with the statutory formalities, who would have the burden of proof if the wills were contested on the grounds of lack of capacity?

Answer:

6.   Mary Anne is 82 years old and lives independently on her 320-acre farm. She has six adult children. She executed a will leaving her farm to her two oldest children, C1 and C2. The remainder of her possessions were to be sold, with the proceeds equally divided between all six children. Mary Anne's attorney had represented her for more than twenty years, and he videotaped the execution of the will because he was almost certain that a will contest would be filed. Also, her doctor conducted a medical exam the day prior to the will execution and noted that Mary Anne was "sharp." He also notes in the medical file that she manages her 320-acre farm and is in great physical condition. Mary Anne made clear in the video that she was aware that C1 and C2 received a larger share of her estate but that it was a gift to C1 and C2 for all the years of dedication when all of her other children had moved away.

Mary Anne abruptly dies of a heart attack shortly thereafter. A will contest is filed, and the four youngest children allege that C1 and C2 exerted undue influence over Mary Anne. What statement most accurately predicts the outcome of the case?

A. The disproportionately large disposition to C1 and C2, as compared with that to their siblings, automatically gives rise to a presumption of undue influence.

B. The disproportionately large disposition to C1 and C2, as compared with that to their siblings, is a suspicious circumstance. The burden will shift to C1 and C2 to prove the disposition was not the product of undue influence.

C. The four youngest children will likely be unable to meet the initial burden requiring there be a confidential relationship and between Mary Anne and C1 and C2.

D. The four youngest children are unlikely to prevail because the testator was represented by independent counsel.

7. Mason is eighty years old. He is a widower. He has severe health issues and is unable to attend to his own physical daily needs, such as bathing and dressing. His child, C, has not visited him or spoken with him in more than a decade. He has no other living family members.

His next-door neighbor, Gladys, took him into her home and attended to his daily needs. Mason lived with her for one year prior to his death and had little contact with the outside world during that time. A few weeks before his death, he asked Gladys to hire an estate planning attorney to come to the house and help him draft and execute a will. Gladys hired a casual acquaintance from her church. The estate planning attorney met with Mason privately, and prepared and helped Mason execute a will leaving his entire estate to Gladys.

If child, C, files a will contest alleging undue influence, which of the following statements is most accurate?

A. Child C has the burden of establishing that undue influence occurred.

B. Child C must satisfy an initial burden, and if successful in doing so, the burden will then shift to Gladys to prove that no undue influence occurred.

C. Gladys has an initial burden of establishing that no undue influence occurred because she was in a confidential relationship with Mason, and she isolated him.

D. Gladys has an initial burden of establishing that no undue influence occurred because she has a preexisting relationship with the attorney hired to prepare Mason's will.

8. Dembe is ninety years old. He lives alone, has no living relatives, and is socially isolated. He relies on his housekeeper and financial planner to manage all his affairs. His financial planner recommended that he hire a prominent estate planning attorney (John) to prepare his estate plan. Under the terms of the will, Dembe's entire estate will pass to John. Under his prior wills, his estate passed to the National Alley Cat Association, the nation's leading cat advocacy organization to help stray and feral cats. Dembe dies, and the National Alley Cat Association is prepared to contest the will. Which of the following statements is most accurate?

    A. Since Dembe and John have an attorney-client relationship, John has the burden of proving he did not exert undue influence over Dembe.

    B. Even though Dembe and John have an attorney-client relationship, John does not have the burden of providing he did not exert undue influence over Dembe because there are no suspicious circumstances surrounding the will.

    C. As the contestant, the National Alley Cat Association has the burden of proving that John exerted undue influence over Dembe.

    D. The National Alley Cat Association has the burden of proving John exerted undue influence over Dembe, and since Dembe and John have an attorney-client relationship, John has no burden of proving there are no suspicious circumstances surrounding the will.

Facts for Questions 9 through 11

Mei has three children: Riko, Sakura, and Tsumugi. She has never previously executed a will. She retained an attorney, Attorney, to prepare a will leaving her estate to Riko and Sakura in equal shares. She would like to disinherit Tsumugi completely.

Attorney prepared a will leaving $300,000 to himself. The residue of the estate was to be divided into two equal shares between Riko and Sakura. Attorney advised Mei that the will was prepared as she instructed. Mei had time to review the will but executed the instrument based upon Attorney's description without first reviewing it. Mei died shortly thereafter.

9. Assuming that Riko, Sakura, and Tsumugi are Mei's intestate heirs, which of the following answers is most accurate?

    A. Mei was fraudulently induced to execute the will, and it is therefore invalid. Riko, Sakura, and Tsumugi will inherit as intestate heirs.

    B. The will is automatically invalid because Mei did not review it.

C. Mei had testamentary capacity and the ability and opportunity to review the will. Therefore, the will is valid as executed, even if Attorney was mistaken as to the contents of the will.

D. Mei was fraudulently induced to execute the will, therefore, the portion of the will procured by fraud will be invalid. The $300,000 gift to Attorney is invalid, and Riko and Sakura will inherit the estate in equal shares.

10. What if Mei had instructed Attorney to include a no-contest clause in the will. The clause states that any person who challenges "all or any part" of the will's validity will not be entitled to receive any benefit from the will. Do Riko and Sakura need to be concerned that they will lose their respective shares of the estate if they challenge the $300,000 gift to Attorney?

Answer:

11. Assume that Attorney did not fraudulently insert a $300,000 gift to himself in the will. Instead, he drafted the will to disinherit Tsumugi and included a no-contest clause. Would the no-contest clause provide an incentive for Tsumugi not to contest the will?

Answer:

12. Ariadne suffers from severe delusions and both audible and visual hallucinations. She is admitted to a local care facility when her family needs additional assistance managing her medical condition. The medical attention and medications provided by the local care facility have always stabilized her condition. Her family is concerned because she has been hospitalized more frequently over the last year, and the medications seem to be taking longer to improve her condition.

Ariadne owns some jewelry, household furnishings, personal effects, and has a small savings account. Her few possessions are extraordinarily valuable to her, and she knows exactly who she wants each item to go to after her death. She contacted an attorney to prepare a will to memorialize these intentions.

Her condition later flared, and she was hospitalized. The medications normally work within a couple of hours, but this time, the medications took a full twenty-four hours to take effect. Her doctors were concerned and asked that she remain hospitalized for one week under observation. While at the hospital, towards the end of the one-week hospitalization, her attorney visited, and she executed her will.

Does she have capacity to execute the will?

A. Yes. Even though she was hospitalized for a mental health condition, since she was not adjudicated as incapacitated, she had the mental capacity to execute the will.

B. Yes. Even though she was hospitalized for a mental health condition, she had a lucid interval during which to execute the will.

C. No. Given the totality of the circumstances at the time the will was executed, she did not have the mental capacity to execute the will.

D. No, unless her attending physician attests to her mental capacity.

13. Freja suffers from dementia. Because she is unable to manage her own affairs, her daughter Alma has been appointed (by a court of proper jurisdiction) to be her conservator (or guardian). Is Freja able to execute a will while she is a conservatee (or ward)?

A. Having been declared incapacitated, Freja—by definition—does not have the mental capacity to execute a will.

B. Having been declared incapacitated raises a rebuttable presumption that Freja does not have the mental capacity to execute a will.

C. The legal standard for incapacity for the appointment of a conservator is different from the legal standard for testamentary capacity. The adjudication does not affect the determination of testamentary capacity.

D. Since she has been appointed a conservator, Alma—rather than Freja—now has the legal authority to execute a will for Freja.

14. Harry is married to Wilhemina. Harry executed a will several years ago that left his estate to his wife, Wilhemina, and their child. Their child died in a tragic accident. After the death of his child, Harry immersed himself in online conspiracy theories. He managed his professional and personal obligations competently, but he became convinced that he was descended from the lost people of Atlantis. Harry believed that if he immersed himself in water for a long period of time, he would harness his ability to breathe underwater. To test his theory, he rented a boat and jumped off the bow with an anchor tied to his leg. Harry drowned.

Wilhemina found a lengthy handwritten note explaining that he had rented a boat and would return later that evening. He said that if for some reason something happened to him, he was revoking any prior testamentary instruments, and he wanted Wilhemina to take everything in his estate. The note was handwritten, signed, and dated.

Do Harry's beliefs about Atlantis (and his ability to breathe underwater) impact his capacity to execute a valid holographic will?

A. While his beliefs are eccentric, nothing about Harry's beliefs impaired his testamentary capacity to leave a holographic will.

B. Harry's beliefs were so against the evidence and reason to the contrary that he was suffering an insane delusion. The result is that the holographic will is invalid.

C. Harry's beliefs were so against the evidence and reason to the contrary that he was suffering an insane delusion. However, since his delusion is unconnected with the disposition of property in the will, the holographic will is valid.

D. Harry's beliefs were so against the evidence and reason to the contrary that he was suffering an insane delusion. However, if he wrote the holographic will during a lucid interval, the will is valid.

15. Reynaldo purchased a painting in 2020 from a garage sale for $50. He purchased the painting because he appreciated the frenzied brush strokes and the arrangement of colors on the canvas. In his will, he leaves his entire estate to his husband Gary—except for the painting, which he leaves to his friend June.

Reynaldo died last week. Gary had an appraiser come to the house to value other property and discovered the painting is worth $2 million. Which of the following statements is most accurate?

A. Reynaldo's beliefs were so against the evidence and reason to the contrary that he was suffering an insane delusion. The result is that his entire will is invalid.

B. Reynaldo's beliefs were so against the evidence and reason to the contrary that he was suffering an insane delusion. The result is that the provision of his will leaving the painting to June is rendered invalid.

C. Reynaldo made a mistake in valuation. The result of the mistake is that the provision of his will leaving the painting to June is rendered invalid.

D. Reynaldo made a mistake in valuation. The mistake will not impact the disposition in his will to June, and she will take the $2 million painting.

Will Execution

1. What is a will?

   Answer:

2. Testator recently died and is survived by an adult child, Alejandro. Testator's apparently valid will (*i.e.*, a document in writing signed by Testator in the presence of three witnesses) leaves all of Testator's estate to his live-in caretaker, Frank. Testator signed the will shortly after his medical records indicate that he had been diagnosed with a degenerative disease that impacts long-term (and eventually short-term) memory. Which answer best explains whether the document will be admitted to probate?

   A. The court will deny the will's probate due to the diagnosis of a degenerative disease in an uncertain stage.

   B. The court will admit the will to probate unless Alejandro proves that Testator lacked the mental capacity to execute a will.

   C. The court will admit the will to probate if Frank can prove that Testator had the capacity to execute a will, notwithstanding the diagnosis of a degenerative illness.

   D. The court will admit the will to probate notwithstanding the diagnosis of a degenerative illness, since during Testator's lifetime, a court had not determined that the illness had rendered Testator incapacitated.

3. Refer to Question 2. Assume, instead, that Alejandro is appointed guardian (conservator) of Testator and then the will is executed. Which answer best explains whether the document will be admitted to probate?

   A. The court will deny the will's probate due to the guardianship.

   B. The court will admit the will to probate unless Alejandro proves that Testator lacked the mental capacity to execute a will.

   C. The court will admit the will to probate if Frank can prove that Testator had the capacity to execute a will, notwithstanding the guardianship.

   D. The court will admit the will to probate, notwithstanding the guardianship.

4. Refer to Question 3. Assume, instead, that the will is executed and, shortly thereafter, Alejandro is appointed guardian (conservator) of Testator. Which answer best explains whether the document will be admitted to probate?

    A. The court will deny the will's probate due to the finding of incapacity in the guardianship proceeding.

    B. The court will admit the will to probate unless Alejandro proves that Testator lacked the mental capacity to execute a will.

    C. The court will admit the will to probate if Frank can prove that Testator had the capacity to execute a will, notwithstanding the guardianship.

    D. The court will admit the will to probate, notwithstanding the guardianship.

5. Refer to Question 4. Assume that the reason that Alejandro was motivated to proceed with the guardianship of Testator was his concern about an improper sexual relationship between Testator and Frank. Which answer best explains whether the document will be admitted to probate?

    A. If Testator had testamentary capacity, evidence of an improper relationship between Testator and Frank is irrelevant.

    B. Evidence of the improper relationship can only be used in the determination of Testator's testamentary capacity.

    C. Even if Testator had testamentary capacity, the will is invalid if Alejandro can prove Frank improperly influenced Testator during the execution of the will.

    D. Even if Testator had testamentary capacity, the will is still valid if Frank can prove that Frank did not improperly influence Testator during the execution of the will.

6. Freja recently died and is survived by her adult child (Arvid) and her grandchild (Branka). Freja's seemingly valid will (*i.e.*, a document in writing signed by Freja in the presence of three witnesses) leaves all of Freja's estate to Branka. Assume that Freja had testamentary capacity, but she was physically too weak to sign her full name on the will. Instead, Freja had only written her first name and omitted her last name in the place designated for her full signature. Will the document be admitted to probate?

Answer:

7. Refer to Question 6. Assume, instead, that Freja was physically too weak to sign her first or last name. She placed a simple handwritten "X" in the place designated for the full signature of the testator. Which answer best explains whether the document will be admitted to probate?

   A. Since Freja did not sign Freja's full name, the will cannot be admitted to probate.

   B. Even though Freja did not sign Freja's full name, the will can be admitted to probate.

   C. Even though Freja did not sign even a part of Freja's full name, the will may be admitted to probate.

   D. Since Freja did not sign even a part of Freja's name, the will cannot be admitted to probate.

8. Refer to Question 6. Assume, instead, that Freja was physically too weak to sign her first or last name. She asked one of the witnesses to sign the instrument on her behalf. The witness signed Freja's name in the designated place while Freja was still in the room, but Freja was not in a position to actually see the witness sign. Which answer best explains whether the document will be admitted to probate?

   A. Since Freja did not sign her full name, the will cannot be admitted to probate.

   B. Since Freja did not sign anything, the will cannot be admitted to probate.

   C. Even though Freja did not sign anything, the will may be admitted to probate.

   D. If Freja could not see the witness sign, no state will allow the will to be probated.

9. Farai died recently survived by an adult child, Chipo. Farai's apparently valid will (*i.e.*, a document in writing signed by Farai in the presence of three witnesses) leaves all of Farai's estate to her live-in significant other, Greyson. Assume that Farai had testamentary capacity, and that the witnesses to the will had no idea that they were witnessing the signing of a will. Can the document be admitted to probate?

   Answer:

10. Refer to Question 9. Assume that Farai had testamentary capacity, the witnesses knew that the instrument was a will, but the witnesses were not actually present when Farai signed the will. Which answer best explains whether the document will be admitted to probate?

   A. In every state in the country, witnessing a will requires that the witnesses be present when the testator signs the will. It is not possible to admit this will to probate.

   B. In every state in the country that requires witnesses, the act of witnessing requires that the witnesses be present when the testator sign the will. It is not possible to admit this will to probate.

   C. No states require that the witnesses be present at the time the testator signs the instrument.

   D. Even if the witnesses did not see the testator sign the will, the will may be admitted to probate.

11. Refer to Question 10. Assume that each witness signed the will but not while the other two witnesses were present. Explain whether the document will be admitted to probate.

   Answer:

12. Benjamin recently died and is survived by an adult child, Abigail. Benjamin's seemingly valid will (*i.e.*, a document in writing signed by Benjamin in the presence of three witnesses) leaves all of Benjamin's estate to his friend, Leah. Assuming he had testamentary capacity, if the witnesses observed a bedridden Benjamin sign the will before the witnesses signed the will on a table with their backs to Benjamin so that he was unable to observe them sign the will, is the will valid?

   A. Since Benjamin did not see the witnesses sign the will, the will cannot be admitted to probate.

   B. If Benjamin observes at least one witness sign the will, it can be admitted to probate.

   C. Even though Benjamin could not see the witnesses sign the will, the will can be admitted to probate.

   D. Even though Benjamin could not see the witnesses sign the will, the will may be admitted to probate.

13. Refer to Question 12. Assume that the witnesses observed Benjamin sign the will, but they themselves did not sign the will until shortly after Benjamin's death. Which answer best explains whether the document will be admitted to probate?

Answer:

14. Refer to Question 12. Benjamin recently died and is survived by an adult child Abigail, and a grandchild Elizabeth. Benjamin's seemingly valid will (*i.e.*, a document in writing signed by Benjamin in the presence of witnesses) leaves all of his estate to Elizabeth. Assume that Benjamin had testamentary capacity and there were two witnesses. Which answer best explains whether the document will be admitted to probate?

   A. A will may be probated with only one witness.

   B. Since there were only two witnesses, the will cannot be admitted to probate.

   C. Because there were at least two witnesses, the will can be admitted to probate.

   D. Because there were at least two witnesses, the will may be admitted to probate.

15. Refer to Question 14. Assume that a form will was used by a non-lawyer friend of Benjamin. The non-lawyer friend filled in all of the blanks in the form, with a typewriter, at Benjamin's direction. The form only allows a testator to sign in the blank space in the first sentence of the will (*i.e.*, "I, _____, hereby declare this document to be my last will."), and then the witnesses signed at the end of the document. Which answer best explains whether the document will be admitted to probate?

   A. Since a will must be signed at its end by the testator, the will cannot be admitted to probate.

   B. Even if the testator did not sign at the end of the will, the will can be admitted to probate.

   C. Even if the testator did not sign at the end of the will, the will may be admitted to probate.

   D. Form wills can never be probated.

16. Anatoliy died recently survived by three descendants—two adult children, C1 and C2, and C1's child Ganna. In 2020, Anatoliy, being disappointed in C2, executed a valid attested will prepared by Anatoliy's lawyer that left his estate to C1. Shortly before Anatoliy's death, while fully competent, he contacted his lawyer to explain that he was now extremely disappointed in C1 and C2. He stated that he wanted all property to pass to Ganna when he died. Anatoliy then instructed the lawyer in the e-mail to "formalize" Anatoliy's wishes. The lawyer prepared a new will for Anatoliy leaving all of his estate to Ganna, but Anatoliy died before he had an opportunity to execute the new will. Who is most likely to succeed to Anatoliy's estate under the circumstances?

Answer:

17. Refer to Question 16. Assume that Anatoliy contacted his lawyer by sending him a typewritten letter that he had dated, signed, and mailed. Who is most likely to succeed to Anatoliy's estate under these circumstances?

   A. Ganna.

   B. C1.

   C. C1 and C2.

   D. C2 and Ganna.

18. Refer to Question 16. Assume that Anatoliy contacted his lawyer by sending him a handwritten note that he had written, dated, signed, and mailed. Who is most likely to succeed to Anatoliy's estate under these circumstances?

   A. Ganna.

   B. C1.

   C. C1 and C2.

   D. C2 and Ganna.

19. Refer to Question 16. Assume that shortly after Anatoliy's death, a typewritten document was found in his safe deposit box. The typewritten document was signed by Anatoliy and dated shortly before his death. The original 2020 will was also found in the safe deposit box. The typewritten document simply stated, "At my death I leave all my property to Ganna."

Who is most likely to succeed to Anatoliy's estate under these circumstances?

   A. Ganna.

   B. C1.

C. C1 and C2.

D. C2 and Ganna.

20. Refer to Question 19. Assume that shortly after Anatoliy's death, a handwritten document was found in his safe deposit box. The handwritten document was signed by Anatoliy and dated shortly before his death. The original 2020 will was also found in the safe deposit box. The handwritten document simply stated, "At my death I leave all my property to Ganna."

Who is most likely to succeed to Anatoliy's estate under these circumstances?

Answer:

21. Refer to Question 20. Assume that the handwritten document signed by Anatoliy in the safe deposit box had been written on hotel stationary. The date was filled in by Anatoliy at the top of the page immediately below the name and address of the hotel, where pre-printed form lettering provided "_____ __, 20___." Anatoliy filled the month and day and last two digits of the year in the preprinted blanks on the stationary.

Who is most likely to succeed to Anatoliy's estate under these circumstances?

A. Ganna.

B. C1.

C. C1 and C2.

D. C2 and Ganna.

22. Noah died recently. Noah was survived by Noah's two adult children, Mateo and Emily, and Mateo's child, Gigi. Shortly before Noah died, angry with both adult children, a competent Noah phoned his lawyer to prepare a will leaving all of his property to Gigi. The lawyer prepared the will and phoned Noah to advise that the will was ready for execution. Dependent on Mateo for transportation, Noah asked Mateo to take him to the lawyer's office in order to take care of "a few matters." Unknown to Noah, Mateo had overheard Noah's telephone conversation with the lawyer and continued to postpone the trip to the lawyer's office. Noah died without ever executing the will. There were no earlier wills. What is the most likely disposition of Noah's estate?

Answer:

23. Olivia died recently, survived by one child, Liam, and Liam's two children, G1 and G2. Shortly before Olivia died, while Liam was out of town, G1, using physical threats, forced a competent but physically weak Olivia to sign a typewritten will that G1 had prepared. Two of G1's friends were present and signed the will as the witnesses. The will purports to devise Olivia's estate to G1 and G2. One of the witnesses has had a change of heart and is willing to testify as to what occurred. Which answer best explains the most likely disposition of Olivia's estate?

    A. The will can be admitted to probate; G1 and G2 take.

    B. The will can be admitted to probate, but Liam may take the entire estate anyway.

    C. The will can be admitted to probate, but Liam may take G1's half of the estate.

    D. The will cannot be admitted to probate; Liam takes.

24. Professor is teaching a class on will formalities. To demonstrate compliance with the state's holographic will statute, Professor turns to the board and writes (in dry-erase marker), "All my property to the law school at which I am employed." Professor signs the board. An hour later, Professor is an automobile accident that proves fatal. Will Professor's employer receive her estate?

    A. Yes, as long as this is Professor's only testamentary instrument, because of the preference for testacy.

    B. Yes, because this writing complies with the holographic wills statute.

    C. No, because this writing lacks *animus testandi* (*i.e.*, testamentary intent).

    D. No, because this writing is undated and therefore does not comply with the holographic wills statute.

25. John lived alone in a two-bedroom apartment. His neighbors had not seen him come or go from his apartment for a week. The authorities entered his apartment to do a wellness check and they found him deceased on the floor, trapped under a heavy bookshelf, with a pen knife clutched in his hand. Scratched into the wood floor (apparently with use of the pen knife) were the following words, "I leave my entire estate to my nephew and nothing to my brother. /initials/."

John was not married and had no children. He was survived by his brother and nephew. It was determined that he passed of natural causes: he was trapped under a heavy bookshelf that had fallen, and he was unable to call for help. John's nephew removed the portion of the flooring with the scratched words and offered the wood planks for probate. Several witnesses testified that the writing on the floor was John's handwriting.

Should the writing on the flooring be admitted to probate?

A. No. The writing is not signed.

B. No. Wood flooring cannot be probated.

C. No. No one witnessed the words being etched into the wood flooring.

D. Yes. It is entirely in John's handwriting.

26. Paul purchased a pre-printed will form from a national office supply chain. The form reads as follows:

> I am _____ of _____ County, _____. This is my Last Will and Testament. I am of sound mind and moral character. I leave all of my real property to _____, and I leave all of my personal property to _____. I name _____ as the executor of my estate. Signed on this _____ day of _____, _____ by _____. At the request of the testator, and in the testator's presence, each of us have sub-scribed as witnesses to this will on this _____ day of _____,

At home, Paul uses a pen to complete the form by handwriting his name and place of domicile in the first sentence's blanks. In the next blanks, he names Adam to receive his real property, Bill to receive his personal property, and Cora to serve as his executor. He takes the form will to his bank. Paul signs and dates it, and the document is then notarized. He returns home and passes away in his sleep later that evening. The will was located on the top of the desk in his office. The testator resides in a jurisdiction that applies UPC rules. Is the will valid?

A. No. The will is not attested.

B. No. The only statements expressing testamentary intent are part of the pre-printed form language of the instrument.

C. Yes. A writing with material provisions in the handwriting of the testator is valid.

D. Yes. A writing that is signed and notarized by the testator is valid.

Will Revocation

In this chapter, assume that any party requesting that a court exercise its "dispensing power" to excuse the testator's "non-compliance" with the statutory requirements of will execution or revocation cannot meet the burden of proof required in UPC §2-503 (or a "substantial compliance" rule in a jurisdiction which has not adopted the Uniform Probate Code). These so-called "harmless error" statutes generally permit a court to admit a will to probate that was not executed with statutory formalities if the proponent can establish by clear and convincing evidence that the testator intended the document to be a will.

1. Xenia died recently survived by two adult children, Yolanda and Zephyr. In 2021, Xenia, being disappointed in Zephyr, executed a valid attested will prepared by her lawyer that left her entire estate to Yolanda. However, the 2021 will was discovered after Xenia's death in her safe deposit box with an "X" marked across the signature of Xenia. Who is likely to receive Xenia's estate?

   Answer:

2. João died recently survived by his only descendants—two adult children, Ana and Clara, and Ana's child, Matilde. In 2015, João, being disappointed in Clara, executed a valid attested will prepared by his lawyer that left his estate to Ana. João's lawyer retained the original of the 2015 will. João later telephoned the lawyer explaining that he wanted all of his property to go to Matilde when João died and instructed the lawyer to (i) retrieve the 2015 will from the firm's vault and destroy it and (ii) draft a new will leaving all of João's property to Matilde. The lawyer immediately photocopied and then destroyed the 2015 will and later prepared the new will, but João did not sign it before he died. Who is likely to receive João's estate?

   A. Ana.

   B. Matilde.

   C. Clara and Matilde.

   D. Ana and Clara.

3. Refer to Question 2. Additionally, assume that João had validly executed the new will leaving all of his property to Matilde and he had physically destroyed the 2015 will. However, shortly prior to João's death, upset over the news that Matilde, a U.S. Marine, had been killed in action in Afghanistan, João destroyed the will in favor of Matilde. Unfortunately, João died prior to receiving the news that Matilde had not died but had been taken prisoner and had just been rescued. Would your answer change?

Answer:

4. In 2001, Magdalena validly executed a typewritten, witnessed will leaving all of her estate to a friend, Arnold.

In 2010, Magdalena validly executed a new typewritten, witnessed will expressly revoking all prior wills and leaving all of Magdalena's property to another friend, Bini.

Before Magdalena's death, while she was angry with Bini, and while several friends were present, a competent Magdalena intentionally destroyed the 2010 will by tossing it in a fire in the fireplace and told the friends that Magdalena wanted the estate to pass to Arnold when Magdalena died.

Magdalena died recently survived by one adult child, Chester, from whom she was estranged, and several cousins. The 2001 will is still located in Magdalena's safe deposit box. Which answer best describes who is most likely to succeed to Magdalena's estate?

A. Chester.

B. Arnold.

C. Bini.

D. The cousins.

5. Building upon the facts of Question 4, assume that Magdalena's 2010 will had not expressly revoked all earlier wills and simply left all of Magdalena's estate to Bini. Who is most likely to succeed to Magdalena's estate?

A. Chester.

B. Arnold.

C. Bini.

D. The cousins.

6. Building upon the facts of Question 5, assume that the 2010 document had not been a typewritten witnessed will, but a document entirely in Magdalena's handwriting and signed by Magdalena. Who is most likely to succeed to Magdalena's estate?

    A. Chester.

    B. Arnold.

    C. Bini

    D. The cousins.

7. Refer to Question 4. Who is likely to succeed to Magdalena's estate if, after the 2001 will had been executed, Magdalena had left the original 2001 will with the lawyer, and the lawyer destroyed the 2001 will in 2015 when the lawyer was cleaning out the lawyer's file room? The lawyer will testify that the lawyer thought retention of the original was unnecessary because the 2001 will had been revoked when the 2010 will was executed by Magdalena.

Answer:

8. Ruby died recently survived by one adult child, Carlysle, and several siblings. In 2015, because Ruby was estranged from Carlysle, Ruby validly executed a typewritten, witnessed will leaving all of Ruby's estate to her girlfriend, Alice. The original 2015 will has not been found. Ruby's lawyer will testify that, after the 2015 will had been executed, Ruby took the original, explaining that she was going to place the original in her desk at home. Which answer best describes who is most likely to succeed to Ruby's estate?

    A. Carlysle.

    B. Alice.

    C. The oldest sibling.

    D. All the siblings.

9. Building upon the facts of Question 8, assume that evidence reveals that a competent but bedridden Ruby had not personally destroyed the 2015 will but had asked Ruby's nurse to destroy the will. The nurse found the 2015 will in a desk in Ruby's study, returned to the bedroom, and while Ruby was watching, tore the will into multiple pieces and tossed the 2015 will into a trash can. Who is most likely to succeed to Ruby's estate?

    A. Carlysle.

    B. Alice.

    C. The oldest sibling.

    D. All the siblings.

10. Dural died recently survived by his two children, C1 and C2, and C2's child, Allorah. Dural had validly executed a will leaving all of his property to Allorah at a time when a competent Dural was angry with C1 and C2. Shortly prior to Dural's death, having been threatened with physical harm by C1, a competent but bedridden Dural directed a nurse to retrieve the will from the study. The nurse brought the will to them, and they tore the will into many pieces. Unknown to C1, the nurse had overheard C1's physical threats. Which answer best explains the most likely disposition of Dural's estate?

    A. The will can be admitted to probate; Allorah takes.

    B. The will cannot be admitted to probate; C1 and C2 take.

    C. The will cannot be admitted to probate, but Allorah may take the entire estate.

    D. The will cannot be admitted to probate, but Allorah may take C1's half of the estate.

11. Aknah died recently survived by a child, Bilal, and Bilal's two children, G1 and G2. Aknah had validly executed a will whereby she left her entire estate to G1 and G2. Shortly prior to Aknah's death, a competent but bedridden Aknah directed her nurse to retrieve the will from her desk located in her study so that she could destroy the will. Unknown to Aknah, G1 overheard her instructions to the nurse and substituted a photocopy of the will for the original will before the nurse could retrieve it. Neither Aknah nor the nurse noticed the "switch." Aknah died shortly after destroying the photocopy of the will. Which answer best explains the most likely disposition of Aknah's estate?

    A. The will may be admitted to probate; G1 and G2 take.

    B. The will cannot be admitted to probate; Bilal takes.

    C. The will can be admitted to probate, but Bilal may take.

    D. The will may be admitted to probate, but Bilal may take G1's half of the estate.

12. Emma died recently. Emma was survived by her children, Charlotte and Drew, and Emma's grandchildren, G1 and G2. Emma had validly executed a typewritten witnessed will leaving all of Emma's property to G1 and G2. Near the time Emma was diagnosed with dementia, Emma, in the presence of two family friends, destroyed her will, explaining to the friends that she had reconciled with Charlotte and Drew. Explain the most likely disposition of Emma's estate.

Answer:

13. Building on Question 12, assume that Emma had testamentary capacity and did not destroy the old will. Instead, Emma handwrote the following note, "I hereby revoke all prior wills and leave all my property to Charlotte." Emma signed the note while two family friends watched, explaining Emma had reconciled with Charlotte. Which answer best explains who is likely to succeed to Emma's estate?

A. G1 and G2.

B. Charlotte and Drew.

C. Charlotte and G2.

D. Charlotte.

14. Building on Question 13, assume that the note written and signed by Emma simply said, "I revoke all of my prior wills." Which answer best explains who is likely to succeed to Emma's estate?

A. G1 and G2.

B. Charlotte and Drew.

C. Charlotte and G2.

D. Charlotte.

15. Aiko died recently. She was survived by her spouse, Stephen, and Aiko's parents, M and F; Aiko never had any children. Her will was validly executed prior to her marriage to Stephen, and Aiko never changed the will. It devises Aiko's entire estate to M and F. What impact, if any, did Aiko's marriage to Stephen have upon the will?

Answer:

16. Refer to Question 15. Assume that the will was executed during the marriage of Aiko and Stephen. What is the likely impact upon the will of Aiko?

    A. The will can be admitted to probate; the entire estate passes to M and F.

    B. The will cannot be admitted to probate; the entire estate passes to Stephen.

    C. The will can be admitted to probate; Stephen will be entitled to his marital share, if any, and M and F will succeed to everything else.

    D. The will cannot be admitted to probate; the estate will be shared by Stephen, M, and F.

17. Sebastián died recently. He was survived by his parents, M and F. Sebastián was divorced from his spouse, Jerome, for two years prior to his death. After the divorce, Sebastián did not change the will that he had executed while still married to Jerome—which left all of his property to his then-spouse. What is the most likely disposition of Sebastián's estate?

Answer:

Will Interpretation & Construction

1. Explain how will interpretation differs from will construction.

   Answer:

2. Oskar died recently. He was survived by an independent adult child, Ella. Oskar's valid, probated will leaves all of his property to Ella, including personal property and un-improved real property. After his death, the court-appointed personal representative determined that the fair market value of Oskar's estate was $1 million. It was also de-termined that Oskar owed unsecured contractual creditors $250,000 and tort creditors $500,000; the expenses of Oskar's last illness were $250,000. Which answer best explains how Oskar's assets will likely be distributed?

   A. All of the assets will be sold to pay the creditors.

   B. Only the personal property can be sold to pay the creditors on a pro rata basis.

   C. All of the assets will be sold to pay only the tort creditors and the last illness expenses.

   D. Only the personal property can be sold in order to pay the tort creditors and the last illness expenses on a pro rata basis.

3. Assume the same facts as Question 2 except that Ella is a minor at the time of Oskar's death. Which answer best explains how Oskar's assets will likely be distributed?

   A. All of the assets will be sold to pay the creditors.

   B. Tort creditors will not be paid if a minor child survives the decedent.

   C. No personal property will be sold to pay creditors if a minor child survives the decedent.

   D. Under the UPC, Ella will be entitled to a homestead allowance, $15,000 in household furnishings and personal effects, and perhaps a reasonable allowance for a period not to exceed one year.

4. Assume the same facts as Question 2 except that Oskar was also survived by his second spouse Willa (who is not a parent of Ella) and the only real estate owned by Oskar is the primary residence of Oskar and Willa. Which answer best explains how Oskar's assets will likely be distributed?

   A. The home will likely be sold to pay the creditors.

   B. The home will not be sold to pay the debts, and Ella will inherit the home.

   C. The home will not be sold to pay the debts, and Willa will inherit the home.

   D. The home will not be sold to pay the debts and will be owned by Ella, but Willa will have a right to live there.

5. Oman died recently. Oman was survived by two independent adult children, Shelly and Drew. Oman's valid will has been admitted to probate; it simply states, "I devise my home to Shelly and the rest, residue, and remainder of my estate to Drew." At the time of Oman's death, the significant assets of the estate consisted of the home (fair market value of $100,000) and shares of a New York Stock Exchange company (fair market value of $100,000). The only debt or expense of Oman's estate is a note signed by Oman and secured by the home; the outstanding balance of the debt at the time of death was $50,000. The will does not direct how the decedent's debts are to be paid. Which answer best explains the most likely disposition of Oman's estate?

   A. Shelly receives the home, subject to the outstanding indebtedness, and Drew receives all of the shares of stock.

   B. Shelly receives the home, free of any indebtedness, and Drew receives only the shares of stock remaining after enough shares are sold to pay the debt.

   C. Half of the debt should be paid by Shelly, or out of the sales proceeds of the home, and the other half of the debt should be paid out of the sales proceeds of part of the stock.

   D. The answer depends on the decisions the creditor makes after Oman's death.

6. Assume the same facts as Question 5. How would your answer differ if the $50,000 debt was not a note secured by the home but an unsecured debt of $50,000 owing by Oman at the time of Oman's death?

   A. Shelly receives the home, free of any indebtedness, and Drew receives only the stock remaining after the debt is paid.

   B. Drew would receive the stock, and the home would be sold in order to pay the debt, with Shelly receiving the balance of the proceeds of the sale after the debt is paid.

C. Half of the debt should be paid by Shelly, or out of the sales proceeds of the home, and the other one-half of the debt should be paid by Drew, or out of the sales proceeds of part of the stock.

D. The answer depends on the intention of the creditor after Oman's death.

7. Bayan (they/them) died recently. Bayan was survived by three independent adult children, Child1, Child2, and Child3. At the time of Bayan's death, their estate consisted of their home and the home's contents (fair market value of $1 million), stocks and bonds (fair market value of $1 million), and $500,000 cash. At the time of their death, there were outstanding unsecured debts of $1 million. Bayan's valid will has been admitted to probate, and the will devises the home and its contents to Child1, $1 million to Child2, and the rest, residue, and remainder of Bayan's estate to Child3. Which of the described assets should be used by the executor to satisfy the debts?

Answer:

8. Assume the same facts as Question 7, except that the will devises $1 million to Child2, the stocks and bonds to Child3, and the rest, residue, and remainder of Bayan's estate to Child1. Which answer best describes the assets the executor should use to satisfy the debts?

A. The home and its contents.

B. Cash.

C. The stocks and bonds.

D. A third of the home and its contents, a third of the cash, and a third of the stocks and bonds.

9. Assume the same facts as Question 7 except that the will devises $1 million to Child2 and the rest, residue, and remainder of Bayan's estate to Child1 and Child3. Which answer best describes the assets the executor should use to satisfy the debts?

A. Cash.

B. Half of the home and its contents and half of the stocks and bonds.

C. The home and its contents.

D. The stocks and bonds.

10. Loujain died recently. She was survived by three independent adult children, Child1, Child2, and Child3. Loujain's valid, probated will, dated 2000, devises all of her 21st Century Fox ("21CF") stock to Child1, Blackacre to Child2, and the rest, residue, and remainder of Loujain's estate to Child3. Following the execution of the will, Loujain sold Blackacre and immediately used the sales proceeds to purchase Whiteacre. Loujain's home was originally located on Blackacre, and then she moved into a house on Whiteacre. In 2018, Disney acquired 21CF. Loujain's 21CF shares were exchange for shares in Disney.

At the time of Loujain's death, her significant assets were Whiteacre, the Disney stock, and just enough cash to pay her debts and the administration expenses. Which answer best describes the disposition of the Disney stock and Whiteacre?

A. The Disney stock passes to Child1, and Whiteacre passes to Child3.

B. The Disney stock passes to Child1, and Whiteacre passes to Child2.

C. The Disney stock passes to Child3, and Whiteacre to passes Child2.

D. The Disney stock and Whiteacre pass to Child3.

11. Grover died recently, survived by his three independent adult children, Child1, Child2, and Child3. His valid will has been admitted to probate. The will devises Grover's Cadillac to Child1, $100,000 to Child2, and the rest, residue, and remainder of his estate to Child3. At the time that Grover executed the will, his significant assets consisted of the Cadillac (fair market value of $50,000), cash ($100,000), stocks and bonds (fair market value of $100,000), and a home (fair market value of $100,000). Immediately prior to his death, the Cadillac had a fair market value of $25,000, there was no cash remaining, the stocks and bonds had declined in value to only $10,000, and the home had declined in value to $65,000. Grover died in a one-car automobile accident while driving the Cadillac, and his insurance company has recently paid the executor of the estate $25,000 in order to "total" the car ($24,000 for replacement value, $1,000 salvage value). The debts, all unsecured, and the administration expenses totaled $50,000. Explain the likely disposition of the remaining assets of Grover's estate.

Answer:

12. Lily died recently. Lily was survived by her three independent adult children, Child1, Child2, and Child3. Lily's valid will has been admitted to probate. The will directs that $10,000 is to be paid to Child1, and the rest, residue, and remainder of her estate is to pass equally to Child2 and Child3. After the execution of the will and six months prior to Lily's death, she made a gift of $10,000 to Child1 and another gift of $10,000 to Child2. At the time of Lily's death, her estate consisted primarily of cash with a total value of $100,000 after the debts were paid. Which answer best describes the most likely disposition of the remaining assets of Lily's estate?

A. $50,000 to Child2 and $50,000 to Child3.

B. $10,000 to Child1, $45,000 to Child2, and $45,000 to Child3.

C. $10,000 to Child1, $40,000 to Child2, and $50,000 to Child3.

D. $45,000 to Child2 and $55,000 to Child3.

13. Assume the same facts as Question 12 except that the $10,000 "given" to Child2 was actually a loan by Lily that had not been repaid by Child2 prior to her death. Also, Lily's estate is insolvent (*i.e.*, her debts exceed the described assets by $10,000). Which answer best describes the effect the outstanding loan will have on the administration of Lily's estate?

A. It has no effect because the death of Lily extinguished the debt.

B. Child2 must repay one-half the debt.

C. Child2 must repay the whole debt.

D. Child2 must pay $10,000 to Child1.

14. Building upon the facts of Question 13, Child2 has been given a $10,000 loan but Lily's estate was solvent (*i.e.*, the value of the non-exempt liquid assets exceed the debts by more than $10,000) at the time of her death. Which answer best describes the effect the outstanding loan will have on the administration of Lily's estate?

A. It has no effect because the death of Lily extinguished the debt.

B. Child2 must repay one-half the debt.

C. Child2 must repay the whole debt.

D. Although Child2 does not have to repay the debt, Child2's share of the estate will be reduced by half of the amount of the debt.

15. Building upon the facts of Question 13, assume that Lily loaned $10,000 to Child2 more than fifteen years prior to Lily's death. Also, Lily's estate is insolvent (*i.e.*, her debts exceed the described assets by $10,000). Which answer best describes the effect the outstanding loan will have on the administration of Lily's estate?

A. It has no effect.

B. Child2 must repay one-half of the debt.

C. Child2 must repay the whole debt.

D. Although Child2 does not have to repay the debt, Child2's share of the estate will be reduced by half of the amount of the debt.

16. Building upon the facts of Question 14, Child2 has been given a $10,000 loan more than fifteen years prior to Lily's death. At the time of her death, Lily's estate was solvent (*i.e.*, the value of the non-exempt liquid assets exceed the debts by more than $10,000). Which answer best describes the effect the outstanding loan will have on the administration of Lily's estate?

    A. It has no effect.

    B. Child2 must repay one-half of the debt.

    C. Child2 must repay the whole debt.

    D. Although Child2 does not have to repay the debt, Child2's share of the estate will be reduced by half of the amount of the debt.

17. Brigitta died recently. At the time she executed her will, Brigitta had three independent adult children, Child1, Child2, and Child3. Brigitta's valid will has been admitted to probate. The will devises Blackacre to Child1, Whiteacre to Child2, and the rest, residue and remainder of Brigitta's estate to Child3.

Child1 predeceased Brigitta. Child2 died one day after Brigitta. Child3 died one week after Brigitta. Brigitta was also survived by several cousins. Each child of Brigitta had a valid, probated will that devised that child's estate to that child's surviving spouse. Neither Child1, Child2, nor Child3 had any children.

What is the most likely disposition of Brigitta's estate?

Answer:

18. Assume the same facts as Question 17, except that Child1, Child2, and Child3 all died before Brigitta. The children's spouses survived Brigitta. Which answer best describes the most likely disposition of Brigitta's estate?

    A. Blackacre passes to Child1's spouse; Whiteacre passes to Child2's spouse; the rest, residue, and remainder passes to Child3's spouse.

    B. Blackacre passes to Child1's spouse; Whiteacre passes to Child2's spouse; the rest, residue, and remainder passes to the cousins.

    C. Blackacre and Whiteacre pass to the cousins; the rest, residue, and remainder passes to Child3's spouse.

    D. The entire estate passes to the cousins.

19. Assume the same facts as Question 17 except that Child1, Child2, and Child3 were survived by one child each (Child1's child is Ana; Child2's child is Ben; and Child3's child is Chuck). Ana, Ben, and Chuck are adults.

    Which answer best describes the most likely disposition of Brigitta's estate?

    A. Blackacre passes to Child1's spouse and Ana; Whiteacre passes to Child2's spouse and Ben; the residue of the estate passes to Child3's spouse.

    B. Blackacre passes to Ana; Whiteacre passes to Ben; the residue of the estate passes to Chuck.

    C. Blackacre passes to Ana; Whiteacre passes to Child2's spouse; the residue passes to Child3's spouse.

    D. Blackacre passes to Ana; Whiteacre passes to Ben; the residue of the estate passes to Child3's spouse.

20. Ibrahim died recently. He was survived by one independent adult daughter, Delilah. Ibrahim has become very close to his friend's three adult children, Aaron, Beula, and Chase. Ibrahim's valid will has been admitted to probate and devises Blackacre to Aaron, Whiteacre to Beula, and the rest, residue, and remainder of the estate to Chase. Aaron, Beula, and Chase predeceased Ibrahim.

    Aaron, Beula, and Chase each died with both a surviving spouse and a child. The wills of Aaron and Beula each devised their estate to their surviving spouse.

    What is the most likely disposition of Ibrahim's estate following formal administration?

    Answer:

21. Amelia died recently. She was survived by an independent adult child, Drew. Another child of Amelia, Samia, died several years before Amelia died; Samia was survived by three children, S1, S2, and S3. Amelia's valid will has been admitted to probate and simply says, "I devise all of my property equally to S1, S2, and S3." S1 died one day before Amelia died; S1 was survived by a spouse who is the sole beneficiary of her will and a child Zephyr. S2 died one day after Amelia died; S2 was survived by his spouse (who is the sole beneficiary of his will) and his child Yala. S3 survived Amelia. Which answer best explains the most likely disposition of Amelia's estate?

    A. The entire estate passes to S3.

    B. A third passes to S1's spouse, a third passes to S2's spouse and a third passes to S3.

    C. A third passes to Zephyr, a third passes to Yala, and a third passes to S3.

    D. Two-thirds pass to S3 and Drew, and one-third passes to S3.

22. Assume the same facts as Question 21 except that S1 and S2 are not survived by children. Which answer best describes the most likely disposition of Amelia's estate?

    A. The entire estate passes to S3.

    B. A third passes to S1's spouse, a third passes to S2's spouse, and a third passes to S3.

    C. One-third passes to S2's spouse, and two-thirds pass to S3.

    D. One-third passes to S3, and two-thirds pass to Drew and S3.

23. Refer to Question 21. How would your answer differ if Samia would have had another child after the execution of the will and before she died? This child, S4, survived Amelia.

    A. My answer would not change.

    B. S4 and S3 would share a third of the estate.

    C. S4 and S3 would share a half of the estate.

    D. Zephyr, Yala, S3, and S4 would share the estate equally.

24. Grace died recently. Grace was survived by an independent adult child, Daria. Another child of Grace, Shelly, died several years before Grace died; Shelly was survived by three adult children, G1, G2, and G3. Grace's valid will has been admitted to probate and simply says, "I devise all of my property to my grandchildren." G1 died one day before Grace died; G1 was survived by her spouse, who is the sole beneficiary of G1's will, and one child Zenia. G2 died one day after Grace died; G2 was survived by his spouse, who is the sole beneficiary of G2's will, and one child Yelania. G3 survived Grace. (The below diagram may be helpful.) Which answer best describes the most likely disposition of Grace's estate?

    A. One-third passes to Zenia, one-third passes to Yelania, and one-third passes to G3.

    B. One-third passes to Zenia, one-third passes to G2's spouse, and one-third passes to G3.

    C. The entire estate passes to G3.

    D. Two-thirds passes to Daria, and one-third passes to G3.

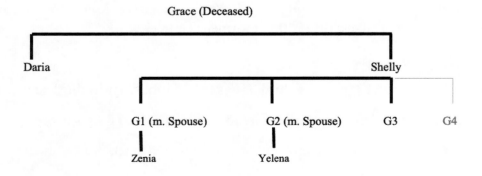

25. Assume the facts of Question 24 and refer to the above diagram. How would your answer differ if Shelly would have had another child, G4, before Shelly died, and G4 had survived Grace?

   A. My answer would not change.

   B. G3 and G4 would share one-third of the estate.

   C. G3 and G4 would share one-half of the estate.

   D. Zenia, Yelania, G3, and G4 would share the estate equally.

26. Assume the facts of Question 24 except that Grace's will states, "I devise all of my property to my grandchildren who survive me." What is the most likely disposition of the estate?

Answer:

27. Grigori died recently. He was survived by an independent adult child, Mischa. Grigori was predeceased by his daughter Polina, who died several years prior to Grigori. Polina is survived by her three children, G1, G2, and G3.

   Grigori's valid will has been admitted to probate and simply says, "I devise all of my property to my grandchildren." G1 died one day before Grigori died. She was survived by her spouse, who is the sole beneficiary of G1's will. G2 died one day after Grigori died. He was survived by his spouse, who is the beneficiary of G2's will. G3 survived Grigori.

   Which answer would best describe the most likely disposition of Grigori's estate?

   A. Two-thirds passes to Mischa and one-third passes to G3.

   B. One-half passes to Mischa and one-half passes to G3.

   C. One-third passes to G1's spouse, one-third passes to G2's spouse, and one-third passes to G3.

   D. The entire estate passes to G3.

28. Ophelia died recently. Ophelia was survived by an independent adult child, Dalia. Another child of Ophelia, Sofie, died several years before Ophelia died; Sofie was survived by her stepchildren, A, B, and C, the children of Sofie's spouse by a prior marriage. Ophelia's valid will has been admitted to probate and simply says, "I devise all of my property to A, B, and C." A died one day before Ophelia died; A was survived by her spouse, who is the sole beneficiary of her will, and also her child Anne. B died one day after Ophelia died; B was survived by her spouse (who is the sole beneficiary of her will), and her child Bob. C survived Ophelia. Sofie never adopted A, B, and C. Which answer best describes the most likely disposition of Ophelia's estate?

A. The entire estate passes to Dalia.

B. Two-thirds pass to Dalia, and one-third passes to C.

C. One-third passes to Anne, one-third passes to Bob, and one-third passes to C.

D. The entire estate passes to C.

29. How would your answer in Question 28 differ if (i) Ophelia's will would have devised the estate to "Ophelia's grandchildren," and (ii) A, B, and C had survived Ophelia by 120 hours? Witnesses will testify that Ophelia referred to A, B, and C as "grandchildren" and treated them as "grandchildren" even after Sofie's death. Which answer best describes the most likely disposition of Ophelia's estate?

Answer:

30. Testator died. He was survived by his only child (Hovan) and his one grandchild (Mari). Both Hovan and Mari are independent adults. The will of Testator is admitted to probate. The testamentary instrument devises Blackacre to Mari, and the rest, residue, and remainder of his estate to a charity. Due to Mari's serious financial difficulties, she filed a valid disclaimer. Mari was not married, and she has no children. What is the likely disposition of Blackacre?

Answer:

31. David died recently. David was survived by his only child, Elliott, an independent adult. A, B, and C were friends of David. David's valid will has been admitted to probate, and the will provides that (i) the stock certificates located in David's safe deposit box are devised to A, (ii) the jewelry listed on David's homeowner's insurance policy is devised to B, (iii) any other personal property is to be distributed by the executor pursuant to the instructions the testator intends to leave in a memo that will be attached to the will, and (iv) the rest, residue, and remainder of David's estate is devised to Elliott. A memo was attached to the will at the time David died. The memo was dated several months after the execution of the will and indicated that certain described items of tangible personal property were to be delivered to C by the executor. This memo was typewritten and signed by David. Which answer best describes the most likely disposition of the stock

certificates located in the safe deposit box, the jewelry listed on the insurance policy, and the items of personal property described in the memo?

A. The stock, jewelry, and personal property pass to Elliott.

B. The stock passes to A; the jewelry passes to B; and the other items of tangible personal property pass to C.

C. The stock passes to A; the jewelry passes to B; and the other items of tangible personal property pass to Elliott.

D. The stock passes to A, and the jewelry and the other items of tangible personal property pass to Elliott.

32. Zephyr (they/them) died recently. They were survived by their adult child, Carol, and Carol's child, Gigi. Zephyr's valid will has been admitted to probate. The will devises Blackacre to Freddie, a friend of Zephyr, and the rest, residue, and remainder of the estate to a charity.

Friends of both Freddie and Zephyr will testify that the two agreed orally—prior to the execution of the will—that Freddie would manage Blackacre during Carol's lifetime. Freddie agreed to pay Carol any income generated by Blackacre, and then at Carol's death, to transfer Blackacre outright to Gigi.

What is the most likely disposition of Blackacre?

Answer:

33. Assume the same facts as Question 32, except that the agreement between Zephyr and Freddie had been memorialized in a written agreement signed by both at the time the will was executed. What is the most likely disposition of Blackacre?

A. An express trust has been created with Freddie as trustee, and Carol and Gigi as beneficiaries.

B. Freddie acquired fee simple title to Blackacre since the terms of the agreement are not in the will.

C. Carol, as Zephyr's sole heir, or the charity will have the court impose a resulting trust on Freddie in favor of Carol since Zephyr's attempt to create an express trust failed.

D. The court will impose a constructive trust on Freddie in favor of Carol and/or Gigi to avoid the unjust enrichment of Freddie.

34. Assume the same facts as Question 32, except that Zephyr's will devised Blackacre "to Freddie, as trustee." Which answer best describes the most likely disposition of Blackacre?

A. An express trust has been created with Freddie as trustee, and Carol and Gigi as beneficiaries.

B. The charity will acquire fee simple title to Blackacre since the terms of the agreement are not in the will.

C. Carol, as Zephyr's sole heir, will have the court impose a resulting trust on Freddie in favor of Carol since Zephyr's attempt to create an express trust failed.

D. The court will impose a constructive trust on Freddie in favor of Carol and Gigi to avoid the unjust enrichment of Freddie and/or the charity.

35. Assume the same facts as Question 34, except that Zephyr's will had devised Blackacre "to Freddie, as trustee," but there is no evidence of any agreement whatsoever between Zephyr and Freddie related to Blackacre. Which answer best describes the most likely disposition of Blackacre following Zephyr's death?

A. An express trust has been created with Freddie as trustee, and the charity as beneficiary.

B. The charity acquires fee simple title to Blackacre.

C. Freddie acquires fee simple title to Blackacre.

D. Carol, as Zephyr's sole heir, will have the court impose a resulting trust on Blackacre in favor of Carol.

36. Jagger died recently. He was survived by his independent adult child, Cecilia, and Cecilia's child, Gloria. The valid will of the decedent has been admitted to probate. The will devises Blackacre to "Ziggy in trust for Cecilia and Gloria," and the rest, residue and remainder of Jagger's estate to a charity. Several friends of both Jagger and Ziggy will testify that the two had orally agreed—prior to the execution of Jagger's will—that Ziggy would manage Blackacre for Cecilia during her lifetime, paying her any income generated and then, at her death, Ziggy would convey Blackacre outright to Gloria. What is the most likely disposition of Blackacre?

Answer:

37. Assume the same facts as Question 36, except that there is no evidence of any agreement between Jagger and Ziggy related to Blackacre. Which answer best describes the most likely disposition of Blackacre following formal administration of Jagger's estate?

   A. An express trust has been created with Ziggy, as trustee, and Cecilia and Gloria, as the beneficiaries.

   B. The charity acquires fee simple title to Blackacre.

   C. Cecilia, as Jagger's sole heir, will have the court impose a resulting trust on Blackacre in favor of Cecilia.

   D. Cecilia and Gloria acquire fee simple title.

38. Xander died recently survived by his sister-in-law's child Gregor. Xander's valid will has been admitted to probate. Xander's will devises Blackacre to Fiona (his close friend), and the rest, residue and remainder of the estate to a charity. Several friends of both Xander and Fiona will testify that the two had orally agreed—prior to the execution of Xander's will—that Fiona would manage Blackacre for Xander's sister-in-law during her lifetime, paying her any income generated and then, at her death, Blackacre is to be conveyed outright to Gregor.

Xander's sister-in-law died one day prior to Xander. She was survived by a spouse, S, as well as her two children (Gregor and Jill). Her valid will has been admitted to probate and leaves all of her property to S.

Which answer best describes the most likely disposition of Blackacre following formal administration of Xander's estate?

   A. An express trust has been created with Fiona as trustee, and Gregor as beneficiary.

   B. Fiona acquired fee simple title to Blackacre since the terms of the agreement are impossible to complete.

   C. Gregor, as Xander's heir, will have the court impose a resulting trust on Fiona in favor of Gregor since Xander's attempt to create an express trust failed.

   D. Gregor will have the court impose a constructive trust on Fiona in favor of Gregor in order to avoid unjust enrichment by Fiona.

39. Assume the same facts as Question 38, except that both Xander's sister-in-law and Gregor died prior to Xander. Xander's sister-in-law was survived by her spouse, S, and her will has been admitted to probate and leaves all of her property to S. Gregor was survived by his spouse, GS, and one child, GG; Gregor's valid will has been admitted to probate and devises all of Gregor's property to GS. Which answer best describes the most likely disposition of Blackacre following formal administration of Xander's estate?

   A. GS will have the court impose a constructive trust on Fiona to avoid unjust enrichment.

   B. GG will have the court impose a constructive trust on Fiona to avoid unjust enrichment.

   C. The charity will have the court impose a constructive trust on Fiona to avoid unjust enrichment.

   D. Fiona retains the fee simple title.

40. Assume the same facts as Question 38, except that both Xander's sister-in-law and Gregor survived Xander. Fiona, however, died one day prior to Xander. Fiona was survived by her spouse, Spouse, and one child, F1. Fiona's valid will has been admitted to probate and devises all of her property to Spouse. What is the most likely disposition of Blackacre following the administration of Xander's estate?

   A. Xander's sister-in-law and Gregor will have the court impose a constructive trust on Spouse to avoid unjust enrichment.

   B. Xander's sister-in-law and Gregor will have the court impose a constructive trust on Fiona's child F1 to avoid unjust enrichment.

   C. Xander's sister-in-law will have the court impose a resulting trust on the charity since the attempt to create an express trust failed.

   D. The charity acquires Blackacre.

41. Assume the same facts as Question 38, except that Xander's sister-in-law, Gregor, and Fiona have all survived Xander.

   You are Fiona's lawyer. She has informed you that while she acknowledges that she had an oral agreement with Xander, she does not want to assume the responsibility of managing Blackacre for anyone. Which answer best describes the legal advice that should be given to Fiona under these circumstances?

   A. You can disclaim, and the title will vest in the charity.

   B. You can disclaim, and the title will vest in Xander's sister-in-law.

C. You can accept the legal title to Blackacre and then simply convey Blackacre to Xander's sister-in-law and Gregor.

D. You can disclaim, and the court will appoint a successor trustee to manage the express trust.

42. Assume the same facts as Question 41, except that the property subject to the oral agreement and devised to Fiona under Xander's will was common stock in a publicly held corporation (and not Blackacre). What advice should be given to Fiona?

Answer:

Limitations on Testamentary Power

1. Explain the concept of testamentary power.

   Answer:

2. Suki, who is not married, died recently survived by two adult children, Ann and Bob. In the presence of several friends, a competent Suki typed a letter addressed to both Ann and Bob stating that at Suki's death, the home and its contents were to pass to Ann. Suki explained to the friends what she was doing and then signed the letter. At all relevant times, Suki was a competent individual, and Suki's friends are willing to testify as to Suki's verbal statements. Ann and Bob did not receive the letter until after Suki's death. Which answer best explains the most likely disposition of Suki's home and its contents?

   A. The house and its contents pass to Ann and Bob.

   B. The house and its contents would pass to Ann.

   C. The house but not its contents would pass to Ann.

   D. The contents but not the house would pass to Ann.

3. Assume the same facts as Question 2 except that the letter was delivered to Ann and Bob prior to Suki's death. Which answer best explains the most likely disposition of Suki's home and its contents?

   A. The house and its contents pass to Ann and Bob.

   B. The house and its contents would pass to Ann.

   C. The house but not its contents would pass to Ann.

   D. The contents but not the house would pass to Ann.

4. Assume the same facts as Question 2 except the letter was entirely in Suki's handwriting and signed. Which answer best explains the most likely disposition of Suki's home and its contents?

   A. The house and its contents pass to Ann and Bob.

   B. The house and its contents would pass to Ann.

   C. The house but not its contents would pass to Ann.

   D. The contents but not the house would pass to Ann.

5. Les and Moe are adult, independent, unmarried brothers. Les and Moe inherited Black-acre as tenants in common when their parent, Dad, died. Following Dad's death, Les and Moe executed a single written document in 2000 meeting the requirements of a valid will. In this document, the first to die devises his interest in Blackacre to the other. In addition, the will devises Blackacre to their niece, Nan, upon the survivor's death. Les has recently died survived by his brother Moe and niece Nan.

   The family has discovered a validly executed will signed in 2010. The testamentary instrument devises the entire estate of Les, including his interest in Blackacre, to friend Fran. Which answer best describes the most likely disposition of Blackacre by reason of the death of Les?

   A. Les's interest passes nonprobate to Moe.

   B. Moe succeeds to Les's interest pursuant to the 2000 will.

   C. Fran succeeds to Les's interest pursuant to the 2010 will.

   D. Fran succeeds to Les's interest pursuant to the 2010 will, and Moe has a breach of contract action against Les's estate.

6. Refer to Question 5. What would your answer be if the 2000 will included a provision stating that Les and Moe agreed never to revoke the 2000 will?

   Answer:

7. Refer to Question 5. What would your answer be if the 2000 document had been a written agreement signed and acknowledged by Les and Moe before a notary public providing that Blackacre would become the survivor's property upon the first of Les and Moe to die?

    A. Les's interest passes nonprobate to Moe.

    B. Moe succeeds to Les's interest upon the probate of the 2000 document.

    C. Fran succeeds to Les's interest pursuant to the 2010 will.

    D. Fran succeeds to Les's interest pursuant to the 2010 will, and Moe has a breach of contract action against the estate of Les.

8. Spouse 1 and Spouse 2 are married with no children. In 2015, they executed new wills. Spouse 1's will leaves all of his property to Spouse 2, so long as Spouse 2 survives him; should Spouse 2 predecease Spouse 1, all property will instead pass to Spouse 2's niece Chelsea. Spouse 2's will leaves all of his property to Spouse 1, so long as Spouse 1 survives him; should Spouse 1 predecease Spouse 2, all property will instead pass to Chelsea.

   Spouse 1 died recently, and his 2015 will has been admitted to probate. Spouse 2 is seeking legal advice. Spouse 2 wants to devise his entire estate to his new boyfriend. What answer best describes the legal advice that should be given to Spouse 2 about leaving his estate to his new boyfriend?

    A. You are free to devise the entire estate to anyone you choose.

    B. You can devise the entire estate to your new boyfriend, but Chelsea may sue you for breach of contract.

    C. You can devise the entire estate to your new boyfriend, but Chelsea may have a breach of contract action against your estate.

    D. You cannot devise the entire estate to your new boyfriend. Chelsea inherited a remainder interest in Spouse 1's estate at his death—and that interest will become possessory at your death.

9. Assume the same facts as Question 8 except that the 2015 wills both contained provisions stating that Spouse 1 and Spouse 2 agreed not to revoke the 2015 wills. What answer best describes the legal advice that should be given to Spouse 2 about leaving his estate to his new boyfriend?

    A. My answer would not change.

    B. You can devise the entire estate to your new boyfriend, but Chelsea may sue you for breach of contract.

    C. You can devise the entire estate to your new boyfriend, but Chelsea may have a breach of contract action against your estate.

    D. You cannot devise the entire estate to your new boyfriend. Chelsea inherited a remainder interest in Spouse 1's estate at his death—and that interest will become possessory at your death.

10. Assume the same facts as Question 9 except that Chelsea died one week after Spouse 1. Chelsea never married and has no children. Chelsea's valid, probated will leaves her estate to her roommate Harvey. What answer best describes the legal advice that can be given to Spouse 2 on these facts?

    A. You can probably devise the entire estate to anyone you choose.

    B. You can probably devise the entire estate to your new boyfriend, but Harvey may sue you for breach of contract.

    C. You can probably devise the entire estate to your new boyfriend, but Harvey may have a breach of contract action against your estate.

    D. You cannot devise the entire estate to your new boyfriend. Chelsea's remainder interest in Spouse 1's estate was devised by Chelsea to Harvey.

11. Assume the same facts as Question 10 except that Chelsea is survived by a child, CC. What answer best describes the legal advice that can be given to Spouse 2 on these facts?

    A. My answer would not change.

    B. You cannot devise the entire estate to your new boyfriend. Chelsea inherited a remainder interest in Spouse 1's estate at his death that she devised to Harvey.

    C. You can devise the entire estate to your new boyfriend, but CC may sue you for breach of contract.

    D. You can devise the entire estate to your new boyfriend, but CC may have a breach of contract action against your estate.

12. Emma and Nadia are two competent, unmarried twin sisters who inherited Blackacre as joint tenants (not tenants in common) when their mother died in 2010. Following the death of their mother, Emma and Nadia executed a single written document in 2011 that satisfied the requirements of will validity in the state of relevant jurisdiction. In this document, the first to die among them would devise her interest in Blackacre to the other. Additionally, the joint will devises Blackacre to their nephew, Charles, upon the death of the second among them.

    Emma has recently died survived by Nadia, Charles, and her sister Gracie (also the mother of Charles). The 2011 joint will included a provision stating that Emma and Nadia agreed never to revoke the 2011 joint will. The family has discovered a validly executed will signed in 2020 by Emma that devises her entire estate—including Blackacre—to her friend Fernando. Which answer best describes the most likely disposition of Blackacre by reason of Emma's death?

    Answer:

13. Assume the same facts as Question 12 except that Emma's 2020 will devised Blackacre to Fernando and the rest of Emma's estate equally to Fernando and Nadia. What answer best describes the likely disposition of Emma's estate?

   A. Emma's interest in Blackacre would pass nonprobate to Nadia.

   B. Emma's interest in Blackacre passes nonprobate to Nadia, but Nadia cannot accept any benefits from Emma's estate unless Nadia conveys Emma's one-half interest to Fernando.

   C. Emma's interest in Blackacre passes nonprobate to Nadia, but Nadia cannot accept any interest in Emma's estate unless Nadia conveys all of Blackacre to Fernando.

   D. Emma's one-half interest in Blackacre passes to Fernando.

14. Assume the same facts as Question 13 except that Nadia died one week before Emma. Nadia also executed a 2020 will, leaving all of her estate to her spouse, Sully, which she married in 2015. She was also survived by a child C1.

   A. Blackacre passes to Fernando, and the balance of Emma's estate passes equally to Fernando and Sully.

   B. Blackacre passes to Fernando, and the balance of Emma's estate passes equally to Fernando and C1.

   C. The entire estate, including Blackacre, passes to Fernando.

   D. Charles will seek specific performance of the original contract between Emma and Nadia.

15. Danny's validly executed will left "all of my property" to his adult child, Adam. On the same day Danny executed the will, he changed the beneficiary of a life insurance policy from his deceased spouse to Danny's other adult child, Bob. Danny's most valuable assets are Blackacre and the $1,000,000 life insurance policy. Explain the most likely disposition of both assets upon Danny's death.

   Answer:

16. Assume the same facts as Question 15 except that the will was executed by Danny five years after he had changed his beneficiary from his deceased spouse to Bob. Would your answer change?

   Answer:

17. Olive's validly executed will, dated 2010, devised any and all life insurance on Olive's life to child, C1, and the rest, residue and remainder of Olive's estate to child C2. C1 and C2 are both adults, and children of a prior marriage of Olive. The only life insurance on Olive's life at the time of her death was a $1 million policy purchased in 2020 and made payable at Olive's death to her spouse, Sunny. Sunny died in 2022, with a valid will that left all to her child by a prior marriage, Celia. Which answer best describes the most likely disposition of the insurance proceeds upon Olive's death?

   A. The insurance company should pay the $1 million to Celia as the devisee under Sunny's will.

   B. The insurance company should pay the $1 million to Celia pursuant to the substituted gift statute.

   C. The insurance company keeps the $1 million since the designated beneficiary died before the insured.

   D. The $1 million becomes part of Olive's probate estate and passes to C1 under her will.

18. Assume the same facts as Question 17 except that the $1 million insurance policy was made payable to Sunny only if she survived Olive, and if not, to C2. Would your answer change?

   Answer:

19. Spouse 1 and Spouse 2 were married and resided in a non-UPC community property state. Spouse 1 has recently died. The significant assets are Blackacre (the separate property of Spouse 1), Whiteacre (the community property of Spouse 1 and Spouse 2), and Greenacre (the separate property of Spouse 2). Spouse 1's valid will has been admitted to probate and devises "all of my property" to Cobb, Spouse 1's child by a prior marriage. Which answer best explains the likely distributions of the three tracts of land?

   A. Blackacre passes to Cobb; Whiteacre and Greenacre are retained by Spouse 2.

   B. Blackacre and Whiteacre pass to Cobb; Greenacre is retained by Spouse 2.

   C. Blackacre and one-half of Whiteacre pass to Cobb; Spouse 2 retains Greenacre and half of Whiteacre.

   D. One-half of both Blackacre and Whiteacre pass to Cobb; Spouse 2 retains Greenacre and half of both Blackacre and Whiteacre.

20. Assume the same facts as Question 19 except that Spouse 1's will devised Whiteacre to Cobb, and the rest, residue, and remainder of Spouse 1's interest to Spouse 2.

Answer:

Surviving Spouses, Former Spouses & Omitted Children

1. Gregor and Shawna have been together for over twenty years, but only married for the last four years. During the marriage, Gregor acquired real and personal property located in the state where they resided; all assets were titled in Gregor's name. He recently died, and his valid will has been admitted to probate. The will leaves all of Gregor's property to Chelsea, the adult child of Gregor and Shawna.

   Assuming all debts and taxes have been satisfied, describe Shawna's interest in the assets.

   Answer:

Note: *Except where specifically indicated, answer the remaining questions in Unit 8 ignoring a surviving spouse's homestead, exempt property, and family allowance rights and assuming the state where they reside is a non-community property state that has adopted the Uniform Probate Code.*

2. Assume the same facts as Question 1 except that Gregor's will leaves Greenacre to Shawna and the "rest, residue, and remainder of my property" to Chelsea. Assuming all debts and taxes have been satisfied, which answer best describes the most likely disposition of Gregor's estate?

   A. Greenacre passes to Shawna, and the remaining assets pass to Chelsea.

   B. Greenacre passes to Shawna, and the remaining assets are shared equally by Shawna and Chelsea.

   C. Greenacre passes to Shawna, and the remaining assets pass 30% to Shawna and 70% to Chelsea.

   D. The value of Greenacre is deducted from Shawna's share of Gregor's estate.

3. Assume the same facts as Question 1 except that Gregor's will leaves all of his property to Shawna. Assuming all debts have been satisfied, which answer best describes the interest of Chelsea in the described assets?

  A. Shawna succeeds to the entire estate.

  B. Chelsea is entitled to an intestate share of the estate, and Shawna owns the balance.

  C. An amount necessary for Chelsea's support during formal administration may be set aside for her, and Shawna owns the balance.

  D. An amount necessary for Chelsea's support for the remainder of her lifetime is set aside, and Shawna owns the balance (if any).

4. Assume the same facts as Question 3 except that Chelsea is a minor at the time of Gregor's death. How would your answer differ?

Answer:

5. Jane and Matt were married for one year. Prior to and during the marriage, Jane acquired real and personal property; all assets were owned by Jane and titled in her name. Jane died recently, and her will has been admitted to probate. The will leaves Greenacre to Charlie and the "rest, residue, and remainder of my property" to Matt. Charlie is Jane's adult child from a prior marriage. Assuming all debts and taxes have been satisfied, which answer best describes the most likely disposition of Jane's estate?

  A. Greenacre passes to Charlie, and the balance will pass to Matt.

  B. Greenacre is divided equally by Charlie and Matt, and the balance of the estate passes to Matt.

  C. Matt must elect to either take his elective share or the amount to which he is entitled under Jane's will.

  D. Charlie must elect to take his intestate share or Greenacre.

6. Blake and Ruby were married for over twenty years. Blake recently died, and his valid will has been admitted to probate. The will leaves his estate to Chomley, his adult child from a prior marriage. Also assume that, at the time of death, Blake was a participant in a pension plan provided by his employer. Additionally, the employer provided each employee with a group life insurance policy as part of its employee benefit package. The employer's records indicate that Blake had not signed the appropriate forms necessary to designate the beneficiaries of the plan and policy in the event of his death. Which answer best describes the most likely disposition of the death benefits payable by reason of the pension plan and the life insurance policy?

A. All benefits pass as part of the probate estate to Chomley.

B. All benefits pass outside of probate to Ruby.

C. The insurance proceeds pass as part of the probate estate to Chomley, and the death benefits pass nonprobate to Ruby.

D. The death benefits pass as part of the probate estate to Chomley, and the insurance proceeds pass nonprobate to Ruby.

7. Assume the same facts as Question 6 except that Ruby and not Blake has died. Ruby's valid will has been admitted to probate, and leaves all of her property to a child by a prior marriage. Explain the most likely effect that Ruby's death will have on Blake's pension plan.

Answer:

8. Judith and Chevy were married. Judith died recently. Her original will left all of her property equally to Chevy and Max, her adult child by a prior marriage. However, Judith revoked the described will (Will 1) shortly before she died and then validly executed a new will (Will 2) leaving "all of my property to Paul." Paul is Judith's friend.

   Will 2 has been admitted to probate. Assuming all debts and taxes have been satisfied, which answer best describes the most likely disposition of Judith's estate.

   A. Paul succeeds to the assets.

   B. Chevy takes an elective share, Max takes an intestate share, and Paul inherits the balance.

   C. Chevy takes an elective share, and Paul inherits the balance.

   D. Max takes an intestate share, and Paul inherits the balance.

9. Assume the same facts as Question 8 except that Judith also signed a form provided by her employer that changed the beneficiary of her ERISA regulated pension plan from Chevy to Paul. Which answer best describes the most likely disposition of the pension plan's death benefit?

   A. It is payable to Paul.

   B. It is payable to Paul and Max.

   C. It is payable to Max.

   D. It is payable to Chevy.

10. Teddy (they/them) died recently, survived by their spouse Sybil and Teddy's parents (Mom and Dad). Teddy never had any children. Their will was validly executed prior to their marriage to Sybil; Teddy never changed the will. It devises Teddy's entire estate to Mom and Dad. What is the most likely disposition of Teddy's estate?

    Answer:

11. Assume the same facts as Question 10 except that Teddy's will was executed after the date of their marriage to Sybil. What is the most likely disposition of Teddy's estate?

    A. The will can be admitted to probate; the entire estate passes to Mom and Dad.

    B. The will cannot be admitted to probate; the entire estate passes to Sybil.

    C. The will can be admitted to probate; Sybil will be entitled to her elective share, if any, and Mom and Dad will succeed to everything else.

    D. The will cannot be admitted to probate; the estate will be shared by Sybil, Mom, and Dad.

12. Andromeda died recently. She was survived by her spouse, Sam, and their two minor children (C1 and C2). Andromeda's will, which was executed after she married Sam but before the birth of the two children, leaves all of her property to Sam. Which answer best describes the most likely disposition of Andromeda's estate?

    A. The will can be admitted to probate; the entire estate passes to Sam.

    B. The will cannot be admitted to probate; the entire estate passes to C1 and C2.

    C. The will cannot be admitted to probate; Sam, C1, and C2 share the estate.

    D. The will can be admitted to probate, but C1 and C2 will be entitled to an intestate share of the estate, and the balance of the entire estate passes to Sam.

13. Assume the same facts as Question 12 except that the will had been executed following the births of C1 and C2. Which answer best describes the most likely disposition of Andromeda's estate?

    A. The will can be admitted to probate; the entire estate passes to Sam.

    B. The will cannot be admitted to probate; the entire estate passes to C1 and C2.

    C. The will cannot be admitted to probate; Sam, C1, and C2 share the estate.

    D. The will can be admitted to probate, but C1 and C2 will be entitled to an intestate share of the estate, and the balance of the estate passes to Sam.

14. Sarah died recently. She was survived by her spouse, Tom, and their minor child C1. She was also survived by C2, the nonmarital child of Sarah and Phillip, conceived during Sarah's extramarital affair. Sarah's will was executed after her marriage to Tom and before the births of C1 and C2. The will leaves all of Sarah's property to Tom. Which answer best describes the most likely disposition of Sarah's estate?

   A. The will can be admitted to probate; the entire estate passes to Tom.

   B. The will cannot be admitted to probate; the entire estate passes to C1 and C2.

   C. The will can be admitted to probate, but C1 and C2 will be entitled to an intestate share of the estate, and the balance of the entire estate passes to Tom.

   D. The will can be admitted to probate, but C2 will be entitled to an intestate share of the estate, and the balance of the entire estate passes to Tom.

15. Trevor died recently. Trevor was survived by his parents, Mom1 and Mom 2. Trevor was divorced from his spouse, Shelly, two years prior to his death. Trevor's valid will leaves his entire estate to Shelly. Trevor executed the will during his marriage, and he failed to change or revoke it. What is the most likely disposition of Trevor's estate?

   Answer:

16. Olivia and Steph were divorced last year after ten years of marriage. Olivia died intestate recently and was survived by her parents, Mom and Dad. Two of the more significant assets existing at the time of Olivia's death were two savings accounts. The bank's records indicate that the first account is a "joint account with survivorship rights" in the names of Olivia and Steph. The second account is "payable on Olivia's death" to Steph. Apparently, Olivia forgot to change the deposit agreements with the bank after the bitter divorce—even though Olivia was awarded ownership of both accounts as part of the divorce settlement and did not have an obligation to leave Steph's name on the accounts. Which answer best describes the most likely disposition of the accounts?

   A. Both accounts pass nonprobate to Steph.

   B. The joint account passes to Mom and Dad, and the payable on Olivia's death (POD) account passes nonprobate to Steph.

   C. The POD account passes to Mom and Dad, and the joint account passes nonprobate to Steph.

   D. Both accounts pass to Mom and Dad.

17. Assume the same facts as Question 16 except that there was also an insurance policy on Olivia's life and a pension plan provided by her employer. The policy was owned by Olivia and still made payable at Olivia's death to Steph. The death benefit of the pension plan was also still payable to Steph. Olivia forgot to change the beneficiary designations, but she was awarded the policy and plan as part of the divorce settlement and was not obligated to designate Steph as the beneficiary of either. What is the most likely disposition of the death benefits?

Answer:

Trusts as Will Substitutes

1. Client explains that she has recently read several books on avoiding probate. These books describe probate as a corrupt system whose primary beneficiaries are lawyers. The books insist that any reasonable person should avoid probate at all costs and that there are never any benefits to property passing through probate. Client also explains that she is a person of "moderate" wealth, recently widowed with three adult children who live in three different states. She is considering moving to one of those states. The solution, as Client understands it, is the "living trust." Is Client's understanding of probate and living trusts accurate? If not, outline for Client a more balanced understanding of the potential advantages and disadvantages of probate compared to "living trusts."

   Answer:

2. Shelby transferred property to Trustee, in trust, to pay Shelby the income for life, and to distribute the trust estate to Bob on her death. Shelby retained the power to revoke or amend the trust. She died intestate, survived by Bob. Bob is not Shelby's intestate heir. The trust instrument was not witnessed and was not otherwise executed in compliance with the statutory formalities for a will. Which of the following best describes the distribution of the trust estate at Shelby's death?

   A. Shelby's trust is invalid. The trust estate must pass through the probate system which means that the trust estate passes to Shelby's intestate heirs.

   B. Shelby's trust is a valid testamentary trust. The trust estate passes through probate to Bob.

   C. Shelby's trust is a valid testamentary trust. The trust estate passes nonprobate to Bob.

   D. Shelby's trust is a valid inter vivos trust, which means that the trust estate passes to Bob outside of the probate system.

3. Assume the same facts as Question 2 except that Shelby has declared herself to be the trustee of the property, rather than naming a third party as trustee. Would the result in Question 2 change?

Answer:

4. Oliver died recently. Oliver was survived by two children, C1 and C2, as well as (i) a great grandchild, Gigi, the only child of C1's deceased child, G1, and (ii) G2, the only child of C2. The family relationships are illustrated below.

Oliver's valid will has been admitted to probate and devises his entire estate to G2. Several years prior to Oliver's death, he had executed a valid inter vivos irrevocable declaration of trust, whereby he declared himself to be the trustee of Blackacre; Frank was named as the successor trustee. At that time, Oliver was married to Wilhamina. The document was duly recorded in the county where Blackacre is located. The terms of the written trust agreement provide that, for the remainder of Oliver's life, he is to receive all of the trust's income; at Oliver's death, all the income is to be paid to Wilhamina; and at the death of the survivor of Oliver and Wilhamina, Blackacre is to be delivered to G1. After the execution of the trust document, but before Oliver died, he and Wilhamina divorced, and G1 died, survived by G1's spouse, S, and G1's only child, Gigi. G1's valid will has been admitted to probate and devises all of his property to S. What is the most likely disposition of the trust estate by reason of Oliver's death?

Answer:

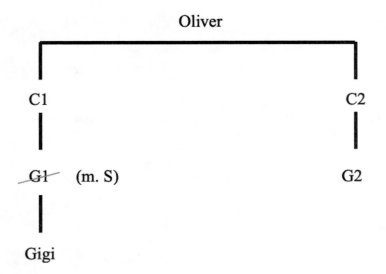

5. Assume the same facts as Question 4 except that the trust agreement, by its own terms, was revocable. Also, there is no evidence that Oliver ever intended to (or actually did) revoke the trust. Would your answer change?

   A. My answer would not change.

   B. Because Wilhamina was no longer Oliver's spouse and G1 predeceased Oliver, Blackacre should be delivered to G2.

   C. Because Wilhamina was no longer Oliver's spouse, Blackacre should be delivered to Oliver's heirs at law.

   D. Because Wilhamina was no longer Oliver's spouse, Blackacre should be delivered to Gigi.

6. Olivia died recently. She was survived by two children, C1 and C2, and two grandchildren, G1 and G2. Prior to her death, Olivia had properly executed a valid, enforceable inter vivos revocable declaration of trust document, whereby she declared himself to be the trustee of the trust. The terms of the trust provide that the income and principal could be used for Olivia's health, education, maintenance, and support during the remainder of her lifetime; at Olivia's death, any real property is to be delivered to G1, and any personal property is to be delivered to G2. There is no evidence that Olivia ever intended to revoke the trust. The trust also provided that, if Olivia was ever unable or unwilling to act, a local bank was named as the successor trustee. At the time the trust document was signed by Olivia, she attached a ten-dollar bill to the trust document. No other assets were made subject to the trust during Olivia's lifetime. Following the execution of the trust document, Olivia validly executed a will, whereby she devised her entire estate to the bank as the successor trustee of the described inter vivos trust. The significant assets of Olivia's estate at the time of her death were Blackacre (fair market value $100,000) and common stocks (fair market value $100,000). Neither the will nor the trust document addresses the payment of Olivia's debts following her death, but there were unsecured debts of $100,000 at Olivia's death. What is the most likely disposition of Blackacre and the stocks by reason of Olivia's death?

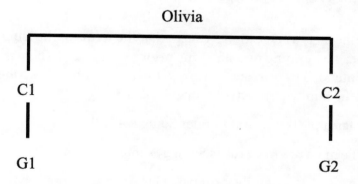

Answer:

7. Assume the same facts as Question 6 except that Olivia was married to Sam at the time that she executed the trust agreement and will and also at the time of her death. Also assume that, prior to Olivia's death, she transferred to herself, as trustee of the trust, $100,000 cash still held in trust at the time of her death. Which answer best describes the legal advice you should give to Sam after he explains to you that he has been apparently disinherited by Olivia?

    A. Don't worry, the trust agreement and will are void.

    B. You are entitled to your marital share of the $100,000, Blackacre, and the stocks.

    C. You are entitled to your marital share of Blackacre and the stocks.

    D. You are entitled to your marital share of Blackacre.

8. Squiggy died last week. One year ago, she typed and signed a letter to her brother, Tom. In the letter, Squiggy wrote that the family farm was being held in an irrevocable trust; Squiggy declared that she was serving as the trustee of the family farm and that she would continue to manage the farm as long as she could, paying herself all the income from the farm each year. However, the letter explained that if Squiggy were ever unable or unwilling to continue as trustee, Tom would serve as trustee until Squiggy died and was to pay Squiggy any income the farm produced. At Squiggy's death, the terms of the letter direct Tom, as trustee, to convey the family farm to Tom, personally. Also, on that same day, Squiggy executed a will, which has now been admitted to probate. Under the terms of the will, Squiggy's estate is devised to Grant, the only child of Squiggy's only child Carol. Despite the letter, record title to the farm remained in Squiggy's name, individually. Both Grant and Carol survived Squiggy. Which answer best describes the most likely disposition of the family farm after Squiggy's death?

    A. The family farm passes to Grant under Squiggy's will.

    B. The family farm passes to Carol as Squiggy's intestate heir.

    C. At Squiggy's death, the family farm passed to Tom as a nonprobate asset.

    D. Tom, as trustee, can convey legal title to Tom, individually.

9. Assume the same facts as Question 8 except that the terms of the letter provide that the trust was revocable by Squiggy at any time prior to her death. There is no evidence that Squiggy ever intended to revoke the trust. Which answer best describes the most likely disposition of the family farm after Squiggy's death?

    A. The family farm passes to Grant under Squiggy's will.

    B. The family farm passes to Carol as Squiggy's intestate heir.

    C. At Squiggy's death, the family farm passed to Tom as a nonprobate asset.

    D. Tom, as trustee, can convey legal title to Tom, individually.

10. In 2024, River created a trust by executing an irrevocable trust agreement with her sister, Theresa. The assets of the trust consist of real and personal property; title is in Theresa's name, as trustee. The beneficiaries are Theresa's adult children, B1 and B2. B1 is entitled to all of the income for the rest of B1's lifetime; at B1's death, Theresa is to deliver the trust estate to B2. After creating the trust, River became very ill and could not work. During River's illness, she fell significantly behind on the payment of many of her debts. Consequently, one of River's creditors has recently obtained a judgment against her and is trying to attach the assets of the trust. Which answer best describes the legal advice you would give to Theresa?

    A. The trust estate is not reachable by River's creditors unless they are tort creditors.

    B. The trust estate is not reachable by River's creditors unless they are a provider of medical services.

    C. The trust estate is not reachable by any of River's creditors.

    D. The trust estate may be reached by River's creditors.

11. Assume the same facts as Question 10 except that the trust agreement by its own terms was revocable by River. Assuming that River has never evidenced any intention to revoke the trust, which answer best describes the legal advice you would give to Theresa?

    A. The trust estate is not reachable by River's creditors unless they are tort creditors.

    B. The trust estate is not reachable by River's creditors unless they are a provider of medical services.

    C. The trust estate is not reachable by any of River's creditors.

    D. The trust estate may be reached by River's creditors.

12. Assume the same facts as Question 11 except that River had just died and that the judgment was obtained by her creditors against her personal representative. Which answer best describes the legal advice you would give to Theresa?

    A. The trust estate is not reachable by River's creditors unless they are tort creditors.

    B. The trust estate is not reachable by River's creditors unless they are a provider of medical services.

    C. The trust estate is not reachable by any of River's creditors.

    D. The trust estate is reachable by River's creditors.

13. Chucky created a revocable trust that becomes irrevocable at his death. He has named himself as trustee. The principal asset of the trust is Chucky's home. The trust provides that at Chucky's death, the home is to be delivered by the successor trustee to his daughter Eliana. Which of the following best describes whether Chucky made a gift for federal transfer tax purposes?

   A. Chucky has not made a gift of the home to Eliana. By retaining the power to revoke the trust, Chucky has not parted with dominion and control over the home.

   B. Chucky has made a gift of his home to Eliana.

   C. Chucky has made a gift of a future interest in his home to Eliana.

   D. Chucky has parted with dominion and control of his home, but a gift made through a trust does not give rise to tax consequences.

14. Assume the same facts as Question 13 except that, prior to Chucky's death, he resigned as trustee. By the terms of the trust, Eliana becomes the successor trustee. Has Chucky made a gift for federal transfer tax purposes?

   Answer:

15. Assume the same facts as Question 14. At Chucky's death, is his home included in his gross estate for federal estate tax purposes?

   A. No, the home is excluded from the gross estate.

   B. Yes, the home is included in the gross estate.

   C. The fair market value of Chucky's retained life estate is included in the gross estate.

   D. The fair market value of Eliana's remainder interest is included in the gross estate.

16. Miley created a revocable trust to pay income to her child, Cal, for Cal's lifetime and then on his death to distribute the principal to Cal's son, George. Miley is the original trustee, and Gringotts Bank is the successor trustee. In the current year, the trust has $5,000 of income, which the trustee distributes to Cal. Which of the following best describes the federal gift tax consequences of the described transactions?

   A. Miley made a gift of the trust corpus to Cal and George when Miley created the trust.

   B. Miley made a gift of a life estate to Cal when Miley created the trust.

   C. Miley made a gift of $5,000 when the income distribution was made to Cal.

   D. Miley did not make a gift to Cal because she has the power to revoke the trust.

17. Assume the same facts as Question 16. Which is the best statement as to how the $5,000 income is taxed for federal *income* tax purposes?

    A. The $5,000 income is taxable to Miley because she retained the power to revoke the trust.

    B. The $5,000 income is taxable to Miley because she retained the power to revoke the trust, but the inclusion will be offset by a deduction for $5,000 because of the distribution to Cal.

    C. The $5,000 income is taxable to "the trust." However, "the trust" will be entitled to an offsetting deduction for the $5,000 distribution to Cal.

    D. Cal will be taxed on $5,000 of income in the year that he receives the $5,000 distribution.

18. Assume the same facts as Question 16. Once a revocable trust has been created and funded by the settlor, the law of trusts governs the administration of the trust estate, and Miley, as trustee, will be held to the same fiduciary standards as Gringotts Bank, if it were serving as the trustee. True or False? Explain your answer.

    Answer:

19. A testator must have testamentary capacity to validly execute a will. Is testamentary capacity required for the creation and funding of a revocable trust intended to be a will substitute?

    Answer:

20. A review of a validly executed and funded inter vivos trust agreement reveals that the terms of the agreement do not specify whether the trust is revocable or irrevocable by the settlor. Both the settlor and the trustee ask, "Is it a revocable trust?"

    Answer:

Express Trusts

1. True or False? An express trust is a legally recognizable entity for state law purposes. Explain your answer.

   Answer:

2. Oskar has one child, a daughter Cici, and one grandchild through Cici named Ginger. Oskar conveyed his property Blackacre to his cousin, Freddie. After the conveyance, Oskar told Ginger that, at the time of the conveyance, he and Freddie discussed the following:

   i) Freddie would manage Blackacre until Oskar's death;

   ii) upon Oskar's death, Freddie would convey Blackacre to Ginger; and,

   iii) Freddie will pay to Oskar any income generated by Blackacre during Oskar's lifetime.

   The deed was duly recorded. No income had been generated since the conveyance. Oskar recently died. Record legal title is in Freddie's name. Freddie denies that he had any agreement with Oskar concerning what Freddie was obligated to do with the property. Which answer best describes the most likely disposition of Blackacre following Oskar's death?

   A. Ginger can have the court enforce the terms of the oral express trust.

   B. Freddie retains Blackacre since the oral express trust is unenforceable.

   C. Cici will have the court impose a resulting trust on Freddie in favor of Cici since Oskar's attempt to create an express trust failed.

   D. Ginger will have the court impose a constructive trust on Freddie in favor of Ginger because Freddie breached the oral agreement.

3. Assume the same facts as Question 2 except that other friends of Oskar were present at the time of the original transaction between Oskar and Freddie, and they are willing and able to testify as to the oral agreement. What is the most likely disposition of Blackacre by reason of Oskar's death?

   Answer:

4. Assume the same facts as Question 3 except that Freddie admits that he and Oskar had the oral agreement but says Freddie will not abide by the agreement since it was not in writing. Which answer best describes the most likely disposition of Blackacre following Oskar's death?

   A. Ginger can have the court enforce the terms of the oral express trust.

   B. Freddie retains Blackacre since the oral express trust is unenforceable.

   C. Cici will have the court impose a resulting trust on Freddie in favor of Cici since Oskar's attempt to create an express trust failed.

   D. Ginger will have the court impose a constructive trust on Freddie in favor of Ginger because Freddie breached the oral agreement.

5. Assume the same facts as Question 3 except that Freddie was also Oskar's long-time accountant and financial advisor. Which answer best describes the most likely disposition of Blackacre following Oskar's death?

   A. Ginger will ask the court to enforce the terms of the oral express trust.

   B. Freddie retains Blackacre since the oral express trust is unenforceable.

   C. Ginger will have the court impose a constructive trust on Freddie in favor of Ginger.

   D. Cici will have the court impose a resulting trust on Freddie in favor of Cici.

6. Lakshmi has one child, a daughter Cici, and one grandchild through Cici named Ginger. Lakshmi has assigned eBay (NASDAQ: EBAY) common stock certificates to his cousin, Freddie. At the time of the assignment, Lakshmi and Freddie orally agreed upon the following:

   (i) that Freddie would hold the stock until Lakshmi's death;

   (ii) upon Lakshmi's death, Freddie would assign the stock to Ginger; and,

   (iii) Freddie will pay to Lakshmi any dividends paid by eBay during Lakshmi's lifetime.

Lakshmi has recently died intestate. The stock has been registered in Freddie's name, and he now denies that he had any agreement with Lakshmi regarding the eBay stock after Lakshmi's death. However, friends of both Lakshmi and Freddie were present at the time of the original transaction and are willing and able to testify that there was the oral agreement. Which answer best describes the most likely disposition of the shares of stock by reason of Lakshmi's death?

A. Ginger will have the court impose a constructive trust on Freddie in favor of Ginger because Freddie breached the oral agreement.

B. Ginger will have the court enforce the terms of the oral express trust.

C. Cici will have the court impose a resulting trust on Freddie in favor of Cici because Lakshmi's attempt to create an express trust failed.

D. Freddie retains the stock since the oral express trust is unenforceable.

7. Star has one child, a daughter Cici, and one grandchild through Cici named Ginger. Star has conveyed Blackacre to her friend, "Freddie, as trustee." At the time of the conveyance, Star and Freddie orally agreed—in the presence of credible, disinterested witnesses—upon the following:

    (i) Freddie would manage Blackacre until Star's death;

    (ii) upon Star's death, Freddie would convey Blackacre to Ginger; and,

    (iii) Freddie will pay to Star any income generated by Blackacre during her lifetime.

The deed was duly recorded. No income has been generated since the conveyance. Star has recently died intestate. Freddie now claims that he is not required to convey the property to Ginger since the terms of the agreement were not in writing. Which answer best describes the most likely disposition of Blackacre by reason of Star's death?

A. Ginger will have the court enforce the terms of the oral express trust.

B. Ginger will have the court impose a constructive trust on Freddie in favor of Ginger because Freddie breached the oral agreement.

C. Cici will have the court impose a resulting trust on Freddie in favor of Cici because Star's attempt to create an express trust failed.

D. Freddie will retain Blackacre since the oral express trust is unenforceable.

8. Assume the same facts as Question 7 except that (i) there is no admissible evidence of the terms of the oral agreement between Star and Freddie about Freddie's obligations concerning the property, and (ii) the duly recorded deed conveyed Blackacre to "Freddie, as trustee for Ginger." Which answer best describes the most likely disposition of Blackacre by reason of Star's death?

    A. Fee simple title is vested in Cici.

    B. Fee simple title is vested in Ginger.

    C. Freddie owns the legal title, and Ginger owns the equitable interests.

    D. Freddie owns the legal title, and Cici owns the equitable interests.

9. Reyes has one child, a daughter Cici, and one grandchild through Cici named Ginger. Reyes has conveyed Blackacre to her friend, "Freddie, as trustee." At the time of the conveyance, Reyes and Freddie orally agreed upon the following:

    (i) that Freddie would manage Blackacre until Reyes's death; and,

    (ii) upon Reyes's death, Freddie would convey Blackacre to Ginger.

    The deed was duly recorded. Record legal title is in Freddie's name. Freddie acknowledges the oral agreement he had with Reyes. However, a creditor of Freddie has obtained a judgment against him and is seeking to satisfy the judgment by attaching Blackacre. Assuming the relevant statute of frauds does not require a trust of real property to be in writing, what legal advice should be given to Freddie?

    Answer:

10. Assume the same facts as Question 9, except that the relevant statute of frauds requires a trust of real property to be in writing. How would your answer differ?

    Answer:

11. Assume the same facts as Question 9 except that a writing signed by Reyes and Freddie evidencing the creation of the trust and its terms has been discovered. However, a creditor of Freddie has a judgment against him and is seeking to satisfy the judgment by attaching Blackacre. Which answer best describes the legal advice that should be given to Freddie?

A. You can convey Blackacre to Ginger pursuant to your agreement with Reyes notwithstanding the judgment against you.

B. You can convey Blackacre to Cici pursuant to the agreement with Reyes, but the creditor will have it set aside as a transfer in fraud of creditors.

C. You can allow the creditor to attach Blackacre notwithstanding your agreement with Reyes.

D. The creditor can attach Blackacre regardless of what you decide to do.

12. Octavia has one child, a daughter Cici, and one grandchild through Cici named Ginger. Octavia and Freddie, a friend of Octavia, entered into a written trust agreement signed by both Octavia and Freddie. Following the execution of the trust agreement, Octavia conveyed Blackacre to Freddie, and the recorded legal title is in his name. The terms of the trust agreement direct Freddie to manage Blackacre until Octavia's death, and then Freddie is to convey the property to Ginger.

   Octavia died intestate recently. Ginger died following the conveyance to Freddie, but prior to Octavia's death. Also assume Ginger died intestate and was survived by her mother Cici and father Doug. Ginger never married and had no descendants. Cici and Doug are divorced. Which answer best describes the most likely disposition of Blackacre by reason of Octavia's death?

   A. Cici will have the court impose a resulting trust on Freddie in favor of Cici.

   B. Cici will ask the court to enforce the terms of the express trust.

   C. Cici and Doug will ask the court to enforce the terms of the express trust.

   D. Freddie retains fee simple title.

13. Assume the same facts as Question 12 except that the terms of the written express trust directed Freddie to deliver Blackacre at Octavia's death to Ginger, if Ginger survived Octavia. Which answer would most likely describe the disposition of Blackacre by reason of Octavia's death?

   A. Freddie retains fee simple title.

   B. Cici will have the court impose a resulting trust on Freddie in favor of Cici.

   C. Cici will have the court enforce the terms of the express trust.

   D. Cici and Doug will have the court enforce the terms of the express trust.

14. Mai Roland is survived by one child, Lenore, and one grandchild, Rolf, through another child of Mai who predeceased her. Mai died recently. Her valid will has been admitted to probate and devises 1,000 shares of the common stock of a publicly held corporation to Lenore "with the request" that Lenore deliver the shares to Rolf, provided that he "graduates from college"; the rest, residue, and remainder of Mai's estate is devised to a charity.

    Rolf was eighteen years old at the time of Mai's death and had not yet graduated from high school. Which answer best explains the likely disposition of the shares of stock by reason of Mai's death?

    A. Lenore is the trustee of an express trust for the benefit of Rolf.

    B. Rolf will have the court impose a constructive trust on Lenore in favor of Rolf to avoid unjust enrichment.

    C. The charity will have the court impose a resulting trust on Lenore in favor of Rolf, since Mai's attempt to create an express trust failed.

    D. Lenore owns the stock.

15. Assume the same facts as Question 14 except that Mai's will devises the 1,000 shares to "Lenore to be delivered to Rolf when he graduates from college." Which answer best explains the likely disposition of the shares of stock by reason of Mai's death?

    A. Lenore is the trustee of an express trust for the benefit of Rolf.

    B. Rolf will have the court impose a constructive trust on Lenore in favor of Rolf to avoid unjust enrichment.

    C. The charity will have the court impose a resulting trust on Lenore in favor of Rolf, since Mai's attempt to create an express trust failed.

    D. Lenore owns the stock.

16. Assume the same facts as Question 15 except that Rolf died after the will was executed by Mai but before she died. Rolf had not yet graduated from college. Which answer best explains the likely disposition of the shares of stock by reason of Mai's death.

    A. Lenore is the trustee of an express trust for the benefit of Rolf's heirs.

    B. The charity owns the stock.

    C. The charity will have the court impose a resulting trust on Lenore in favor of the charity because Mai's attempt to create an express trust failed.

    D. Lenore owns the stock.

17. Hector died recently. He is survived by one child, daughter Jan, and Jan's son (his grand-child) Ed. Prior to Hector's death, he told several friends that he was holding Blackacre as trustee for the benefit of Ed, and when Ed reached age 21, Hector was going to convey legal title to Ed. Record legal title then and now is in Hector's name. There is no written evidence of Hector's stated intent. When Hector died, Ed was age 18. Jan now claims Blackacre as Ed's heir. Assuming the statute of frauds does not require a trust of real property to be in writing, what is the most likely disposition of Blackacre by reason of Hector's death?

    Answer:

18. Assume the same facts as Question 17 except that the property involved is 1,000 shares of stock in a publicly held corporation. Which answer best explains the most likely disposition of the 1,000 shares of stock?

    A. The court should appoint a successor trustee of the express trust to manage the stock until Ed attains age 21.

    B. The trust is unenforceable; the stock passes to Jan.

    C. Ed will have the court impose a constructive trust on Jan to avoid unjust enrichment by Jan.

    D. The personal representative of Hector's estate should retain the stock until Ed attains age 21 and then deliver it to Ed.

19. Assume the same facts as Question 17 except that a written memorandum stating Hector's intent and signed by Hector has been discovered. Record legal title to Blackacre remains in Hector's name. Which answer best describes the most likely disposition of Blackacre by reason of Hector's death?

    A. The court should appoint a successor trustee of the express trust to manage Blackacre until Ed attains age 21.

    B. The trust is unenforceable; Blackacre passes to Jan.

    C. Ed will have the court impose a constructive trust on Jan to avoid unjust enrichment by Jan.

    D. The personal representative of Hector's estate should retain Blackacre until Ed attains age 21 and then deliver Blackacre to Ed.

20. Assume the same facts as Question 19 except that shortly prior to Hector's death, he conveyed Blackacre as a gift to his friend George. George was unaware of the trust. Which answer best describes the legal advice you would give to Ed?

A. That's life; there's nothing you can do.

B. You should file suit against Hector's estate for breach of fiduciary duty.

C. You should have the court impose a constructive trust on George because Hector breached a fiduciary duty.

D. You should file suit against George for conspiring with Hector to breach a fiduciary duty.

21. Maricella died recently. She is survived by one adult child, daughter Celia, and Celia's daughter (Maricella's grandchild) Liz. Prior to Maricella's death, in a written document that she signed, she declared that she was serving as the trustee of Blackacre. The document also explains that she would manage Blackacre so long as she was willing and able to do so; if Maricella would ever be unable or unwilling to continue to serve as trustee, her friend Freddie would serve as trustee until Maricella's death. The document also provides that Freddie, as trustee, was to convey Blackacre to Freddie at the time of Maricella's death. Additionally, prior to her death, Maricella or Freddie—whoever was serving as trustee—was to pay to Maricella any income Blackacre generated. The terms of the written document also provide that the trust was irrevocable.

Maricella's valid will, executed the same day as the described written document, has been admitted to probate and devises all of her estate to Liz. Record title to Blackacre stayed in Maricella's name until she died. Which answer best describes the most likely disposition of Blackacre by reason of Maricella's death?

A. Because the document was not executed with testamentary formalities, Blackacre passes to Liz.

B. Because the document was not executed with testamentary formalities, Blackacre passes to Celia.

C. Blackacre passes to Freddie by reason of Maricella's death.

D. Freddie, as trustee, can convey legal title to Freddie, individually.

22. Assume the same facts as Question 21 except that the terms of the described written document provide that the trust was revocable by Maricella at any time prior to her death. There is no evidence that Maricella ever intended to revoke the trust. Which answer best describes the most likely disposition of Blackacre by reason of Maricella's death?

A. Because the document was not executed with testamentary formalities, Blackacre passes to Liz.

B. Because the document was not executed with testamentary formalities, Blackacre passes to Celia.

C. Blackacre passes to Freddie by reason of Maricella's death.

D. Freddie, as trustee, can convey legal title to Freddie, individually.

23. Orin was the settlor of a valid, enforceable irrevocable express trust. The trustee is Tomás; the beneficiaries are two adults, Uma and Gary. According to the terms of the trust agreement, Uma is entitled to all the trust income for the rest of Uma's lifetime; at her death, the trustee is to distribute the trust estate to Gary. Tomás has recently learned that Uma has assigned her interest in the trust to Quinn (they/them). Quinn is demanding that the trustee distribute the trust income to them. Which answer best describes the legal advice that should be given to Tomás?

A. The assignment is valid; you should distribute the income to Quinn as long as Uma is alive.

B. The assignment is void; you should continue to pay Uma for the remainder of her lifetime.

C. Since the assignment is not enforceable against the trust, you should continue to pay the income to Uma for the rest of her lifetime.

D. Uma's interest in the trust has terminated; the remaining trust assets should be delivered to Gary.

24. Assume the same facts as Question 23 except that the trust agreement only authorizes Tomás to deliver to Uma as much income as she needs for her health, support, education, or maintenance. Which answer best describes the legal advice that should be given to Tomás?

A. The assignment is valid; you should pay all the income to Quinn for the rest of Uma's lifetime.

B. The assignment is valid; you should distribute to Quinn whatever income you would have distributed to Uma for her health, support, education, or maintenance.

C. The assignment may be valid if Quinn paid Uma good and valuable consideration in exchange for the assignment.

D. The assignment may be valid if Quinn provided services for Uma's health, support, education, or maintenance.

25. Assume the same facts as Question 23 except that the trust agreement authorized Tomás to distribute to Uma only as much income as Tomás, in his discretion, deems appropriate. What legal advice should be given to Tomás under the circumstances?

Answer:

26. Assume the same facts as Question 23 except that it was Gary, not Uma, who assigned Gary's interest in the trust estate to Quinn. Which answer best describes the legal advice that should be given to Tomás under the circumstances?

   A. The assignment is void; you should continue to pay the income to Uma and deliver the trust estate to Gary when Uma dies.

   B. The assignment is valid; Tomás should deliver the trust estate to Quinn now.

   C. The assignment is valid; Tomás should deliver the trust estate to Quinn when Uma dies.

   D. The assignment is enforceable only against Gary; you should continue to pay the income to Uma and deliver the trust estate to Gary when Uma dies.

27. Assume the same facts as Question 26 except that the trust agreement includes a provision that prohibits both voluntary and involuntary assignments of beneficial interests by beneficiaries. Which answer best describes the legal effect of the assignment?

   A. The assignment is unenforceable against Tomás who can deliver the trust estate to Gary when Uma dies.

   B. The assignment is valid; Tomás should deliver the trust estate to Quinn when Uma dies.

   C. The assignment is valid only if Quinn paid good and valuable consideration for the assignment.

   D. The assignment is voidable at the election of Gary.

28. Assume the same facts as Question 23 except that both Uma and Gary assigned their interests in the trust estate to Tomás, not Quinn. Which answer best explains the most likely disposition of the trust estate under those circumstances?

   A. The assignment can be set aside by Orin.

   B. The assignment is valid; Tomás is now the beneficiary of the trust.

   C. The assignment is valid; Tomás acquires fee simple title to the trust estate.

   D. The assignment may be voidable by Uma and Gary.

29. Agnar created a valid, enforceable irrevocable express trust. Ylfa is the trustee; Carrie and Ginny are the beneficiaries. The trust agreement provides that Ylfa is to pay to Carrie only as much income as Ylfa, in her discretion, determines is appropriate, as long as Carrie is alive; at her death, Ylfa is to deliver the remaining trust estate to Ginny. Ylfa has been making distributions of income to Carrie, and Carrie believes the amount is not enough; Ginny believes the amount is too much. Which parties have standing to challenge the distributions made by Ylfa?

Answer:

30. Assume the same facts as Question 29 except that the terms of the trust granted the trustee "absolute, uncontrolled discretion." Which parties have standing to challenge the distributions made by Ylfa?

A. Ylfa is not answerable to the beneficiaries.

B. The court will have to substitute its judgment for that of Ylfa's judgment.

C. Ylfa must prove that she did not abuse her discretion.

D. Carrie or Ginny must prove that Ylfa abused her discretion.

31. Assume the same facts as Question 29 except that the trust agreement authorized Ylfa to distribute to Carrie only as much income as was necessary for her health, support, education, or maintenance. Which answer best describes the burden of proof in litigation involving the appropriate amount?

A. Ylfa must prove that Ylfa did not abuse Ylfa's discretion.

B. Ylfa must prove the amount distributed was needed for Carrie's health, support, education, or maintenance.

C. Carrie or Ginny must prove the amount was not the amount needed for Carrie's health, support, education, or maintenance.

D. Carrie or Ginny must prove that Ylfa abused her discretion.

Creditor Rights

1. Jeremiah created a valid, enforceable irrevocable express trust last year by a written agreement. The assets of the trust consist of real and personal property. The trustee is Ted; the beneficiaries are Clay and Gertrude. Clay is entitled to all the income for the rest of Clay's lifetime; at Clay's death, Ted is to deliver the trust estate to Gertrude. A creditor of Jeremiah has recently obtained a judgment against him and is trying to attach the assets of the trust. Which answer best describes the legal advice you would give to Ted?

    A. The trust estate is not reachable by Jeremiah's creditors.

    B. The trust estate is not reachable by Jeremiah's creditors unless they are tort creditors.

    C. The trust estate may be reached by Jeremiah's creditors.

    D. The trust estate is reachable by Jeremiah's creditors.

2. Assume the same facts as Question 1, except that the trust agreement by its own terms was revocable by Jeremiah; however, Jeremiah has never evidenced any intention to revoke the trust. Which answer best describes the legal advice you would give to Ted?

    A. The trust estate is not reachable by Jeremiah's creditors.

    B. The trust estate is not reachable by Jeremiah's creditors unless they are tort creditors.

    C. The trust estate may be reached by Jeremiah's creditors.

    D. The trust estate is reachable by Jeremiah's creditors.

3. Assume the same facts as Question 2 except that Jeremiah had just died and that the judgment was obtained by Jeremiah's creditor against his personal representative. Which answer best describes the legal advice you would give to Ted?

    A. The trust estate is not reachable by Jeremiah's creditors.

    B. The trust estate is not reachable by Jeremiah's creditors unless they are tort creditors.

    C. The trust estate may be reached by Jeremiah's creditors.

    D. The trust estate is reachable by Jeremiah's creditors.

4. Assume the same facts as Question 1 except that the irrevocable trust agreement was pursuant to an oral understanding between Jeremiah and Ted. Which answer best describes the legal advice you would give to Ted under the circumstances?

    A. The trust estate is not reachable by Jeremiah's creditors.

    B. The trust estate is not reachable by Jeremiah's creditors unless they are tort creditors.

    C. The trust estate may be reached by Jeremiah's creditors.

    D. The trust estate is reachable by Jeremiah's creditors.

5. Assume the same facts as Question 1 except that the creditor was a creditor of Ted, not Jeremiah, and has obtained a judgment against Ted arising out of a situation totally unrelated to the trust property. Which answer best describes the legal advice that you would give to Ted in view of these circumstances?

    A. The trust estate is not reachable by your creditors.

    B. The trust estate is not reachable by your creditors unless they are tort creditors.

    C. The trust estate may be reachable depending upon the facts and circumstances.

    D. The trust estate is reachable to satisfy your creditors.

6. Assume the same facts as Question 5 except that the trust agreement was pursuant to an oral agreement between Jeremiah and Ted, and Ted wishes to protect the interests of Clay and Gertrude. What legal advice would you give to Ted?

    Answer:

7. Kirabo created a valid, enforceable, irrevocable express trust last year by a written agreement. The assets of the trust consist of real and personal property. The trustee is Vanna; the beneficiaries are Bran and Caitlin. Bran is entitled to the income for the rest of his lifetime; at his death, Vanna is to deliver the estate to Caitlin. A former business associate of Bran has obtained a judgment against him related to a business transaction unrelated to the trust while the trust was in existence. Which answer best describes the legal advice you would give to Vanna under the circumstances?

    A. The trust estate can be attached to satisfy the debt.

    B. Trust income can be attached to satisfy the debt.

    C. Trust income can be attached only if the claim is tortious in nature.

    D. The trust income cannot be attached to satisfy the debt.

8. Assume the same facts as Question 7 except that the trust agreement only authorizes Vanna to distribute to Bran as much income as Vanna, in her discretion, determines is appropriate. Which answer best describes the legal advice you would give to Vanna under the circumstances?

    A. The trust estate can be attached to satisfy the debt.

    B. Trust income can be attached to satisfy the debt.

    C. Trust income can be attached only if the claim is tortious in nature.

    D. The trust income cannot be attached to satisfy the debt.

9. Assume the same facts as Question 7 except that Vanna, according to the terms of the trust agreement, can only distribute to Bran such amounts of income as are necessary for his health, education, maintenance, or support. Which answer best describes the legal advice you would give to Vanna under the circumstances?

    A. The trust estate can be attached to satisfy the debt.

    B. Trust income can be attached to satisfy the debt.

    C. Trust income can be attached only if the claim is tortious in nature.

    D. The trust income cannot be attached to satisfy the debt.

10. Assume the same facts as Question 9 except that the creditor is a hospital that provided medical services to Bran. Which answer best describes the legal advice you would give to Vanna under the circumstances?

    A. The trust estate can be attached to satisfy the debt.

    B. Trust income can be attached to satisfy the debt.

    C. Trust income can be attached only if the creditor has exhausted Bran's individual assets.

    D. The trust income cannot be attached to satisfy the debt.

11. Assume the same facts as Question 7 except that the creditor is a creditor of Caitlin, not Bran, and has a judgment against Caitlin. Which answer best describes the legal advice that should be given to Vanna under the circumstances?

    A. The trust estate can be attached to satisfy Caitlin's debt.

    B. Caitlin's interest in the trust estate can be attached to satisfy her debt.

    C. The trust estate must be sold in order to pay the debt.

    D. The trust income can be attached.

12. Assume the same facts as Questions 7 and 11. How would your answers differ if the trust agreement included a provision stating expressly that the beneficiaries' interests in the trust could not be attached to satisfy any debt of a beneficiary?

Answer:

13. Assume the same facts as Question 11 except that the only provision in the trust agreement relating to creditors of beneficiaries is one that provides that, if a creditor of Bran's ever attempts to attach his interest, the interest terminates and passes to Caitlin; if a creditor of Caitlin ever attempts to attach the interest of Caitlin, the interest terminates and passes to a charity. Which answer best describes the legal advice you give Vanna if a creditor seeks to attach Caitlin's interest?

    A. The provision is valid; the trustee should terminate the trust by delivering the property to the charity.

    B. The provision is valid; the trustee should terminate the trust by delivering the property to Bran.

    C. The provision is valid; Caitlin's interest has passed to the charity.

    D. The provision is not valid; the creditor can attach Caitlin's interest in the trust.

14. Kermit is involved in some shady business dealings. He anticipates a multimillion-dollar lawsuit will be filed at some point in time, but he is aware of no potential lawsuits as of today. Which of the following approaches has the best chance of keeping $10 million of his assets out of the hands of some future judgment creditor?

    A. Placing $10 million into an irrevocable spendthrift trust with himself as the income beneficiary and his children as the remainder beneficiaries.

    B. Placing $10 million into an irrevocable trust with his children as the only beneficiaries.

    C. Placing $10 million into a revocable spendthrift trust with his children as the only beneficiaries.

    D. Drafting a will that leaves the entirety of his estate to his children.

Powers of Appointment

1. Explain the difference between general powers of appointment and non-general powers of appointment.

   Answer:

2. Ophelia created a valid, enforceable irrevocable express trust. The terms of the written trust agreement direct the trustee, Xia, to pay the income to Arnold for the rest of his lifetime; at the time of Arnold's death, Xia is directed to deliver the trust estate to Arnolds's children if he appoints to them by will. In default of appointment, Xia is to deliver the trust estate to a charity. At the time the trust was created, Arnold had three children, C1, C2, and C3. Following the creation of the trust, Arnold validly executed a will in which he expressly appoints the trust estate to C1 and C2. Which answer best describes the current beneficiaries of the trust?

   A. Arnold.

   B. Arnold, C1, C2, C3, and the charity.

   C. Arnold and the charity.

   D. Arnold, C1, C2, and the charity.

3. Assume the same facts as Question 2 except that Arnold has recently died, survived by his children, C1, C2, and C3. Arnold's will has been admitted to probate. Which answer best describes who is likely to succeed to the trust estate by reason of his death?

   A. The charity.

   B. C1 and C2.

   C. C1, C2, and the charity.

   D. C1, C2, and C3.

4. Assume the same facts as Question 2 except that Arnold's will has been admitted to probate, but also assume that the will does not make any reference to Arnold's power of appointment or the trust estate; it simply devises all of his property to his children. Which answer best describes the most likely disposition of the trust estate?

   A. Xia should distribute it to the charity.

   B. Xia should distribute it to Arnold's children.

   C. The children can have the court impose a constructive trust on the charity to avoid unjust enrichment.

   D. The children can have the court impose a resulting trust on the charity to avoid unjust enrichment.

5. Assume the same facts as Question 3 except that the will described in Question 2 does not comply with a technical requirement of the relevant wills act. What is the most likely disposition of the trust estate?

   Answer:

6. Ophelia created a valid, enforceable irrevocable express trust. The terms of the written trust agreement direct the trustee, Xia, to pay the income to Arnold for the rest of Arnold's lifetime; at the time of Arnold's death, Xia is directed to deliver the trust estate to his children if Arnold appoints to them by will. In default of appointment, Xia is to deliver the trust estate to a charity.

   At the time the trust was created, Arnold had three children, C1, C2, and C3. Following the creation of the trust, Arnold validly executed a will in which he expressly appoints the trust estate to C1 and C2. Arnold then expressly revoked this will and exercised the power of appointment in favor of S, the spouse that Arnold married shortly before his death. The revoked will also devised his probate estate to S.

   Arnold has recently died, survived by his children, C1, C2, and C3, and his spouse S. What result?

   Answer:

7. Assume the same facts as Question 6 except that Arnold never executed a will and died intestate. Which answer best describes the most likely disposition of the trust estate?

   A. Xia should distribute it to the charity.

   B. Xia should distribute it to the children.

   C. The children can have the court impose a constructive trust on the charity to avoid unjust enrichment.

   D. The children can have the court impose a resulting trust on the charity to avoid unjust enrichment.

8. Abraxas died years ago. Abraxas' valid will was admitted to probate and devised Blackacre to Bette for life, remainder to such person or persons as Bette appoints by will, including Bette's estate, and, in default of appointment, to a charity. Bette died recently survived by Bette's spouse, Sam, and her child, Chuck. Bette's valid, probated will specifically appoints Blackacre to Chuck and devises all of Bette's estate to Sam. Which answer best describes the most likely disposition of Blackacre?

   A. It passes to the charity.

   B. It passes to Chuck.

   C. It passes to Chuck, subject to Sam's marital share.

   D. It passes to the charity, subject to Sam's marital share.

9. Assume the same facts as Question 8 except that Bette's will simply devises all of her property to Chuck. There is no reference in her will to Blackacre or Bette's power of appointment. Which answer best describes the most likely disposition of Blackacre by reason of Bette's death?

   A. It passes to Chuck.

   B. It passes to Chuck, subject to Sam's marital share.

   C. It passes to the charity.

   D. It passes to the charity, subject to Sam's marital share.

10. Assume the same facts as Question 8 except that Chuck predeceased Bette survived by Chuck's parents (Bette and Sam). What is the most likely disposition of Blackacre?

Answer:

11. Assume the same facts as Question 8 except that Chuck predeceased Bette survived by Chuck's spouse, CS, and his child, CC. Which answer best explains the most likely disposition of Blackacre by reason of Bette's death?

    A. It passes to CC.

    B. It passes to CS.

    C. It passes to Sam.

    D. It passes to the charity.

12. Assume the same facts as Question 8 except that at the time of Bette's death, her liabilities exceeded her assets. Explain the rights of Bette's creditors, if any, in and to Blackacre.

    Answer:

13. Ten years ago, Anurak created an irrevocable, valid inter vivos express written trust declaration with himself named as trustee. At the time the trust was created, Anurak was solvent and remained solvent right after the trust was funded. The terms of the trust declare the trust to be a "spendthrift" trust and authorize Anurak to distribute to himself as much income and/or principal as he needs for his health, support, education, or maintenance. In addition, Anurak may appoint all or any part of the trust estate to any one or more of his children by deed during his lifetime or at his death by will. At the time of Anurak's death, the successor trustee is to distribute any remaining trust assets to a charity.

    No trust assets have been distributed to Anurak or his children. He is now in financial difficulties due to bad investments made last year. Anurak's creditors are seeking assets to attach. These creditors are seeking your legal advice about the trust and its trust estate. Which answer best describes the legal advice you should give the creditors regarding Anurak's interest in the trust?

    A. You cannot reach any part of the trust estate.

    B. You may be able to reach whatever assets Anurak may distribute to his children.

    C. You may be able to attach only what Anurak distributes to himself.

    D. You can attach all or any part of the trust estate.

14. Assume the same facts as Question 13 except that Anurak's parent created the trust for the benefit of Anurak. What legal advice would you give to his creditors? Would that advice differ if the trust agreement included a "spendthrift" provision?

Answer:

15. Refer to both Questions 13 and 14 and assume Anurak's financial difficulties were resolved prior to his death. At the time of his death, will the trust estates of the two trusts be included in Anurak's gross estate for federal estate tax purposes?

A. Both trust estates will be included in Anurak's gross estate.

B. Both trust estates will be excluded from Anurak's gross estate.

C. The trust estate described in Question 13 is excluded and the other is included.

D. The trust estate described in Question 14 is excluded and the other is included.

Death & Taxes

1. Politicians debate the advisability of the government imposing a "death tax." Republicans typically argue in favor of its repeal; Democrats typically favor its retention. Explain what is the "death tax."

   Answer:

2. Bijan died. His valid will was admitted to probate ten years ago and devised Blackacre to Amira for life, remainder to such of Amira's children as she appoints by will, and in default of appointment, to another child of Bijan, Cira. The rest, residue, and remainder of Bijan's estate was devised to Cira. Additionally, during his lifetime, Bijan had created a valid, irrevocable inter vivos express trust which directed the trustee, Trustee, to pay the income to Amira during her lifetime; at her death, Trustee is directed to distribute the principal to anyone, including Amira's estate, as she may appoint by will, and in default of appointment, to Big State University. Amira died with a valid will expressly exercising both powers in favor of her children. Which answer best explains whether Blackacre and the trust estate of the trust are included in Amira's gross estate for federal transfer tax purposes?

   A. Both Blackacre and the trust estate will be included in Amira's gross estate.

   B. Neither Blackacre nor the trust estate will be included in Amira's gross estate.

   C. Blackacre, but not the trust estate, will be included in Amira's gross estate.

   D. The trust estate, but not Blackacre, will be included in Amira's gross estate.

3. Assume the same facts as Question 2 except that Amira died intestate, survived by her spouse, Sarah, and her children. Which answer best explains whether Blackacre and the trust estate of the trust will be included in Amira's gross estate for federal transfer tax purposes?

   A. Both Blackacre and the trust estate will be included in Amira's gross estate.

   B. Neither Blackacre nor the trust estate will be included in Amira's gross estate.

   C. Blackacre, but not the trust estate, will be included in Amira's gross estate.

   D. The trust estate, but not Blackacre, will be included in Amira's gross estate.

4. Assume the same facts as Question 3 except that the trust estate has a fair market value of $10,000,000. Will the inclusion of the trust estate in Amira's gross estate generate any federal transfer tax liability?

    Answer:

5. Assume the same facts as Question 3. Amira's probate estate includes her home and its contents, an auto, and her investments. State law directs that the home, its contents, and the auto are to be set aside for Sarah's use during formal administration. Which probate assets are included in Amira's gross estate?

    A. The entire probate estate.

    B. The investments, but not the home, its contents, and the auto.

    C. The investments and the auto, but not the home and its contents.

    D. None are part of the probate estate since Amira died intestate.

6. Assume the same facts as Question 5 except that Amira had a valid will that devised her probate estate to her spouse, Sarah. Which probate assets are included in Amira's gross estate?

    Answer:

7. Stella created two valid, enforceable irrevocable inter vivos express trusts. Beatrice is the trustee of the first trust, and as trustee of the trust, Beatrice is authorized to distribute to herself such amounts of the income and principal as Beatrice needs for her health, support, education, or maintenance. At Beatrice's death, the successor trustee is directed to deliver the remaining trust estate to anyone in the world who Beatrice appoints, other than her estate or creditors, and in default of appointment, to Beatrice's sibling, Remy. Stella created the second trust with Beatrice as trustee. According to the terms of the second trust agreement, Beatrice, as trustee, can distribute to herself such amounts of income and principal as she needs for her own comfort or welfare. At Beatrice's death, the successor trustee is directed to deliver any remaining trust estate of the second trust to Remy. Beatrice has recently died, intestate, survived by her children, C1 and C2. Which answer best explains whether the trust estates of the two trusts will be included in Beatrice's gross estate for federal transfer tax purposes?

A. Both trust estates will be included in Beatrice's gross estate.

B. Neither trust estate will be included in Beatrice's gross estate.

C. The trust estate of trust one, but not of trust two, will be included in Beatrice's gross estate.

D. The trust estate of trust two, but not of trust one, will be included in Beatrice's gross estate.

8. Olive created a valid, irrevocable inter vivos express trust with Big Bank and Trust serving as trustee. The terms of the written trust agreement direct the trustee to pay to Beneficiary all of the income and such amounts of principal as the trustee determines is appropriate for Beneficiary's comfort or welfare; at Beneficiary's death, the bank is directed to deliver the trust estate to the children of Beneficiary. Additionally, when Olive died, her valid will was admitted to probate and devised certain property to the bank with directions for the bank to pay to Beneficiary such amounts of income or principal as the bank, in its discretion, determines is appropriate; at Beneficiary's death, the bank is directed to deliver any remaining trust estate to his children. Beneficiary died recently and was survived by his spouse, Shea, and two children, C1 and C2. Which answer best describes whether the trust estates of the inter vivos trust and the testamentary trust will be included in Beneficiary's gross estate for federal transfer tax purposes?

A. The trust estates of both trusts will be included in Beneficiary's gross estate.

B. The trust estates of both trusts will not be included in Beneficiary's gross estate.

C. The trust estate of the inter vivos trust, but not the testamentary trust, will be included in Beneficiary's gross estate.

D. The trust estate of the testamentary trust, but not the inter vivos trust, will be included in Beneficiary's gross estate.

9. Taxpayer died recently. Taxpayer was survived by her spouse, Spouse (a U.S. citizen and resident). Taxpayer's valid will has been admitted to probate and devises her entire probate estate to Spouse. At the time of Taxpayer's death, she owned (1) several tracts of real estate; (2) certain common stocks; (3) numerous items of tangible personal property; and (4) a checking account. The value of the probate estate at Taxpayer's death is $6,000,000. The gross estate for transfer tax purposes consists entirely of these probate assets. Estimate the amount of federal estate tax that will be due by reason of Taxpayer's death.

Answer:

10. Assume the same facts as Question 9. If Spouse dies later in the same year with a gross estate for estate tax purposes of $17,000,000 (the $6,000,000 Spouse inherited from Taxpayer, plus $11,000,000 Spouse already owned), estimate the amount of federal estate tax that will be due.

Answer

11. Owen died recently. Prior to his death, Owen had conveyed to his first child (C1) a remainder interest in Blackacre, expressly retaining a life estate. Owen conveyed to his second child (C2) an executory interest in Whiteacre that becomes possessory at Owen's death. Both deeds were duly recorded prior to Owen's death. Which answer best explains whether Blackacre and Whiteacre will be included in Owen's gross estate for federal transfer tax purposes?

   A. Both Blackacre and Whiteacre will be included in Owen's gross estate.

   B. Neither Blackacre nor Whiteacre will be included in Owen's gross estate.

   C. Whiteacre, but not Blackacre, will be included in Owen's gross estate.

   D. Blackacre, but not Whiteacre, will be included in Owen's gross estate.

12. Assume the same facts as Question 11 except that Owen had deposited $10,000 into a savings account in his own name "payable on Owen's death to C1" and another $10,000 into a checking account in the names of Owen and C2 "with rights of survivorship." Which answer best explains whether these accounts would be included in Owen's gross estate for federal transfer tax purposes?

   A. The checking account and the savings account would be included in Owen's gross estate.

   B. Neither the checking account nor the savings account would be included in Owen's gross estate.

   C. The checking account, but not the savings account, would be included in Owen's gross estate.

   D. The savings account and one-half of the checking account would be included in Owen's gross estate.

13. Assume the same facts as Question 11 except that, at Owen's death, he owned two life insurance policies. One is a term policy made payable at Owen's death to his estate, and the other is a whole-life policy made payable to A at Owen's death. Which answer best explains whether the policies would be included in Owen's gross estate for federal transfer tax purposes?

A. Both policies would be included in Owen's gross estate.

B. Neither policy would be included in Owen's gross estate.

C. The whole-life policy, but not the term policy, would be included in Owen's gross estate.

D. The term policy, but not the whole-life policy, would be included in Owen's gross estate.

14. Assume the same facts as Question 13 except that (i) four years prior to Owen's death, Owen had assigned the ownership of the term policy to C2 (who then changed the beneficiary to C2) and (ii) two years prior to Owen's death, Owen had assigned the ownership of the whole-life policy to C1. Will the policies be included in Owen's gross estate for federal transfer tax purposes?

Answer:

15. Assume the same facts as Question 14 except that, in addition to assigning the life insurance policies to C1 and C2, Owen had also given shares of common stock worth $500,000 to each of C1 and C2 when Owen had assigned the policies. Which answer best explains whether the shares of stock would be included in Owen's gross estate for federal transfer tax purposes?

A. The stock given to both C1 and C2 would be included in Owen's gross estate.

B. The stock would not be included in Owen's gross estate.

C. The stock given to C1, but not C2, would be included in Owen's gross estate.

D. The stock given to C2, but not C1, would be included in Owen's gross estate.

16. Omre died recently. He was survived by two children, C1 and C2, and three grandchildren, G1, G2, and G3. Omre's gross estate for federal transfer tax purposes has been valued at $6,000,000. At the time of his death, Omre owed to third parties debts secured by real estate included in his gross estate of $600,000 and unsecured debts of $100,000. Which answer describes the proper amount that can be deducted from Omre's gross estate to determine the amount of his taxable estate for federal transfer tax purposes?

A. $700,000.

B. $600,000.

C. $100,000.

D. None.

17. Assume the same facts as Question 17. Also, assume that the expenses of Omre's last illness amounted to $30,000, his funeral expenses amounted to $10,000, and the expenses incurred in the administration of his estate are $10,000. Estimate the amount of federal estate taxes that will be due.

Answer:

18. Taxpayer married Spouse shortly before Taxpayer died. Taxpayer was survived by Spouse and Taxpayer's adult child by a prior marriage, C. Taxpayer's will has been admitted to probate and devises property valued at $6,000,000 to Spouse, property valued at $4,000,000 to C, and property valued at $10,000,000 to Big State University (a non-profit university). Which answer best describes the amount that can be deducted from Taxpayer's gross estate to determine the amount of their taxable estate for federal transfer tax purposes?

A. $6,000,000.

B. $4,000,000.

C. $16,000,000.

D. $14,000,000.

19. Assume the same facts as Question 18 except that the estate is valued at $11 million at the death of the Taxpayer. $1 million was devised to a trustee in trust for Spouse with directions for the trustee to distribute to Spouse such amounts of income and principal as they would need for their health, support, education, or maintenance. At Spouse's death, the trustee is to deliver the remaining trust estate to C. The other $10 million was devised in trust to a trustee with directions to pay to Spouse all of the trust income for the remainder of their lifetime, and at Spouse's death, the principal is to be delivered to C. Which answer best describes the part, if any, of the $11 million that can be properly deducted from Taxpayer's gross estate to determine the amount of their taxable estate for federal transfer tax purposes?

A. $11,000,000.

B. $10,000,000.

C. $1,000,000.

D. $0.

20. Assume the same facts as Question 19. Explain whether or not the trust estates of the described trusts would be included in Spouse's gross estate at the time of their later death.

Answer:

Jurisdiction, Practice, Procedure

1. Briefly explain the probate exception to federal jurisdiction of federal courts.

   Answer:

2. Sarah, an unmarried resident of the State of X, died recently in X. Sarah was survived by several members of her family residing in several different states. Immediately prior to Sarah's death, she owned items of tangible personal property (such as household furnishings, jewelry, clothing, and other personal effects) located in a rented apartment in the State of X, an automobile registered and located in the State of X, a checking account at a local branch of a national bank in X, shares of stock in a corporation incorporated in the State of Y, and other items of tangible personal property located in Sarah's parents' house in the State of Z. Which answer best describes the law to apply in determining the proper succession to the described assets?

   A. Federal law will determine who succeeds to the ownership of the described personal property.

   B. The law of X determines the succession to the tangible personal property located in X; federal law determines the succession of the bank account; the law of Y governs the succession of the shares of stock; and the law of Z governs the succession of the tangible personal property located in Z.

   C. The law of X governs not only the succession of the tangible personal property located in X but also the checking account; the law of Y will govern the succession of the shares of stock; and the law of Z will govern the succession of the tangible personal property located in that state.

   D. The law of X will determine who succeeds to the ownership of the described personal property.

3. Assume the same facts as Question 2 except that Sarah also owned three tracts of land—one tract located in each of the states of X, Y, and Z. Which answer best describes the law that will govern the proper succession to the three tracts?

A. The law of X governs the succession of all three tracts.

B. The law of X governs the succession of the land in X; the law of Y will govern the succession of the land in Y; and the law of Z will govern the succession of the land in Z.

C. Federal law governs the succession of the three tracts to the extent of any inconsistencies existing among the laws of X, Y, and Z.

D. Federal law governs the succession of all three tracts of land because Sarah and the heirs resided in different states.

4. Jerry, an unmarried resident of the State of X, died while vacationing in the State of Y. In addition to the tangible personal property in Jerry's physical possession at the time of his death, Jerry owned real and personal property located in the State of X, but his more valuable assets were real and personal property located in the State of Z. Jerry was survived by several members of his family who all reside in the State of X. Which answer best describes which states' courts have subject matter jurisdiction over the decedent's property?

A. X has exclusive jurisdiction over the assets within its boundaries; Y has exclusive jurisdiction over the assets within its boundaries; and Z has exclusive jurisdiction over the assets within its boundaries.

B. X and Z have exclusive jurisdiction over the real property located within their respective boundaries, but X has exclusive jurisdiction over all personal property wherever located.

C. Each state has jurisdiction over the assets located within its boundaries, but X also has jurisdiction over the personal property located in Y and Z.

D. Each state has jurisdiction over the assets located within its boundaries, but X also has jurisdiction over all assets located in Y and Z.

5. Assume the same facts as Question 4. Which answer best describes which law a court should apply in determining whether the decedent died testate or intestate?

A. The law of X.

B. X's law for the property located in X; Y's law for the property located in Y; and Z's law for the property located in Z.

C. The law of X for all the assets except for the real property located in Z.

D. The law of X for all the assets except for the real and personal property located in Z.

6. Genevieve has recently died. Her will was drafted by Lawyer (who is, in fact, a lawyer). The will names a local bank as executor. Genevieve's will disinherited her youngest son, Sonny. Genevieve and Lawyer had several discussions about disinheriting Sonny in which she explained why she wanted to disinherit Sonny, but the will was silent as to any reason or cause. Genevieve was married to Spouse when the will was executed and when she died, and Spouse is the parent of Sonny. Spouse has never been represented by Lawyer, was not aware that Lawyer was hired by Genevieve, and was livid that Sonny had been disinherited. Lawyer believes that, if Spouse knew the reasons for Sonny's disinheritance, he would not be as upset. However, Lawyer was told by Genevieve that she did not want him to disclose her reasoning after her death for any reason. Which of the following is the best statement as to Lawyer's obligations with respect to the information?

A. So long as Genevieve was living, Lawyer was obligated not to disclose confidential information. However, the lawyer-client relationship does not survive death, which means Lawyer can now use professional discretion with respect to disclosing the information.

B. Since Sonny is the object of the information, Sonny may consent to the disclosure by Lawyer to Spouse. However, if Sonny does not consent, Lawyer may not disclose the information.

C. Since Spouse was married to Genevieve when the will was drafted, Spouse has the right to any information disclosed to Lawyer since spouses do not have the right to keep legally relevant information confidential from each other.

D. Since the bank is the personal representative of Genevieve's estate, only the bank has the right to the information and the right to consent to Lawyer's disclosure of the information.

7. Lawyer is a solo practitioner who has been diagnosed with the early stages of a degenerative, terminal illness. Lawyer's primary practice area is in probate and estate planning. Lawyer has always worked alone, but she is concerned about what will happen to her clients and files when she eventually becomes too sick to work. She has made arrangements with another lawyer, John, to review all of Lawyer's files when she is no longer able to work. Lawyer's clients have never met John. Does Lawyer's arrangement with John violate her duty to preserve the confidentiality of the clients' information?

A. Yes, unless her clients have explicitly authorized the arrangement.

B. Yes, because John is not a partner, associate or employee of Lawyer.

C. No. Unless her clients have explicitly prohibited her from making such an arrangement, Lawyer is authorized to make these arrangements since a reasonable client would approve the arrangement to safeguard his or her own interests.

D. No, unless (i) the client explicitly authorizes the arrangement or (ii) the court approves the arrangement.

8. Chuck makes an appointment with Lawyer. Lawyer has never met Chuck until this meeting. Chuck provides Lawyer with his prior estate planning documents and detailed information about his financial situation. Chuck also explains that he has no close relatives in the community. As Chuck begins discussing his plans for his estate, Lawyer becomes concerned that Chuck may not have the requisite capacity to execute an estate plan. By the end of the meeting, Lawyer is concerned that Chuck may cause substantial harm to himself or another. What should Lawyer do under these circumstances?

   A. Depending on the seriousness of what Lawyer has learned, Lawyer may initiate a guardianship or other appropriate protective court proceeding. Alternatively, Lawyer may consult with appropriate third parties who may have the ability to protect Chuck without such a court proceeding, such as family members or social workers. Lawyer may disclose information that the Lawyer has learned during discussions with Chuck to the extent necessary to protect Chuck's interests.

   B. Chuck is Lawyer's client. Lawyer may not disclose any of the information or use it in a guardianship or similar proceeding without Chuck's consent.

   C. Lawyer may initiate a guardianship or other appropriate protective court proceeding with respect to Chuck only if the court approves the disclosure of the information and determines the extent to which disclosing it is necessary to protect Chuck's interests.

   D. Based on what Lawyer has learned, Lawyer may initiate a guardianship or other appropriate protective court proceeding. However, Lawyer may not consult with any third parties other than the appropriate court. Lawyer may disclose information Lawyer learned during discussions only with the court, but only in the context of a guardianship or other appropriate proceeding, and only to the extent necessary to the proceeding.

9. Attorney receives a phone call from Cassandra. Attorney has represented Cassandra on various matters in the past. Cassandra explains that Cassandra's mother, Mother, is in a nursing home and that Mother is physically weak but mentally alert. Cassandra explains that Mother would like to update her will. Attorney makes an appointment to visit with Cassandra and Mother at the nursing home. During the meeting, Attorney observes that Mother is unable to rise from the bed or speak much above a whisper. Attorney is not able to understand what Mother is saying, so Attorney relies on Cassandra to explain what Mother is saying about the changes she would like in her will. When Cassandra explains something to Attorney, Cassandra turns to Mother and asks, "Mom, is that right?" Mother invariably nods her head that it is. Part of what Mother apparently wants to change in her will relates to ongoing litigation with Mother's siblings involving some real estate. Through Cassandra, Mother tells Attorney several facts that have not been revealed in the litigation but are prompting Mother to change her estate plan.

Does Cassandra's presence during these discussions affect the applicability of Attorney's attorney-client evidentiary privilege with Mother?

A. Since Cassandra is a third-party present during the disclosure of the information, there is no attorney-client privilege with respect to the information.

B. Since both Cassandra and Mother are Attorney's clients, the attorney-client privilege remains applicable to the information.

C. Since Cassandra's participation in the discussion between Attorney and Mother is necessary to Attorney's representation of Mother, the attorney-client privilege remains applicable to the information.

D. Cassandra's participation in the discussion has prevented the attorney-client relationship from being formed between Attorney and Mother.

10. Assume the same facts as Question 9. Mother has two children, Cassandra and Bob. Later in the meeting, Cassandra relays Mother's desire that Bob be disinherited. This change would directly benefit Cassandra. Again, Mother nods her head in approval. Attorney is personally aware of the justified reasons for Mother wanting to disinherit Bob. What should Attorney do under the circumstances?

Answer:

11. Husband and Wife are married. Husband made an appointment with Lawyer to discuss estate planning. At the first meeting, Husband, Wife, and Lawyer discuss the estate planning in detail but never discuss who Lawyer represents. In the absence of an agreement otherwise, who does Lawyer represent?

A. Lawyer is presumed to represent Husband and Wife jointly.

B. Lawyer is presumed to represent Husband and Wife separately.

C. Lawyer is presumed to represent Husband and Wife jointly and separately.

D. Lawyer represents the client who made the appointment.

12. Assume the same facts as Question 11. What should Lawyer explain to Husband and Wife about the ethical rules of jointly representing a married couple in estate planning?

Answer:

13. Assume the same facts as Question 11. After Lawyer begins working on the couple's joint estate plan, Husband calls Lawyer. Husband reveals that he had a romantic relationship outside of his marriage with Wife, and Wife is unaware of the relationship. Does Lawyer have a duty to disclose this information to Wife?

   A. Yes, because Lawyer must disclose to each of them the content of all communications with the other.

   B. Yes, unless Wife has waived the right to be provided information Husband provides to Lawyer.

   C. No, if Lawyer concludes the communication is not relevant to the legal representation.

   D. No, because it is confidential information provided by Lawyer's client.

14. Assume the same facts as Question 13. The estate planning involves coordinating the clients' nonprobate and probate assets. In order to minimize legal fees, Husband and Wife had agreed with Lawyer that they would each be responsible for making any changes necessary to coordinate their respective nonprobate assets with the agreed upon estate plan and that Lawyer would have no responsibility with respect to the nonprobate assets.

Husband calls Lawyer and says the following: "Do not tell Wife, but I changed the beneficiary of my largest insurance policy to my girlfriend Gwen."

What should Lawyer do with respect to this information?

   A. As Husband is the client and has instructed Lawyer to keep the information confidential, Lawyer must not reveal it to Wife.

   B. Lawyer needs to advise Husband that Lawyer is under an obligation to disclose this information to Wife or withdraw from representation unless Husband discloses it.

   C. Lawyer should withdraw from representation and refuse to discuss the matter any further with either Husband or Wife.

   D. Husband and Wife agreed that Lawyer would have no responsibility for the nonprobate assets. Thus, Lawyer has no responsibility to disclose any information related to the nonprobate assets.

15. Chris is Lawyer's client. She has been Chris' attorney for many years. Each year on Lawyer's birthday, Chris gives her a gift. Is it ethical for Lawyer to accept such gifts?

   A. No, because lawyers may not accept gifts from clients.

   B. No, because it is presumptively fraudulent.

C. Yes, so long as Lawyer does not suggest the gift or engage in any type of undue influence to obtain the gift.

D. Yes, because there are no restrictions on social gifts or other activities between lawyers and their clients.

16. Assume the same facts as Question 15. During an appointment to update Chris' estate planning, Chris tells Lawyer that he would like for the will to include a $50,000 gift to Lawyer as appreciation for her kindness over the years. Lawyer tries to tell Chris that this is not necessary, but Chris insists. What would you do if you were Lawyer?

Answer:

17. Assume the same facts as Question 16, except that the discussion concerning the $50,000 bequest did not happen and Chris wants to remove his daughter as executor of his estate and name Lawyer instead. What would you do if you were Lawyer?

Answer:

18. Elizabeth is the executor of Decedent's estate. Elizabeth has approached Attorney to assist Elizabeth during the estate administration process. Absent any agreement otherwise, who would be Attorney's client?

A. Elizabeth.

B. Decedent's estate.

C. The beneficiaries of Decedent's estate.

D. Elizabeth and the beneficiaries of Decedent's estate.

19. Assume the same facts as Question 18. Assume Attorney is Elizabeth's child who has recently passed the bar exam and needs clients to pay off her student loans. What should Attorney do under the circumstances?

Answer:

20. Assume the same facts as Question 19, except that Attorney is Elizabeth's law partner (and not Elizabeth's child). Elizabeth is an insurance defense lawyer with the firm and a sibling of Decedent. What would you do if you were Attorney?

Answer:

21. Chelsea hires Attorney to draft her will. Attorney becomes so familiar with Chelsea's estate during the estate planning process that Chelsea asks Attorney to serve as executor of the estate. Is it ethical for Attorney to draft a will naming herself (Attorney) as the executor of the estate?

  A. Yes, so long as while serving as executor Attorney does not charge the estate for being both the executor and the executor's attorney.

  B. Yes, but Attorney should make sure Chelsea understands there is no necessity of Attorney being named. Attorney should also discuss what her fees would be while serving as executor, including any fees as attorney and not just as executor.

  C. No, because Attorney cannot draft a will in which Attorney receives any substantial interest.

  D. No, unless the will requires that Attorney serve as executor without compensation.

22. Assume the same facts as Question 21. Assume that Chelsea would like Attorney to serve as a trustee of a testamentary trust created in Chelsea's will for Decedent's children. If the will contains an exculpatory clause for trustees, will a court enforce it if Attorney serves as trustee?

Answer:

23. Lawyer prepares Cian's will. After the will is executed, Cian asks if Lawyer would keep the will in the firm's vault for safekeeping. Is it proper for the firm to retain the will?

Answer:

Practice Final Exam

1. Yorick died recently. He was survived by both of his parents. Yorick divorced Henry two years prior to his death. After the divorce, Yorick did not change the validly executed will that Yorick had signed while married to Henry. The will included a pecuniary bequest of $10,000 to Child, Henry's child by a prior marriage. What effect did the divorce have on the pecuniary bequest of $10,000 to Child?

   Answer:

2. Esmerelda and Frodo were siblings and had owned investment real estate as joint tenants with rights of survivorship since before Esmerelda's marriage to Spouse. Under Esmerelda's valid will, her entire probate estate is devised to her Spouse. Esmerelda died recently. Which of the following best describes the proper disposition of the land?

   A. Spouse receives Esmerelda's interest in the real estate. However, it is subject to the claims of Esmerelda's creditors.

   B. Spouse receives Esmerelda's interest in the real estate free and clear of Esmerelda's creditors' claims.

   C. Frodo receives Esmerelda's interest in the real estate. However, it is subject to the claims of Esmerelda's creditors.

   D. Frodo receives Esmerelda's interest in the real estate free and clear of Esmerelda's creditors' claims.

3. Atticus conveyed Blackacre to himself, in trust, to pay himself the income for life, and for the trust estate to pass to Vivi at Atticus' death. Atticus retained the power to revoke or amend the trust. He died intestate, survived by Vivi. She is not Atticus' intestate heir. The recorded deed was not witnessed and was not otherwise executed in compliance with the statutory formalities for a will. Which of the following best describes the distribution of the trust estate at Atticus' death?

   A. Atticus' trust is invalid. The trust estate must pass through the probate system which means that the trust estate passes to Atticus' intestate heirs.

   B. Atticus' trust is a valid testamentary trust. The trust estate passes probate to Vivi.

   C. Atticus' trust is a valid testamentary trust. The trust estate passes nonprobate to Vivi.

   D. Atticus' trust is a valid inter vivos trust. The trust estate passes to Vivi outside of the probate system.

4. Azra and Bobbi were two unmarried cousins. They inherited Blackacre as tenants in common when their grandparent, Omma, died. Following Omma's death, Azra and Bobbi executed a single written document in 2020 meeting the requirements of a valid will. In this document, the first to die devises her interest in Blackacre to the other. In addition, the will devises Blackacre to their alma mater, Starfleet University, upon the survivor's death. Azra has recently died, survived by Bobbi. The family has discovered a validly executed will signed in 2022 by Azra that devises Azra's entire estate, including Blackacre, to Fred, a friend. Which answer best describes the most likely disposition of Blackacre by reason of Azra's death?

   A. Azra's interest passes nonprobate to Bobbi.

   B. Bobbi succeeds to Azra's interest pursuant to the 2020 will.

   C. Fred succeeds to Azra's interest pursuant to the 2022 will.

   D. Fred succeeds to Azra's interest pursuant to the 2022 will, and Bobbi has a breach of contract action against Azra's estate.

5. Gigi died recently. Gigi was survived by her spouse, Spouse, and their two minor children, Romeo and Juliet. Gigi's will, which was validly executed after Gigi married Spouse but before the births of Romeo and Juliet, leaves all of Gigi's property to Spouse. Which answer best describes the most likely disposition of Gigi's estate?

   A. The will can be admitted to probate; the entire estate passes to Spouse.

   B. The will cannot be admitted to probate; the entire estate passes to Romeo and Juliet.

   C. The will cannot be admitted to probate; Spouse, Romeo, and Juliet share the estate.

   D. The will can be admitted to probate, but Romeo and Juliet will be entitled to an intestate share of the estate, and the balance of the entire estate passes to Spouse.

6. Hector died recently, survived by his adult child Doug. Another child of Hector, Shelly, died several years before Hector died; Shelly was survived by her child Gidget. Hector's valid will has been admitted to probate and says, "I devise all of my property to my grandchild, Gidget." Gidget, who was married to Spouse and also the mother of two children, GGC1 and GGC2, filed a valid disclaimer in the probate proceedings of Hector's estate, believing it was a way to make a gift to Gidget's children without incurring gift tax. Which answer best describes the effect the disclaimer would have on the disposition of Hector's estate?

   A. The estate would pass to Gidget's spouse.

   B. The estate would pass to GGC1 and GGC2 as distributees under the will.

   C. The estate would pass to GGC1 and GGC2, but as a gift by Gidget to GGC1 and GGC2.

   D. The estate would pass to Doug.

7. Assume the same facts as Question 6 except that Gidget is the stepchild (not biological child) of Shelly. Hector's will devised the estate to Gidget. Which answer best describes the effect the disclaimer would have on the disposition of Hector's estate?

   A. The estate would pass to Doug.

   B. The estate would pass to Doug and to Gidget's spouse.

   C. The estate would pass to Gidget's spouse.

   D. The estate would pass to GGC1 and GGC2.

8. Octavio died recently. He was survived by two adult children, Clover and Emery. Octavio never signed a will but verbally told several friends over an extended period of time that he wanted Clover to have his home and its contents when he died. At all relevant times, Octavio was a competent individual, and his friends are willing to testify as to Octavio's verbal statements. No document appearing to be a will was found after Octavio's death. Which answer best explains the most likely disposition of Octavio's home and its contents?

   A. Clover inherits both the home and its contents.

   B. Clover inherits the contents but not the home.

   C. Clover inherits the home but not its contents.

   D. Clover and Emery inherit both the home and its contents.

9. Assume the same facts as Question 8 except that moments before Octavio died, while still competent, he told his doctor and two nurses that he really wanted Clover to have his home and its contents when he died. Which answer best explains the most likely disposition of Octavio's home and its contents?

   A. My answer would not change.

   B. Clover inherits both the home and its contents.

   C. Clover inherits the contents but not the home.

   D. Clover inherits the home but not its contents.

10. Assume the same facts as Question 8 except that Clover can produce credible witnesses who will testify that Octavio verbally told Clover that if she dropped out of school, returned home, and cared for Octavio in his declining years, she would receive the home and its contents at Octavio's death. In reliance on this promise, she dropped out of school, returned home, and cared for him. How would your answer change (if at all)?

Answer:

11. Assume the same facts as Question 8 except that Clover can produce a written agreement—signed by Clover and Octavio—whereby Octavio promised to devise his home and its contents to Clover, if she dropped out of school, returned home, and cared for Octavio in his declining years. In reliance on this written agreement, Clover dropped out of school, returned home, and cared for him. Which answer best explains the most likely disposition of Octavio's home and its contents?

   A. My answer would not change.

   B. The home and its contents passed to Clover.

   C. The contents, but not the home, passed to Clover.

   D. Clover would have a contract claim against Octavio's estate.

12. Oliwier and Tom, a friend of Oliwier, entered into a written trust agreement. They both signed the agreement. Shortly thereafter, Oliwier conveyed Blackacre to Tom; record legal title is in Tom's name. The terms of the trust agreement direct Tom to manage Blackacre until Oliwier's death; at that time, Tom is to convey Blackacre to Oliwier's grandchild, Greg. Prior to Oliwier's death, any income generated was to be delivered to Oliwier, but no income was generated.

Greg died in January of this year. Greg was survived by his spouse (Spouse) and child (Greg Junior). Greg's valid will was admitted to probate and devises his entire estate to

Spouse. Oliwier died in June of this year. Oliwier died intestate and was survived by his estranged child (Chucky) and Greg Junior. Which answer best describes the most likely disposition of Blackacre by reason of Oliwier's death?

A. Chucky will ask the court to impose a resulting trust on Tom in favor of Chucky.

B. Spouse will ask the court to enforce the express trust on Tom in favor of Spouse.

C. Greg Junior will ask the court to enforce the express trust on Tom in favor of Greg Junior.

D. Tom retains fee simple title.

13. Assume the same facts as Question 12 except that—unknown to both Oliwier and Tom at the time of the written agreement and conveyance—Greg was already dead. Which answer best describes the most likely disposition of Blackacre by reason of Oliwier's death?

A. Chucky will ask the court to impose a resulting trust on Tom in favor of Chucky.

B. Chucky will ask the court to impose a constructive trust on Tom in favor of Chucky.

C. Greg Junior will ask the court to impose a constructive trust.

D. Spouse will ask the court to impose a constructive trust.

14. Assume the same facts as Question 12 except that Greg has not died. Which answer best describes the most likely disposition of Blackacre by reason of Oliwier's death?

A. Greg can have the court enforce the terms of the written express trust.

B. Greg can have the court impose a constructive trust on Tom in favor of Greg.

C. Chucky can have the court to impose a resulting trust on Tom in favor of Chucky.

D. Tom retains fee simple title.

15. Assume the same facts as Question 14 except that prior to his death, Oliwier asked Tom (in a letter delivered to Tom and signed by Oliwier) to convey Blackacre back to him. The letter explained that because Oliwier was very disappointed in Greg, he did not want Greg to have Blackacre after his death. Tom complied with Oliwier's request and conveyed Blackacre back to him. Oliwier then sold Blackacre to GFP, a good-faith purchaser. Is there any liability for Tom, Oliwier's estate, or GFP as a result of the described transactions?

Answer:

16. Rose created a valid, enforceable irrevocable express trust. The terms of the written trust agreement direct the trustee, Tom, to pay the income to Alice for the rest of her lifetime; at the time of Alice's death, Tom is directed to deliver the trust estate to any one or more of Rose's lineal descendants as Alice appoints by will. In default of appointment, Tom is to deliver the trust estate to a named charity.

At the time the trust was created, Alice was not married and did not have any children. Later, Alice married her spouse who had three children from a prior marriage, C1, C2 and C3. Shortly before Alice died, she validly executed a will in which Alice expressly appoints the trust estate to C1, C2, and C3. Alice's will has been admitted to probate. Which answer best describes who is likely to succeed to the trust estate by reason of Alice's death?

A. The charity.

B. C1, C2, C3.

C. Alice's estate.

D. Rose's heirs/devisees.

17. Adam and Blake lived together in a long-term, committed relationship. They never married but were the parents of a child, Cora. Adam died and was survived by Blake and Cora. Adam's will has been admitted to probate and devises property valued at $6,000,000 to Blake, property valued at $4,000,000 to Cora, and property valued at $10,000,000 to Starfleet University. Which answer best describes the amount that can be deducted from Adam's gross estate to determine the amount of Adam's taxable estate for federal transfer tax purposes?

A. $4,000,000.

B. $6,000,000.

C. $10,000,000.

D. $16,000,000.

18. Assume the same facts as Question 17 except that Adam and Blake are a same-sex couple married in the State of X. They need to relocate to the State of Y for Adam's job. A joint resolution filed in the State of Y House of Representatives would amend the state constitution to declare that the State of Y only recognizes marriages between "one human biological male and one human biological female." Shortly after their move to the State of Y, Adam dies. Which answer best describes the amount that can be deducted from Adam's gross estate to determine the amount of the taxable estate for federal transfer tax purposes?

A. $4,000,000.

B. $6,000,000.

C. $10,000,000.

D. $16,000,000.

19. Mara, an unmarried resident of the State of X, died while on a temporary work assignment in the State of Y. In addition to the tangible personal property in Mara's physical possession at the time of her death, Mara owned real and personal property located in State X, but Mara's more valuable assets were real and personal property located in the State Z. Mara was survived by several members of her family who all reside in State X. Assuming the amount of property (and/or its value) in each state justifies the trouble and expense of a formal administration, describe the states where formal administration of the decedent's estate would be proper.

Answer:

20. Jude created an inter vivos irrevocable trust for the benefit of Mae. Tom is the trustee. Tom hires an attorney, Lawyer, to advise Tom during the administration of the trust. Who is Lawyer's client?

A. The trust.

B. Tom.

C. Mae.

D. Tom and Mae.

Answers

Intestacy

1. **Answer (C) is correct.** The validly executed will of Basilio has a clause expressly disinheriting an heir. At common law, this type of clause is ineffective unless paired with provisions that distribute the entire estate of the decedent. In other words, this type of disinheritance clause is not enforced if the decedent is partially intestate. However, the Uniform Probate Code authorizes a testator to disinherit an heir for purposes of intestate and testate distribution under UPC § 2-101(b). The deceased brother's interest in Basilio's estate will pass to his child (Fermina). Alba's children will be treated as though Alba has disclaimed her interest. Consequently, Fermina will take one-half of the widgets, and the children of Alba will divide the other one-half of the widgets. UPC §§ 2-103(c); 2-106; 2-1106(b)(3)(A). Compare, however, if Alba predeceased Basilio. The disinheritance clause in the will would have no effect, and Fermina, Danita, and Edgar will each take equal 1/3 shares under UPC §§ 2-103(c) and 2-106.

2. **Answer (A) is correct.** The estate of Gisela will pass to her mother, Lena. UPC § 2-103(b).

   Answer (C) is incorrect. The surviving relatives of Petra are irrelevant because Gisela was not survived by Petra.

   Answers (B) and (D) are incorrect. Gisela's brother, Finn, would only take if Lena had not survived.

3. **Answer (B) is correct.** A legal separation is not a divorce under UPC § 2-802. Gisela is Petra's surviving spouse for purposes of intestacy distribution. Because Elias is the child of both Gisela and Petra, Gisela will take the entire intestate estate. UPC § 2-102(1)(B).

   Answer (A) is incorrect. In some non-UPC states, Elias will inherit some portion of Petra's estate. However, Elias will never take to the exclusion of Petra's surviving spouse.

   Answers (C) and (D) are incorrect. Every state has a set of laws that direct what happens to property when someone dies without a valid will in place to direct the disposition of their property ("intestate"). These laws vary dramatically from state to state, but the spouse and children of the decedent will take to the exclusion of anyone else. Petra's parents will not take via intestacy because her spouse (Gisela) and child (Elias) have survived her.

4. **Answer (A) is correct.** The parties with standing to contest the probate of a will include the decedent's heirs at law. Kirra and Coen are Yindi's parents and her only heirs at law absent extraordinary circumstances. *See* UPC §§ 2-103, 2-114. The result is likely to be the same in a non-UPC state.

   Answers (B) and (C) are incorrect. Yindi's parents are her heirs. Absent valid disclaimers by Yindi's parents, her siblings are not heirs. *See* UPC § 2-103. It does not matter if the siblings are full-blood siblings (sharing the same mother and father as Yindi, Siblings 1 and 2) or half-blood siblings (sharing only one common parent with Yindi, Siblings 3 and 4).

   Answer (D) is incorrect. One's status as an heir is not dependent upon the actual personal relationship that existed prior to the decedent's death. *But see* UPC § 2-114.

5. **Answer (D) is correct.** The parties with standing to contest the probate of a will include the decedent's heirs at law. *See generally* McGovern § 13.3. Notwithstanding their divorce, Kirra and Coen were Yindi's parents and her only heirs at law absent extraordinary circumstances. *See* UPC §§ 2-103, 2-114. The result is likely to be the same in a non-UPC state.

   Answer (A) is incorrect. Other than a decedent's surviving spouse, a person related to the decedent only by marriage is not an heir at law.

   Answers (B) and (C) are incorrect. Since Kirra and Coen both survived Yindi, neither the ancestors of Kirra and Coen nor the descendants of those ancestors are Yindi's heirs at law. Yindi's friend, the sole beneficiary named in her will, does not stand to take more if the will is set aside and therefore does not have standing to file a contest.

6. **Answer (D) is correct.** Inheritance rights attach when there is a legally recognized parent-child relationship. Generally, when a child is adopted, the child's relationship with their biological parents is severed and the child is treated as "reborn" into the family of the adoptive parent for purposes of inheritance. For a comprehensive discussion of this issue, see Danaya C. Wright, *Inheritance Equity: Reforming the Inheritance Penalties Facing Children in Non-Traditional Families*, 25 Cornell J.L. & Pub. Pol'y 1 (2015).

   We live in a world where multiple-marriage is common, and two-thirds of remarriages involve children. As many as two-thirds of legally recorded adoptions involve a stepparent. *See* Cynthia R. Mabry & Lisa Kelly, Adoption Law: Theory, Policy, and Practice 1 (2d ed. 2010). It is not uncommon for both biological parents to remain in the child's life as active co-parents, with the stepparent adopting the child to legally recognize the new blended family that has been created. It is also not uncommon for states to waive many of the requirements for a stepparent adoption that exist in a stranger adoption.

   The issue of stepparent adoption is addressed from state to state in wildly disparate ways. Some states do not differentiate for stepparent adoption, and any right to inherit through the natural parent is severed. In a UPC state, when there is a stepparent adoption, the adopted child may still inherit *through* both natural parents. This does not work in the inverse, however, and the natural parent being "replaced" by the stepparent may not inherit *through* the adopted child. *See* UPC §§ 2-119(b).

This question focuses upon the rights of Coen (natural father) to inherit from Yindi when she has been adopted by Alinta (stepparent). Kirra and Alinta are Yindi's heirs. Coen would not have a right to inherit from Yindi if she died intestate. *See* UPC §§ 2-118, 2-119. Accordingly, Coen would not have standing to contest the probate of the will. The same result is likely to occur in a non-UPC state. *See* McGovern § 2.10. *See, e.g.,* Alaska Stat. § 13.12.114(b)(2); Ariz. Rev. Stat. Ann. § 14-2114(B); Haw. Rev. Stat. § 560:2-114(B); S.D. Codified Laws § 29a-2-114(b)(1); Vt. Stat. Ann. Tit. 15A, § 4-102 (examples of states which indicate the adoption of a spouse of the child's natural parent does not affect the right of the child to inherit from or through the other natural parent).

Answer (A) is incorrect. The adoption process typically eliminates the biological parent's status as an heir of the adopted child.

Answer (B) is incorrect. Alinta adopted Yindi and is therefore treated as her parent. Consequently, Kirra is not Yindi's sole heir at law.

Answer (C) is incorrect. It is worth noting that inheritance statutes are often based upon a family paradigm that assumes a traditional nuclear family. Times are changing. This is an area of inheritance in which the law may start to change. As of the date of publication, however, it is inaccurate to state that Coen will "likely" have standing.

7. **Answer (A) is correct.** The issue of stepparent adoption is addressed from state to state in wildly disparate ways. Some states do not differentiate for stepparent adoption, and any right to inherit through the natural parent is severed. In a UPC state, when there is a stepparent adoption, the adopted child may still inherit *through* both natural parents. *See* UPC §§ 2-119(b).

This question focuses upon the rights of Yindi to inherit from and through her natural father. Notwithstanding (i) the divorce of Kirra and Coen and (ii) Yindi's adoption by Kirra's new spouse Alinta, Yindi is still considered to be a child of Coen for intestacy purposes. *See* UPC §§ 2-118, 2-119. As noted above, the same result may not occur in a non-UPC state.

Answers (B), (C), and (D) are incorrect. Because Coen was survived by Yindi, Coen's parents and siblings are not heirs.

8. Because Alinta is also the mother of children of a prior marriage, Alinta is Kirra's sole heir only if the value of the probate estate is less than $225,000. *See* UPC § 2-102 and its comments. If the value of Kirra's probate estate exceeds $225,000, Yindi is entitled to a share of Kirra's probate estate.

For purposes of intestacy, Yindi has been adopted by Alinta and is therefore a child of Kirra and Alinta. Kirra's stepchildren, S1 and S2, have not been adopted and are excluded. Yindi and Alinta will share equally the estate in excess of $225,000. *See* McGovern § 2.10.

In states that have not adopted the Uniform Probate Code, Alinta may be the sole heir due to Alinta's adoption of Yindi. Why? Because the surviving spouse is the common parent of Kirra's only child. Also note that in some community property states, the decedent's half of the community property passes to the surviving spouse only if all the decedent's descendants are also descendants of the surviving spouse.

9. **Answer (D) is correct.** *See* UPC § 2-102(4). Alinta, as surviving spouse, is no longer the common parent of Kirra's only child. This reduces the intestate share to which she is entitled in a UPC state. Please note that the statutory results will likely differ in a non-UPC state.

   Answers (A), (B), and (C) are incorrect. These answers are incorrect for the statutory reasons given.

10. Yes. There are a number of reasons that property may pass by intestate succession even though the decedent has a valid, unrevoked will at time of death. The devisees named in the will may elect not to have the will admitted to probate. The will may not effectively devise the entire probate estate. The devisees could disclaim their interests in the estate. Even if admitted to probate, the devisees may not have survived the testator by the required period of survivorship. In addition, a will can still be a valid testamentary instrument even if it does not contain directions concerning the distribution of the estate. *See* Andersen § 2.

11. **Answer (B) is correct.** Aoife's siblings, who are either born to, or adopted by, either Father or Mother, are Aoife's heirs at law and will share equally in the estate. *See* UPC §§ 2-103, 2-107. In a minority of non-UPC states, half-blood siblings may take only half of what full or whole-blood siblings would inherit, or alternatively, half-blood siblings may be excluded entirely from taking if there is a living full-blood sibling. *See* McGovern § 2.2.

   Answer (A) is incorrect. S4 is related to Aoife by marriage and excluded as an heir unless Mother adopted S4.

   Answer (C) is incorrect. S3 is a child of Mother and is an heir.

   Answer (D) is incorrect. S2 and S3, children of Father and Mother, respectively, are also heirs of Aoife per UPC § 2-107. However, in some non-UPC jurisdictions, a half-blood sibling is not an heir if there is a whole-blood sibling. *See* McGovern § 2.2. In a jurisdiction with this half-blood sibling rule, Answer (D) will be correct.

12. **Answer (D) is correct.** Because Aaron was survived by children, Aaron's heirs are C1 and C2, who would share Aaron's probate estate equally. C3 is a stepchild and excluded, unless Aaron had adopted C3 (or unless the intestate is not survived by a spouse, issue, parents, grandparents or their issue). *See* UPC §§ 1-201(5), 2-103. The result is likely to be the same in a non-UPC state. *See* McGovern § 2.2.

    Answers (A), (B), and (C) are incorrect. Neither Batsheva nor C3 is an heir at law. Batsheva is excluded because Aaron was survived by children.

13. C4 is likely to be an heir. *See* UPC § 2-117. State statutes which have excluded non-marital children from inheriting from their biological fathers in the past have been held to violate the Equal Protection Clause of the Fourteenth Amendment of the U.S. Constitution. *See Trimble v. Gordon*, 430 U.S. 762, 776 (1977). UPC § 2-115(5) directs that the parent-child relationship may be established under relevant state law. The Legislative Note within this section explains that in states that have passed the Uniform Parentage Act (2000, as amended), the "relevant state law" within paragraph (5) should be replaced with § 201(b)(1), (2), or (3) of the Act. States have procedures which allow a child to establish that a man was the child's biological father either before or after the man's death. These statutes typically allow the child to establish paternity after the father dies even if the father never acknowledged the child as his own. *See* McGovern § 2.9.

14. **Answer (D) is correct.** C4 is Aart's only heir. The identity of a child's other parent or the parent who was awarded custody is irrelevant. However, to be an heir, one must not only survive the intestate, but survive by 120 hours. If one survives the intestate but dies within 120 hours, that person is deemed to have died before the intestate. *See* UPC §§ 2-103, 2-104. Some states which have not enacted the Uniform Probate Code nonetheless have statutes that require an heir to survive by 120 hours. *See* McGovern § 2.2.

    Answer (A) is incorrect. C1 did not survive Aart. Even if applicable state law did not require an heir to survive by 120 hours, the common law required an heir to survive the intestate by an "instant" of time.

    Answers (B) and (C) are incorrect. Typically, state statutes require heirs to survive the decedent by 120 hours. Prior to the enactment of statutes that require survivorship by 120 hours, many states had statutes that would have created the presumption that C2 died before Aart. Absent proof to the contrary, in those states, C3 and C4 would be Aart's heirs.

15. **Answer (C) is correct.** Because of the "120-hour rule" of UPC § 2-104(b), C4 would appear to be Aart's only heir. However, the "representation rule" of UPC § 2-106 would substitute G2 and G3 as heirs in place of C2 and C3. Accordingly, Aart's probate estate would be delivered equally to G2, G3, and C4's devisee, S4. If G2 and G3 are minors, their respective shares would be delivered to a guardian or other surrogate pursuant to

local law. The result would be the same in most states that have not enacted the Uniform Probate Code. *See* McGovern § 2.2.

Answers (A) and (B) are incorrect. The "120-hour rule" excludes C2 and C3 as heirs. Consequently, their devisees are not entitled to any part of Aart's estate.

Answer (D) is incorrect. C4 survived Aart by 120 hours and was one of the heirs. At C4's death, C4's interest passed to S4 subject to formal administration of C4's estate.

16. **Answer (C) is correct.** An individual in gestation at the time of the intestate's death is treated as living at the time of the intestate's death if the individual lives for at least 120 hours after birth. *See* UPC § 2-104(b). G6, having been adopted by C3, is an heir of Aart as well. *See* UPC §§ 2-118, 2-119. Consequently, G5 and G2, as well as G6 and G3, succeed to the one-third interests that their parents would have been entitled to had the parents survived Aart by 120 hours. *See* UPC §§ 2-104(b), 2-106, 2-118, 2-119. The result would be the same in some states that have not enacted the Uniform Probate Code. *See* McGovern §§ 2.2, 2.10.

    Answers (A), (B), and (D) are incorrect. These answers are incorrect for the reasons given.

17. G2, G5, G3, G6, and G4 will share the estate equally. None of the children of Aart survived Aart. UPC § 2-106(b) adopts the system of representation called "per capita at each generation" (*i.e.*, equal shares to those equally related). Consequently, the grandchildren share equally in Aart's probate estate since none of the children survived Aart.

    The result will likely differ in a state that provides for a "per stirpes" system of taking by representation (instead of UPC § 2-106). If the applicable statute is a strict "per stirpes," one-third would pass to G2 and G5, one-third would pass to G3 and G6, and one-third would pass to G4. *See* McGovern § 2.2.

18. **Answer (D) is correct.** According to UPC § 2-106, Aart's probate estate is divided into five equal shares for each grandchild who survived Aart (G2, G3, G5, G6) and for the deceased grandchild who left a descendant who survived Aart (G4). The result may differ in a non-UPC state. *See* McGovern § 2.2.

    Answers (A) and (B) are incorrect. GG succeeded to the interest in Aart's estate that G4 would have inherited had G4 survived Aart.

    Answer (C) is incorrect. This answer would be correct in a state with a strict "per stirpes" system of representation.

19. **Answer (D) is correct.** Camille's probate property passes ("escheats") to the state where Camille resided since there are no heirs as defined in UPC §§ 2-102, 2-103. *See* UPC § 2-105; *see also* McGovern § 2.2.

Some states that have not enacted the Uniform Probate Code have adopted a similar "parentelic" system; however, not all parentelic systems are the same. Other states have adopted a "next of kin" system to apply in this situation. *See* McGovern § 2.2.

Answers (A), (B), and (C) are incorrect. Neither A nor B is an heir.

It is worth noting, however, that in some states, both A and B would be the heirs of Camille. In other states, only A would be an heir.

20. **Answer (C) is correct.** According to UPC § 2-103, a descendant of deceased grandparents takes by representation. Accordingly, C would inherit Camille's probate estate. The caveat, of course, is that the result may differ in a non-UPC state. Intestacy statutes vary. *See* McGovern § 2.2.

    Answers (A) and (B) are incorrect. The state takes only if there is no taker under UPC § 2-103.

    Answer (D) is incorrect. The cousin died before Camille died.

21. Early common law prohibited aliens from acquiring land by descent, a rule followed in some states. The modern view is that non-citizens can acquire property unless a state's statute provides otherwise. *See* Atkinson § 24. UPC § 2-111 does not disqualify an heir because he or she is an alien.

    The result may differ in a non-UPC state. However, even if a state purports to limit an alien's inheritance, federal law may override it if the United States has a treaty with the alien's country. *See* Atkinson § 24.

22. Both A and B are Diego's heirs. The legal issue here is whether the gift is an advancement of B's inheritance and should therefore be considered in determining B's share of Diego's probate estate. If considered an advancement, the value of Blackacre would be added to the value of the probate estate to determine the "hotchpot estate," and B's share of the probate estate would be reduced using the "hotchpot" method. B would not be required to reimburse A or to restore Blackacre to the probate estate. *See* McGovern § 2.6.

    On these facts, Blackacre is unlikely to be considered an advancement. UPC § 2-109 and similar statutes enacted in most non-UPC states require written evidence of the intent that a gift is to be treated as an advancement. *See* McGovern § 2.6.

23. **Answer (C) is correct.** C2 would appear to be Helga's only heir. However, the "representation rule" of UPC § 2-106 would substitute G1 as an heir in place of C1. If G1 is a minor, G1's share would be delivered to a guardian or other surrogate pursuant to state law. *See* McGovern § 2.2.

    Answers (A), (B), and (D) are incorrect. These answers are incorrect for the reasons given.

24. **Answer (C) is correct.** C2's spouse acquired C2's interest in Helga's estate. The "representation rule" of UPC § 2-106 substitutes G1 as an heir in place of C1. Accordingly, Helga's probate estate should be delivered equally to G1 and C2's devisee, S2. If G1 is a minor, G1's share would be delivered to a guardian or other surrogate pursuant to state law.

The result would be the same in most states that have not enacted the Uniform Probate Code. *See* McGovern § 2.2.

Answers (A), (B), and (D) are incorrect. These answers are incorrect for the reasons given.

25. **Answer (A) is correct.** Absent written evidence that Helga intended the conveyance to be an advancement (or that C2 acknowledged the gift was an advancement), S2 not only inherited Blackacre when C2 died but also succeeded to C2's interest in Helga's probate estate. *See* UPC § 2-109. The result may differ in states that have not enacted the Uniform Probate Code or a statute similar to UPC § 2-109. *See* McGovern § 2.6.

Answers (B) and (C) are incorrect. For the gift to be treated as an advancement and either reduce or eliminate C2's interest in Helga's probate estate, written evidence of Helga's intent to treat the gift as an advancement (or that C2 acknowledged that the gift was an advancement) must be produced. Many states, including non-UPC states, no longer assume gifts are considered advancements. *See* Naomi R. Cahn, et al., Wills, Trusts, and Estates in Focus 58 (2019).

Answer (D) is incorrect. Even if the gift is treated as an advancement, Blackacre was owned by C2 and passed to S2 at C2's death subject to formal administration of C2's estate. Neither C2 nor S2 is under a legal obligation to reimburse Helga's other heirs or restore Blackacre to Helga's probate estate.

26. **Answer (A) is correct.** Even if there is written evidence of Helga's intent to treat the gift as an advancement to C1, C1 died before Helga, and G1 succeeded to the interest in Helga's probate estate that C1 would have inherited had C1 survived Helga. *See* UPC §§ 2-103, 2-106. Accordingly, Blackacre is not taken into account in determining G1's share of Helga's probate estate. *See* UPC § 2-109(c). The result may differ in states that have not enacted the Uniform Probate Code or a statute similar to UPC § 2-109. *See* McGovern § 2.6.

Answers (B) and (C) are incorrect. Absent written evidence that Helga not only intended for the gift to C1 to be an advancement, but that Helga also intended for the advancement to be taken into account in the event C1 predeceased Helga, the gift is not treated as an advancement. It is possible, in some non-UPC states, for the value of Blackacre to be treated as an advancement to be taken into account in calculating G1's share. In this case, G1 is said to be "burdened by representation."

Answer (D) is incorrect. Even if the gift was an advancement, neither C1, C1's heirs and devisees, nor C1's descendants taking by representation have a legal obligation to restore Blackacre to Helga's probate estate.

27. **Answer (A) is correct.** Since the gift was to G2, it has no effect on C2's inheritance from Helga that passed to S2 when C2 died. The gift is not an advancement. *See* UPC § 2-109; McGovern § 2.6.

Answers (B), (C) and (D) are incorrect. The facts do not create an advancement situation under the Uniform Probate Code, similar statutes in non-UPC states, or the common law. Even a written agreement between Helga and G2 defining the transaction as an advancement may not be binding on C2. Had C2 been a party to the agreement and agreed the gift would be taken into account in determining C2's share of Helga's probate estate, S2 may be bound by the agreement, or estopped to deny that the advancement to G2 should not be taken into account in determining C2's share of Helga's probate estate.

28. Absent written evidence that Helga intended the gift to be an advancement to G2, the gift is not taken into account in determining G2's share of Helga's probate estate. *See* UPC § 2-109.

The same result is likely to occur even in those states that have not enacted the Uniform Probate Code, or an approach to advancement that reverses the common law. At common law, the advancement had to be made to one who would have been an heir at the time of the gift in order for a presumption of advancement to exist. *See* Atkinson § 129. On these facts, G2 was not an "heir apparent" at the time of the gift.

29. **Answer (A) is correct.** At the time of the assignment, C1 did not have a property interest in Matteo's probate estate that C1 could transfer. C1 had an expectancy, not a property interest. Matteo still owned fee simple title. *See* Atkinson § 131. When C2 died, C2's interest in Matteo's estate passed to C2's spouse. The same result would likely occur in states that have not enacted the Uniform Probate Code.

Answers (B) and (C) are incorrect. C1 did not own a property interest in Matteo's property that could be given or sold to the assignee. Had C1 survived Matteo by more than 120 hours, the assignee may have been able to enforce the assignment against C1 and C1's estate, if the assignment had been supported by fair consideration.

Answer (D) is incorrect. The assignee may be a creditor of C1 or C1's estate, but Matteo's estate is not legally obligated to C1's assignee.

30. **Answer (B) is correct.** As soon as Matteo died, Matteo's heirs succeeded to their respective interests in Matteo's estate subject to the 120-hour rule, as well as the debts and other obligations of Matteo and Matteo's estate. *See* UPC § 2-101. Accordingly, C2's expectancy in Matteo's property became a property interest at the time of Matteo's death and could be assigned by C2 to the third party. Of course, the third-party assignee could not acquire an interest greater than the one C2 owned at the time of the assignment.

Answer (A) is incorrect. C2 has assigned C2's interest in Matteo's probate estate.

Answer (C) is incorrect. An assignment does not need good and valuable consideration to be effective. It may have been a gift.

Answer (D) is incorrect. The third-party assignee is not a creditor of Matteo; the third-party assignee acquired whatever interest in Matteo's probate estate that C2 inherited.

31. At the time of the assignment, C2 had an expectancy in Matteo's property. Such an expectancy is not a future interest in Matteo's property; it's not even a property interest. Therefore, the assignment did not transfer any property interest in Matteo's property to the assignee. At Matteo's death, C2's expectancy, in effect, matured into a property interest. State law may provide the third party with a remedy to enforce the assignment as a contract, if the third party paid good and valuable consideration. If no consideration was paid by the third party to C2, the transaction may be viewed as an unenforceable promise of C2. *See* Atkinson § 131. If the assignment was a conveyance of real property, the doctrine of "after acquired title" may be applicable. *See* PATTON AND PALOMAR ON LAND TITLES § 219 (3d ed. 2021).

32. **Answer (A) is correct.** Because C1 predeceased Matteo, C1 is not an heir and did not acquire a property interest in Matteo's probate estate that could be attached by a creditor of C1. *See* McGovern § 2.2.

    Answers (B), (C), and (D) are incorrect. These answers are incorrect for the reasons given.

33. **Answer (A) is correct.** Because C1 did not survive Matteo by 120 hours, C1 is not an heir. Thus, no part of Matteo's probate estate is reachable by C1's creditor. *See* McGovern § 2.2.

    Answers (B) and (C) are incorrect. These answers are incorrect for the reasons given.

    Answer (D) is incorrect. The creditor is not a creditor of Matteo and does not have to follow the procedures required of Matteo's creditors.

34. **Answer (B) is correct.** Because C1 survived Matteo by 120 hours, the lien can attach to C1's interest in Matteo's probate estate that passed to S1 when C1 died. *See* McGovern § 2.2. However, C1's interest in Matteo's estate is still subject to administration by Matteo's personal representative, as well as Matteo's debts and other obligations. The creditor cannot acquire an interest greater than the one C1 inherited.

    Answer (A) is incorrect. The lien can attach to C1's interest in Matteo's probate estate.

    Answer (C) is incorrect. The nature of the debt is irrelevant.

    Answer (D) is incorrect. The creditor is not a creditor of Matteo and does not have to follow the procedures required of Matteo's creditors.

35. The early common law did not allow a decedent's heirs to refuse to accept their inheritances. Modern statutes in most states, such as UPC §§ 2-1102, 2-1105, 2-1106, authorize an heir to disclaim the heir's interest in the decedent's estate so that the property to

which the heir would have been entitled passes as if the heir had predeceased the decedent. Statutes in some states, such as UPC § 2-1105, permit an heir's court-appointed surrogate, guardian, conservator, or personal representative to execute the disclaimer. However, the law varies from state to state on the effect the disclaimer will have on the disclaimant's creditors. *See* UPC § 2-1113 and its comments. Federal law will control if the disclaimant is in bankruptcy. *See* McGovern § 2.8.

36. **Answer (A) is correct.** Assuming the disclaimer satisfied the requirements of both applicable state law and the relevant provisions of the Internal Revenue Code, the interest in Marit's probate estate that C2 would have inherited had it not been for the disclaimer passes from Marit to G2. *See* UPC § 2-1106(b)(3). No part of the disclaimed property is included in C2's gross estate for estate tax purposes, and C2 is not deemed to have made a gift to G2 for gift tax purposes. *See* I.R.C. § 2518; McGovern § 2.8.

    Answers (B), (C), and (D) are incorrect. These answers are incorrect for the reasons given.

37. In most states, if Marit's probate estate is otherwise solvent (*i.e.*, the assets exceed the liabilities), whether or not the debt is valid and enforceable, the concept of "retainer" provides that C1's share of Marit's estate should be reduced by $6,000 so that the other heir's share of the probate estate is increased by a like amount in order to create equality among the heirs. *See* Atkinson § 141. However, UPC § 3-903 gives the borrower the benefit of any defense which would be available in a direct proceeding for recovery of the debt. If Marit's estate is insolvent (*i.e.*, the liabilities exceed the assets) and the debt is a valid and enforceable obligation of C1, C1 should pay into Marit's estate $12,000 in order for the personal representative to have funds to pay Marit's debts. If C1 does not pay what is owed, Marit's personal representative should pursue the $12,000 debt against C1. *See* Atkinson Ch. 13. If the debt is no longer enforceable (*i.e.*, collection is barred by the statute of limitations), C1 has no obligation to pay any amount into Marit's estate.

38. **Answer (A) is correct.** It is generally accepted that delivery and acceptance are necessary for a valid inter vivos gift. Neither the cash nor the deed was delivered to C1 during Marit's lifetime. Accordingly, unless relevant state law relaxes the delivery and acceptance requirements of a gift under "gift causa mortis" theory, both the house and cash would pass to Marit's heirs. *See* Atkinson § 45.

    Answers (B) and (D) are incorrect. The concept of "gift causa mortis" has been limited in most jurisdictions to gifts of personal property only.

    Answer (C) is incorrect. If the described assets were still part of Marit's probate estate, the assets would pass to Marit's heirs. However, if Marit made an inter vivos gift of the assets prior to Marit's death, the assets would have already been owned by the donee prior to Marit's death. Delivery during the donor's lifetime is an essential element of a gift. Since the deed was not delivered while Marit was alive, the house is still part of the probate estate. However, states that recognize the concept of "gift causa mortis" may relax the delivery and acceptance requirements. Accordingly, in those states, the cash may have been given to C1.

39. **Answer (B) is correct.** UPC § 2-803(b) provides that an heir who feloniously and intentionally kills the intestate forfeits the heir's intestate share. It also provides that the intestate's probate estate passes as if the killer disclaimed the killer's interest in the intestate's estate. Accordingly, the interest C1 would have received passes from Marit to G1.

Answer (A) is incorrect. Since C1 is deemed to have disclaimed the interest, the interest is not forfeited to the state.

Answer (C) is incorrect. UPC § 2-803(b) provides that C1's interest passes as if C1 had disclaimed C1's interest. However, in some states, the state "slayer rule" directs that C1's interest might be forfeited and C1's interest would pass to Marit's other heirs. Accordingly, in those states, C2 would take C1's interest, and G1 is excluded since C1, in fact, survived Marit. *See* McGovern § 2.7.

Answer (D) is incorrect. UPC § 2-803(b) provides a legal remedy that avoids having to resort to equitable principles. However, in those states that have not enacted a slayer statute, the other heirs may be able to resort to the constructive trust as a remedy to prevent unjust enrichment.

Probate & Nonprobate Assets

1. The first step in this type of question is to marshall the assets of the decedent. What assets are part of the probate estate and what assets pass outside of probate? Daisy's probate estate includes only her interest in Whiteacre.

Under the common law, Daisy's life estate interest in Blackacre extinguishes at the moment of her death. Avery's remainder interest became fee simple title by the terms of the original grant, and Huxton therefore takes no interest in Blackacre. *See* Atkinson § 2.8. Huxton inherits Daisy's remainder interest in Whiteacare, which was not expressly made subject to the condition that Daisy survive Brooklyn. Huxton does not come into possession of Whiteacre because it is still subject to Brooklyn's life estate. *See* Atkinson § 27. It is worth noting that if the interest in Whiteacre had been held in trust, UPC § 2-707 may reach a different result. *See* Andersen § 45.

Absent a statute, a disposition of property intended to take effect at the transferor's death, which is not executed with testamentary formalities, must be sustained under the theory of contract, gift, or trust. *See* Atkinson, ch. 4. However, legislation exists in most states that validates many types of nonprobate dispositions of property that become effective at the transferor's death. *See* Andersen ch. 5, at 303. In other words, property passing pursuant to will substitute passes outside of probate.

Consequently, at the time of Daisy's death, Huxton acquires no interest in either the savings account or insurance policy—neither asset is part of Daisy's probate estate at the time of her death. Chester becomes the owner of the savings account, and the insurance policy is payable to Ellis, with both the disposition of the savings account and insurance policy controlled by the contract creating each. *See* Andersen ch. 5, at 440. The savings account and life insurance policy are examples of "nonprobate" or "nontestamentary" dispositions.

2. Answer (B) is correct. Daisy's probate estate includes only Daisy's interest in Whiteacre. Blackacre, the account, and the policy proceeds are not part of the probate estate. Since Daisy's will has been admitted to probate, Huxton has been divested, and Grady succeeds to the ownership of the assets included in Daisy' probate estate. *See* Atkinson § 1; Andersen ch. 5.

Answers (A), (C), and (D) are incorrect. Because Daisy died testate, Grady succeeded to the ownership of the probate assets in the same way Huxton inherited the assets in the probate estate when Daisy died intestate. Of the four described assets, only

Daisy's interest in Whiteacre is included in the probate estate and subject to formal administration.

3. **Answer (D) is correct.** Grady inherits Whiteacre, the account, and the policy proceeds; these assets became part of Daisy's probate estate and are subject to formal administration. The intended beneficiary must survive the transferor to be entitled to the account or insurance proceeds. *See* Andersen ch. 5. Blackacre is not included in Daisy's probate estate. Why? Because when Daisy died, Daisy's life interest in Blackacre terminated. Avery's heirs or devisees own Blackacre because Avery had a vested remainder.

   Answers (A), (B), and (C) are incorrect. Daisy's probate estate includes Whiteacre, the account, and the policy proceeds because Brooklyn, Chester, and Ellis died before Daisy. Blackacre passed to Avery's successors in interest at Daisy's death because Daisy only had a life estate, which is not included as a part of Daisy's probate estate.

4. **Answer (A) is correct.** The fact that Daisy had entered into contracts with the bank and insurance company that control the dispositions of the assets at Daisy death did not give Chester and Ellis ownership interests in the assets during Daisy's lifetime. Daisy retained ownership during her lifetime. The intended beneficiary must survive the transferor in order to be entitled to the account or insurance proceeds. *See* UPC §§ 6-101, 6-212 (amended 2019), U.L.A. (1969); Andersen § 19. UPC § 2-702 requires the beneficiary to survive Daisy by 120 hours unless the governing document provides otherwise. The account and proceeds became part of Daisy's probate estate. *See* Andersen § 18(B).

   Answers (B), (C), and (D) are incorrect. Chester and Ellis were "third-party beneficiaries" of the contracts prior to their deaths. Their deaths terminated their contractual rights under the contracts. Since Chester and Ellis had mere "expectancies" and not future interests, the heirs or devisees of Chester and Ellis did not inherit any interest in the account or policy.

5. **Answer (A) is correct.** The fact that Daisy had entered into contracts with the bank and insurance company that control the dispositions of the assets at Daisy's death did not give Chester and Ellis ownership interests in the assets during Daisy's lifetime. Daisy retained ownership during her lifetime. The intended beneficiary must survive the transferor in order to be entitled to the account or insurance proceeds. *See* answer to immediately preceding question. The fact that the intended beneficiary has children is irrelevant if the beneficiary is not related to Daisy. *See* UPC § 2-706. The account and proceeds became part of Daisy's probate estate. *See* Andersen § 18(B).

   Answers (B), (C), and (D) are incorrect. Chester and Ellis were "third-party beneficiaries" of the contracts prior to their deaths. Their deaths terminated their contractual rights under the contracts. Since Chester and Ellis had mere "expectancies" and not future interests, the heirs or devisees of Chester and Ellis did not inherit any interest in the account or policy.

6. **Answer (D) is correct.** Because Chester and Ellis are descendants of Daisy, UPC § 2-706 created substituted gifts in favor of the children of Chester and Ellis. The assets pass nonprobate to the children. *See* Andersen § 45(B)(2)(b). In a non-UPC state, the relevant statute must be examined to see if it is applicable to nonprobate dispositions.

   Answers (A), (B), and (C) are incorrect. These answers are incorrect for the reasons given.

7. **Answer (B) is correct.** The proper execution of a life insurance beneficiary designation form creates a contractual right in the designated beneficiary to receive the proceeds of the policy at the insured's death. The beneficiary designation confers a contractual right on the beneficiary subject to the terms of the policy, which usually reserve to the owner the right to change the beneficiary and require that the beneficiary survive the insured. Since it confers a contractual right, life insurance beneficiary designations do not need to comply with the statutory formalities of a will. The proceeds pass to the beneficiary outside of probate pursuant to the terms of the policy. Thus, B2 held the right to collect the proceeds when Imani died. *See* Andersen § 20.

   Answers (A), (C), and (D) are incorrect. Because it is the present assignment of a contractual right, a life insurance beneficiary designation does not need to comply with the statutory formalities required for a will. There is no distinction between initial beneficiary designations and subsequent designations. When the insured dies, the proceeds are paid to the current beneficiary pursuant to the terms of the policy.

8. No. Traditionally, the terms of the policy control. The most recent beneficiary designation executed in compliance with the terms of the policy conferred the contractual right to receive the proceeds to B2. Imani's will does not override the terms of the life insurance policy. *See* Andersen § 20. If B2 were a beneficiary under the will, B2 may be put to an equitable election to deliver the proceeds as directed in the will in exchange for the devise to B2 in the will. *See* Atkinson § 138. The Uniform Probate Code expressly prohibits the use of wills to change rights of survivorship or pay-on-death designations in bank accounts. *See* UPC § 6-213(b). Although the Uniform Probate Code does not take a position on the use of wills to change beneficiary designations on other nonprobate assets, the general rule in most jurisdictions is that wills are ineffective to do so. In some jurisdictions, wills have been found to determine the beneficiary of some nonprobate assets. For discussion of these so-called "super wills," see Dukeminier 475–76.

9. **Answer (C) is correct.** The deed made a present and irrevocable gift of a nonpossessory future interest to GS. As a lifetime gift, the deed was not a will and did not need to comply with the statutory formalities for a will. It removed the farm from Jojo's probate estate. Since no survivorship language was used, at GS's death, his remainder interest passed to Spouse pursuant to his will. *See* Andersen § 17.

Answer (A) is incorrect. GS's interest in the farm was not conditioned on his surviving Jojo. Survivorship language was not used. Jojo reserved only a life estate, and thus she had no interest in the farm at her death that would pass through probate.

Answer (B) is incorrect. While revocable deeds are legally permissible, this was not a revocable deed. Jojo made a completed and irrevocable gift to GS. She could not revoke it by her will or otherwise.

Answer (D) is incorrect. This answer is incorrect for the reasons explained above.

10. Jojo and GS became joint tenants with rights of survivorship by reason of the deed in most states. At GS's death, his interest in the farm passed nonprobate to Jojo and not under his will to Spouse. When Jojo died, the farm was devised to GD. *See* Andersen § 18.

11. **Answer (B) is correct.** UPC § 2-706 is essentially an anti-lapse statute for life insurance beneficiary designations and many other types of nonprobate transfers. It operates to designate an alternate beneficiary when the named beneficiary predeceases the decedent. UPC § 2-706 provides that when a beneficiary fails to survive the decedent, and the beneficiary is a grandparent (or descendant of grandparent) or a stepchild of decedent, the interest shall pass to the beneficiary's surviving descendants. *See* UPC § 2-706(a). UPC § 2-706 applies its substituted taker provisions to many nonprobate transfers similar to the way anti-lapse provisions apply to wills under UPC § 2-603. Thus, given the family relationship, Grandchild is entitled to receive an equal share of the proceeds. *See* Andersen § 45. Note that the anti-lapse type provisions in some states do not apply to nonprobate transfers.

   Answer (A) is incorrect because the provisions of UPC § 2-706 apply. Note that the anti-lapse type provisions in some states do not apply to nonprobate transfers.

   Answers (C) and (D) are incorrect. The substituted taker provisions entitle Grandchild to an equal share.

12. **Answer (B) is correct.** UPC § 2-706 is essentially an anti-lapse statute for life insurance beneficiary designations and many other types of nonprobate transfers. It operates to designate an alternate beneficiary when the named beneficiary predeceases the decedent. UPC § 2-706 provides that when a beneficiary fails to survive the decedent, and the beneficiary is a grandparent (or descendant of grandparent) or a stepchild of decedent, the interest shall pass to the beneficiary's surviving descendants. *See* UPC § 2-706(a). As a result, the interest of C2 will pass to C2's descendants by right of representation, or in this case, Grandchild.

   Answers (A), (C) and (D) are incorrect. These answers are incorrect for the reasons explained.

13. **Answer (B) is correct.** The Uniform Probate Code provides that a multi-party account (*e.g.*, a "joint account") is presumed to belong to the parties in proportion to their net contributions, which is the contributions of the parties plus their pro rata share of interest and dividends appropriately reduced by withdrawals. This presumption can be overcome by clear and convincing evidence that one of the parties intended a different result. *See* UPC § 6-211; McGovern § 5.5, at 306-07. And thus, in the case of Quill and Xavier, the account proceeds will belong 66.66% to Quill and 33.33% to Xavier.

    Answers (A), (C), and (D) are incorrect. These answers are incorrect for the reasons explained.

14. Unless there is specified nonsurvivorship language in the terms of the account, on the death of Quill, the surviving party (here, Xavier) owns the account. *See* UPC § 6-212(a). Some state statutes require specific "survivorship" language in the terms of the account. In those states, the heirs or devisees of the deceased party inherit the owner's interest in the account. *See* Andersen § 18(B).

15. Yes, as the surviving spouse, Yolanda would own the amount Quill owned immediately before death. *See* UPC §§ 6-211, 6-212(a); Andersen § 18(B).

16. Xavier and Yolanda would each own whatever they owned before Quill's death plus an equal share of what Quill owned. *See* McGovern § 5.5, at 306-07.

17. Unless there is specified nonsurvivorship language in the terms of the account, Yolanda, as the surviving party, owns the account even though she never contributed to the account. *See* UPC § 6-212(a); Andersen § 18(B). Some state statutes require specific "survivorship" language in the terms of the account. In those states, the heirs or devisees of the owner of the account inherit the owner's interest.

18. Yes, according to UPC § 6-102. *See* Andersen § 18(B).

19. Before Mary's death, Nasir has no right to the account. *See* UPC § 6-211(c). However, after Mary's death, Nasir is entitled to whatever remains in the account. *See* UPC § 6-212(b); McGovern § 5.5, at 306-07; Andersen § 18(B).

20. **Answer (A) is correct.** Nonprobate assets are also included in the decedent's gross estate. *See* I.R.C. §§ 2036–2040 (2022).

    Answers (B) and (C) are incorrect. One cannot avoid inclusion in the gross estate by making this type of nonprobate disposition of the property.

    Answer (D) is incorrect. Even though the checking account is in the names of both Pablo and Stella, 100% of the account is included in Pablo's gross estate because he created and funded the account. *See* I.R.C. § 2040 (2022).

21. **Answer (A) is correct.** An insurance policy on the decedent's life is included in the decedent's gross estate if (i) the policy is payable to the decedent's probate estate or (ii) the decedent owned the policy immediately prior to death. *See* I.R.C. § 2042 (2022).

    Answers (B), (C), and (D) are incorrect. Pablo owned both policies at the time of death. Accordingly, the proceeds of each are included in the gross estate.

22. **Answer (A) is correct.** The two plans add $1,500,000 to Zelda's gross estate even though C will have to report the $1,500,000 as income when received. *See* I.R.C. § 2039 (2022).

23. **Answers (B), (C), and (D) are incorrect.** Both plans are included in the gross estate. C will be entitled to an income tax deduction for any estate taxes attributable to the plans. *See* I.R.C. § 691 (2022).

Testamentary Capacity & Will Contests

1. Fraud requires that a wrongdoer knowingly or recklessly make a false representation to the testator about a material fact and that the testator relied upon that misrepresentation as concerns some type of testamentary disposition. Undue influence occurs when a testator's free will is supplanted by that of a wrongdoer, causing the testator to make a will that he, she, or they would not otherwise make. Fraud requires a misrepresentation, but undue influence does not.

2. **Answer (D) is correct.** UPC § 2-501 requires a person to be of "sound mind" when executing a will. The test for mental capacity requires the testator to be capable of knowing and understanding in a general way the nature and extent of their property, the natural objects of their bounty, and the disposition that they are making of their property. RESTATEMENT (THIRD) OF PROP.: WILLS & DONATIVE TRANSFERS § 8.1 (2003). The testator must also be capable of relating these elements to one another and forming an orderly plan as concerns the disposition of their property. It is not necessary that Daisy know the exact valuation of each asset that she owns.

    Answers (A) and (B) are incorrect. UPC § 2-501 requires a person to be of "sound mind" when executing a will. The test for mental capacity requires the testator to be capable of knowing and understanding in a general way the nature and extent of their property but does not require actual knowledge of the nature and extent of all property. RESTATEMENT (THIRD) OF PROP.: WILLS & DONATIVE TRANSFERS § 8.1 (2003). A mistaken belief is irrelevant.

    Answer (C) is incorrect. The test for mental capacity requires the testator to be capable of knowing and understanding in a *general* way the nature and extent of their property. RESTATEMENT (THIRD) OF PROP.: WILLS & DONATIVE TRANSFERS § 8.1 (2003).

3. **Answer (D) is correct.** UPC § 2-501 requires a person to be of "sound mind" when executing a will. The test for mental capacity requires the testator to be capable of knowing and understanding in a general way the nature and extent of their property, the natural objects of their bounty, and the disposition that they are making of their property. RESTATEMENT (THIRD) OF PROP.: WILLS & DONATIVE TRANSFERS § 8.1 (2003). The testator must also be capable of relating these elements to one another and forming an orderly plan as concerns the disposition of their property. This definition relates to the

capability to know, not actual knowledge. The facts of this question are strikingly similar to *Williams v. Vollman*, 738 S.W.2d 849 (Ky. Ct. App. 1987). In *Williams*, the court found an elderly testator competent to execute a will even though he was unaware of the deaths of his wife and daughter because the information had been withheld from him. *See* Restatement (Third) of Prop.: Wills & Donative Transfers § 8.1 reporter's note 16 (2003).

Answers (A) and (B) are incorrect. UPC § 2-501 requires a person to be of "sound mind" when executing a will. The test for mental capacity requires the testator to be capable of knowing and understanding in a general way the natural objects of their bounty but does not require actual knowledge. Restatement (Third) of Prop.: Wills & Donative Transfers § 8.1 (2003). A mistaken belief is irrelevant.

Answer (C) is incorrect. The test for mental capacity does not specifically refer to family members, but it does require that the testator be capable of knowing the natural objects of their bounty. UPC § 2-501; Restatement (Third) of Prop.: Wills & Donative Transfers § 8.1 (2003).

4. The result would not change. The capacity requirements for a will and any revocable will substitutes are the same. Restatement (Third) of Prop.: Wills & Donative Transfers § 8.1(a) (2003).

5. The contestants of a will have the burden of establishing lack of present testamentary intent or capacity, undue influence, fraud, duress, mistake, or revocation. *See* UPC § 3-407.

6. **Answer (C) is correct.** A confidential relationship is created in three types of relationships: fiduciary, reliant, or dominant-subservient. A fiduciary relationship is a relationship that arises from a settled category of fiduciary obligation (*i.e.*, an attorney is in a fiduciary relationship with their client). A reliant relationship exists if the contestant proves the relationship was based on special trust and confidence (*i.e.*, a relationship between a doctor and patient). A dominant-subservient relationship exists if the contestant establishes that the donor was subservient to the alleged wrongdoer's dominant influence (*i.e.*, a relationship between a caregiver and a feeble donor). Dukeminier at 288; Restatement (Third) of Prop.: Wills & Donative Transfers § 8.3 cmt. g (2003). Here, there are no facts to indicate Mary Anne had a fiduciary, reliant, or dominant-subservient relationship with either C1 or C2, therefore, no confidential relationship existed. There are no facts to indicate that C1 and C2 did not behave appropriately. Further, the disposition to C1 and C2 is not suspicious or unnatural when supported with the explanation from testator.

Answers (A) and (B) are incorrect. A disproportionately large disposition to one sibling does not, in and of itself, give rise to a presumption of undue influence. Nor is it a suspicious circumstance that will automatically cause a burden to shift.

Answer (D) is incorrect. It is possible to successfully allege undue influence even when a testator is represented by independent counsel.

7. **Answer (B) is correct.** The general rule is that the contestant to a will has the burden to prove undue influence. UPC § 3-407. In many jurisdictions, however, the burden shifts if the alleged wrongdoer was in a confidential relationship with the testator and there are suspicious circumstances. RESTATEMENT (THIRD) OF PROP.: WILLS & DONATIVE TRANSFERS § 8.3 cmt. f (2003). As Mason's caretaker, Gladys is in a confidential relationship with Mason. Child C may be successful in arguing suspicious circumstances on these facts because of Mason's isolation, the large disposition to his neighbor instead of his child, and the fact that the attorney had a preexisting relationship with Gladys. The burden would then shift to Gladys to establish that no undue influence occurred.

    Answer (A) is incorrect. Although the contestant bears an initial burden, a hallmark of undue influence cases is burden shifting to the alleged wrongdoer after an initial burden is met. RESTATEMENT (THIRD) OF PROP.: WILLS & DONATIVE TRANSFERS § 8.3 cmt. b, cmt. f (2003).

    Answers (C) and (D) are incorrect. Although the burden may shift to Gladys, the contestant bears the initial burden in an undue influence case. RESTATEMENT (THIRD) OF PROP.: WILLS & DONATIVE TRANSFERS § 8.3 cmt. b, cmt. f (2003).

8. **Answer (A) is correct.** The general rule is that the contestant to a will has the burden to prove undue influence. UPC § 3-407. In many jurisdictions, however, the burden shifts if the alleged wrongdoer was in a confidential relationship with the testator and there are suspicious circumstances. Confidential relationships, for these purposes, generally arise in one of three contexts: (a) fiduciary (e.g., lawyer-client); (b) dominant-subservient (e.g., some romantic or family relationships); (c) reliant (e.g., nurse-patient). On these facts, John was in a confidential relationship with Dembe because he is Dembe's lawyer. Because of the suspicious circumstances, John has the burden of proof to offer evidence that Dembe was free from undue influence when he executed the will. RESTATEMENT (THIRD) OF PROP.: WILLS & DONATIVE TRANSFERS § 8.3 cmt. h, illus. 3 (2003).

    Answer (B) is incorrect. The suspicious circumstance is the change in disposition from the National Alley Cat Association (under the prior testamentary instrument) to an attorney with whom Dembe has established a new relationship. John is not the natural object of Dembe's bounty. RESTATEMENT (THIRD) OF PROP.: WILLS & DONATIVE TRANSFERS § 8.3 cmt. h, illus. 3 (2003).

    Answers (C) and (D) are incorrect. The general rule is that the contestant of the will, the National Alley Cat Association, would have the burden of establishing undue influence. In many jurisdictions, however, the burden shifts if the alleged wrongdoer was in a confidential relationship with the testator and there are suspicious circumstances. The attorney-client relationship is a confidential relationship, and as explained above, there are suspicious circumstances. The burden will therefore shift to John. John would have to come forward with evidence that Dembe was free from undue influence when he executed the will. RESTATEMENT (THIRD) OF PROP.: WILLS & DONATIVE TRANSFERS § 8.3 cmt. h, illus. 3 (2003).

9. **Answer (D) is correct.** A testamentary disposition is procured by fraud if the wrong-doer knowingly or recklessly made a material misrepresentation to the testator that was intended to deceive, and the material misrepresentation influenced or caused the testamentary disposition. Attorney knowingly lied to Mei about the contents of the will, intending to induce Mei's execution of the will. Only the provision induced by the fraud will be struck from the will, or here, the $300,000 gift to Attorney. The will was otherwise prepared as Mei requested and intended. The result is that the provision to Attorney will be ignored, but the will otherwise will be probated as written. RESTATEMENT (THIRD) OF PROP.: WILLS & DONATIVE TRANSFERS § 8.3 cmt. j, illus. 8 (2003).

   Answer (A) is incorrect. If a devise in a will is procured by fraud, only that devise is invalid. RESTATEMENT (THIRD) OF PROP.: WILLS & DONATIVE TRANSFERS § 8.3 cmt. d (2003).

   Answer (B) is incorrect. The failure to review a will does not invalidate the will.

   Answer (C) is incorrect. It is generous to suggest that Attorney was mistaken as to the contents of the will, but in fairness, this is not a case of mistake. Attorney fraudulently induced Mei to execute this will. RESTATEMENT (THIRD) OF PROP.: WILLS & DONATIVE TRANSFERS § 8.3 cmt. d, cmt. j (2003).

10. UPC § 3-905 provides that a provision in a will purporting to penalize any interested party for contesting a will is unenforceable if probable cause exists for instituting proceedings. Probable cause to institute proceedings arises when there is evidence that would lead a reasonable person, properly informed and advised, to conclude there is a substantial likelihood that a challenge would be successful. RESTATEMENT (THIRD) OF PROP.: WILLS & DONATIVE TRANSFERS § 8.5 cmt. c (2003). On these facts, there is a substantial likelihood that a challenge by Riko and Sakura would be successful, and so the no-contest clause will not penalize Riko and Sakura if they lose the contest.

11. This is an "unbaited" no-contest clause, meaning Tsumugi does not receive any benefit under the will. He stands to lose nothing if he contests this instrument. Therefore, the no-contest clause provides no incentive for him not to contest the will.

   A no-contest clause discourages the contest of a will when a person is placing something at risk by contesting the will. The no-contest clause trap must be baited with a benefit in the will. *See* Dukeminier at 302-03.

12. **Answer (B) is correct.** A person who is mentally incapacitated part of the time but who has lucid intervals during which they have testamentary capacity can make a valid will during such an interval. RESTATEMENT (THIRD) OF PROP.: WILLS & DONATIVE TRANSFERS § 8.1 cmt. m (2003).

Answer (A) is incorrect. The fact that she has not been found by a court to be incapacitated is not determinative of testamentary capacity. RESTATEMENT (THIRD) OF PROP.: WILLS & DONATIVE TRANSFERS § 8.1 cmt. h (2003).

Answer (C) is incorrect. "Totality of the circumstances" is not part of the test for determining testamentary capacity. The test for testamentary capacity requires that the testator be capable of knowing and understanding in a general way the nature and extent of their property, the natural objects of their bounty, and the disposition that they are making of their property. RESTATEMENT (THIRD) OF PROP.: WILLS & DONATIVE TRANSFERS § 8.1 (2003). The testator must also be capable of relating these elements to one another and forming an orderly plan as concerns the disposition of their property. *Id.*

Answer (D) is incorrect. The fact that her physician has not attested to her mental capacity is not determinative of testamentary capacity. RESTATEMENT (THIRD) OF PROP.: WILLS & DONATIVE TRANSFERS § 8.1 cmt. c (2003).

13. **Answer (B) is correct.** An adjudication of mental incapacity does not conclusively establish that the testator lacks testamentary capacity, but it raises a rebuttable presumption to this effect, shifting the burden of proof to the proponent of the instrument to show the testator possessed testamentary capacity. RESTATEMENT (THIRD) OF PROP.: WILLS & DONATIVE TRANSFERS § 8.1 cmt. h (2003).

Answer (A) is incorrect. Freja does not "by definition" lack capacity. An adjudication of mental incapacity does not conclusively establish that the testator lacks testamentary capacity.

Answer (C) is incorrect. An adjudication of mental incapacity does indeed affect a determination of whether the testator possessed testamentary capacity. It raises a rebuttable presumption that the testator lacked capacity. RESTATEMENT (THIRD) OF PROP.: WILLS & DONATIVE TRANSFERS § 8.1 cmt. h (2003).

Answer (D) is incorrect. In a deviation from the law in many states, UPC § 5-411 does permit a court to authorize a conservator to make a will for the incapacitated person. However, even though Alma may be able to petition the court to do so, she does not necessarily have the exclusive power to make a will for Freja — who still may possess the requisite mental capacity to do so herself.

14. **Answer (C) is correct.** An insane delusion is a belief that is so against all evidence and reason that it must be the product of derangement. RESTATEMENT (THIRD) OF PROP.: WILLS & DONATIVE TRANSFERS § 8.1 cmt. s (2003). However, a person who suffers from an insane delusion is not necessarily deprived of the capacity to make a will. Such a person's will would only be invalid to the extent that it was the product of the insane delusion. *Id.*; Dukeminier at 273-74. Harry's insane delusion about Atlantis did not affect his will since he left his entire estate to his wife as was consistent with his prior estate plan.

Answer (A) is incorrect. Harry's insane delusion about Atlantis did not affect his will since he left his entire estate to his wife as was consistent with his prior estate plan. If Harry left his entire estate to someone dedicated to the study of Atlantis, for example, the will would be invalid.

Answer (B) is incorrect. When a person suffers from an insane delusion, their will is only invalid to the extent that it was the product of the insane delusion.

Answer (D) is incorrect. A person who is mentally incapacitated part of the time but who has lucid intervals during which they have testamentary capacity can make a will during the lucid interval. RESTATEMENT (THIRD) OF PROP.: WILLS & DONATIVE TRANSFERS § 8.1 cmt. m (2003). However, since the delusion does not appear to have affected the disposition of Harry's property, the will is valid despite the delusion. RESTATEMENT (THIRD) OF PROP.: WILLS & DONATIVE TRANSFERS § 8.1 cmt. s (2003). Thus, there is no need to argue that he wrote the will during a lucid interval in order to establish that it is valid (*i.e.*, even if Harry believed he was a descendant of Atlantean royalty and could breathe underwater, he still left his estate to his wife rather than any of his imagined underwater kin).

15. **Answer (D) is correct.** An insane delusion is a belief that is so against all evidence and reason that it must be the product of derangement. RESTATEMENT (THIRD) OF PROP.: WILLS & DONATIVE TRANSFERS § 8.1 cmt. s (2003). The difference between a mistake and an insane delusion is that a mistake is susceptible to correction and an insane delusion is not. Dukeminier at 273-74. There are no facts indicating that Reynaldo's mistake as to valuation is the product of derangement and not susceptible to correction. Consequently, the mistake will not impact the disposition of the painting to June.

    Answers (A) and (B) are incorrect. There are no facts indicating that Reynaldo's mistake as to valuation is the product of derangement and not susceptible to correction. The mistake in valuation appears to be the product of an innocent mistake rather than an insane delusion.

    Answer (C) is incorrect. When there is a mistake in valuation, it does not render a will provision invalid. Dukeminier at 273.

Will Execution

1. Generally, a will is a testamentary instrument that directs how the testator's property is to be distributed after the testator's death. It may also be used to designate who the testator wishes to serve in fiduciary capacities (*e.g.*, executor, trustee, etc.). A will is not valid unless it was executed by the testator who had testamentary capacity following required statutory formalities. If not revoked by the testator prior to death, the will can be admitted to probate by a court of competent jurisdiction to be effective as a testamentary disposition. *See* McGovern Ch. 4.

2. **Answer (B) is correct.** A testator must be at least 18 years of age and be of sound mind to validly execute a will. *See* UPC § 2-501. In a contested probate proceeding, Frank will have the burden to prove the facts of (i) Testator's death, (ii) the court's venue, and (iii) the due execution of the will. However, Alejandro will have the burden to prove Testator did not have testamentary capacity. *See* UPC § 3-407. In some jurisdictions, Frank would have the burden to prove Testator had testamentary capacity at the time Testator executed the will. *See* Atkinson §§ 100, 101.

   Answer (A) is incorrect. A diagnosis of a degenerative illness alone is not likely to be considered prima facie evidence of the lack of Testator's testamentary capacity.

   Answer (C) is incorrect. According to the Uniform Probate Code, the burden of proof on the issue of testamentary capacity is on the contestant.

   Answer (D) is incorrect. The test for the capacity necessary to execute a will differs from the test for incapacity in a guardianship or conservatorship proceeding. Courts consider a variety of factors to determine whether a testator had testamentary capacity, such as the testator's ability to understand the nature of a testamentary act, to remember the "natural" objects of the testator's bounty, and to understand the nature and extent of the testator's property. *See* McGovern § 7.1.

3. **Answer (B) is correct.** Alejandro has the burden to prove Testator lacked testamentary capacity when the will was executed. *See* UPC § 3-407. However, introduction of evidence that Testator had previously been found to be incapacitated in a guardianship proceeding may be evidence that Testator lacked testamentary capacity. *See* McGovern § 7.2. In some non-UPC jurisdictions, the burden of proof is on Frank to prove Testator had testamentary capacity. *See* Atkinson §§ 100, 101.

   Answers (A), (C), and (D) are incorrect. These answers are incorrect for the reasons given.

4. **Answer (B) is correct.** Alejandro has the burden to prove Testator lacked testamentary capacity when the will was executed. *See* UPC § 3-407. The fact that Testator was found to be incapacitated in a guardianship proceeding after the will was executed may be evidence of incapacity but is not conclusive. Different tests for capacity are used in guardianship proceedings and probate proceedings. Note that in some non-UPC jurisdictions, Frank would have the burden to prove that Testator had testamentary capacity. *See* Atkinson §§ 100, 101.

    Answers (A), (C), and (D) are incorrect. These answers are incorrect for the reasons given.

5. **Answer (C) is correct.** The will of a testator with the requisite testamentary capacity can still be denied probate if the devisee improperly influenced the testator during the execution of the will. Accordingly, Alejandro has the burden to prove Frank's undue influence. *See* UPC § 3-407. Non-UPC states typically place the burden on the contestant for the issue of undue influence. *See* McGovern § 7.3.

    Answers (A) and (B) are incorrect. Undue influence is an issue separate and distinct from testamentary capacity, although evidence of one is relevant to the other.

    Answer (D) is incorrect. The burden of proof is typically on the contestant even in a state where the burden of proof on capacity is on the proponent.

6. A will must be in writing and signed by the testator. *See* UPC § 2-502. However, a testator does not need to sign the testator's legal name or even the name typically used by the testator. The rule is that whatever is intended to serve as a signature will suffice. Accordingly, if Freja wrote her first name and intended it to be her signature, the will is signed. If the evidence shows that Freja intended to write both first and last names, but was unable to complete the task, some courts have held the will was not signed. *See* McGovern § 4.2. It is worth noting that this rule generally remains the same even in non-UPC states.

7. **Answer (C) is correct.** Whatever a testator intends to be a signature can be a signature. It is not unusual for a testator to make a "mark" on the will rather than sign the testator's name. If the "mark" was intended to be a signature, the will has been signed. *See* McGovern § 4.2. Accordingly, Branka has the burden to prove due execution, including the signature requirement. *See* UPC § 3-407. In non-UPC states, the burden of proof is typically placed upon the proponent of the will. *See* Atkinson §§ 100, 101.

    Answers (A), (B), and (D) are incorrect. If it can be proven that Freja intended the mark to be her signature, the will can be admitted to probate.

8. **Answer (C) is correct.** UPC § 2-502(a)(2) authorizes what is commonly called a "proxy signature." If the testator's name is signed by another in the testator's conscious presence

and at the testator's direction, the will can be admitted to probate. Accordingly, Branka has the burden to prove the requisites of a "proxy signature." While most states that have not enacted the Uniform Probate Code permit "proxy signatures," they may differ on what is required for a "proxy signature" to be effective. *See* McGovern § 4.2.

Answer (A) is incorrect. A will can have a proxy signature.

Answer (B) is incorrect. Branka will have to prove by a preponderance of the evidence that the witness signed Freja's name at Freja's direction and in Freja's conscious presence.

Answer (D) is incorrect. UPC § 2-502(a)(2) requires that the witness sign Freja's name at Freja's direction in Freja's "conscious presence." This requirement is met on these facts. In some non-UPC states, however, the proxy signature may need to have been done in Freja's "visual presence" or "line of sight." If so, since Freja could not see the witness sign the will, the will may not be valid.

9. UPC § 2-502 does not require that the testator "publish" the document as a will. Accordingly, it is not necessary to prove that the witnesses were aware the document they were signing was Farai's will. If Greyson can prove that the witnesses signed after they observed Farai sign the document, or that the witnesses signed after Farai acknowledged her own signature, the will can be admitted to probate, even if they were not aware what they signed was actually a will.

In non-UPC states, the technical requirements for will execution vary. For example, the testator may be required to "publish" the will. In some states, the testator must—at a minimum—acknowledge to the witnesses that the document is the testator's document. Also, some states require that the testator request the witnesses sign the document. *See* McGovern § 4.3.

10. **Answer (D) is correct.** UPC § 2-502(a)(3)(A) does not require the witnesses observe a testator signing the will. The Uniform Probate Code only requires that each witness observe one of the following: (i) the testator sign the will, (ii) the testator acknowledge the testator's signature, or (iii) the testator acknowledge the document as the testator's will. If it can be established that the witnesses signed the will within a reasonable time after they observed the testator acknowledging the testator's signature or the will itself, the will can be admitted to probate.

In a non-UPC state, the state's attestation requirements may be significantly different. *See* McGovern § 4.3.

Answers (A), (B), and (C) are incorrect. The will formalities vary—sometimes dramatically—from state to state. *See* James Lindgren, *Abolishing the Attestation Requirement for Wills*, 68 N.C. L. Rev. 541 (1990). It is therefore important to be wary of any answer choice on the topic of will execution that uses language such as "all states," "no states," "always," or "never."

11. The Uniform Probate Code does not require that each witness sign in the presence of the other witnesses so long as they otherwise comply with UPC § 2-502(a)(3)(A). Some non-UPC states require the witnesses to sign in each other's presence. *See* McGovern § 4.3.

12. **Answer (C) is correct.** UPC § 2-502(a)(3)(A) does not require that the witnesses sign the will in the presence of the testator. Assuming the other requirements of UPC § 2-502 can be proven by Abigail, the will can be admitted to probate. *See* UPC § 3-407. Many non-UPC states require that the witnesses sign the will in the presence of the testator. *See* McGovern § 4.3.

    Answers (A), (B), and (D) are incorrect. The Uniform Probate Code does not require that the testator observe the witnesses sign the will. In those jurisdictions that require that the witnesses sign in the presence of the testator, research may be necessary to determine if the law of the state requires "conscious" presence or "visual" or "line of sight" presence. If so, the will may not be valid.

13. The Uniform Probate Code does not require that the witnesses sign the will in the testator's presence, and the comments to UPC § 2-502 suggest that they can even sign the will after the testator's death. Accordingly, if Leah can prove that the witnesses did sign within "a reasonable time" after they observed Benjamin sign the will, or Benjamin acknowledge his signature, or Benjamin acknowledge the document as his will, the will may be admitted to probate.

    Many non-UPC states have enacted statutes that require the witnesses to sign in the testator's presence. It is up to the trier of fact to determine if this presence requirement has been met, and it may depend upon whether the court is applying the inflexible "line of sight test" or the less rigid "conscious presence test." The line of sight test is only met if the testator is able to see the witnesses in the act of signing. The conscious presence test requires only a general comprehension of the other party's actions, even if they are not clearly visible in line of sight.

    This question speaks to the issue of post-death subscription or witnessing. Two competing rules have emerged with regard to post-death subscription. The first rule, from *In Re Estate of Flicker*, 339 N.W.2d 914 (Neb. 1983), provides that the will speaks as of decedent's death and must be properly executed before then. The conflicting rule comes from *In Re Estate of Peters*, 526 A.2d 1005 (N.J. Q1987). Interpreting the Uniform Probate Code, the New Jersey court believed that a witness was allowed to sign "within a reasonable period of time" of observing the testator sign, regardless of whether the testator is still living. TL;DR: In a UPC state, post-death subscription is permitted.

14. **Answer (C) is correct.** The Uniform Probate Code only requires two witnesses. *See* UPC § 2-502(a)(3). If the will is otherwise valid, the will can be admitted to probate with only two witnesses. The Uniform Probate Code was amended in 2008 to also allow notarized wills without any witnesses. *See* McGovern § 4.3.

Answers (A, (B), and (D) are incorrect. The Uniform Probate Code does not require three witnesses. In those jurisdictions that do require more than two witnesses, research may be necessary to see if the state has a "harmless error" statute, or if the courts have otherwise relaxed the doctrine of "strict compliance."

15. **Answer (C) is correct.** Unlike statutes in some states, the Uniform Probate Code does not require that the testator sign the will at the end of the document. *See* UPC § 2-502(a)(2). Elizabeth must prove that Benjamin intended the writing of his name in the first line to be his signature. *See* UPC § 3-407. In a non-UPC state, research may be necessary to determine if the applicable statute requires the testator's signature to appear at the end of the will. If so, the will may not be valid.

    Answers (A) and (B) are incorrect. The fact that the testator did not sign at the end is not necessarily a bar to the will's probate in most states. Nevertheless, the fact the testator wrote the testator's name in the body of the will may not constitute a "signature."

    Answer (D) is incorrect. Beware of the fill-in-the-blank or form will that states it is "valid in all fifty states." It is not uncommon for a fill-in-the-blank will to cost far more to probate than a professionally drafted instrument. Form wills can and may be probated, but the treatment of these wills varies dramatically from state to state.

16. C1 will likely inherit the entire estate. Anatoliy did not comply with the statutory requirements of revocation or execution. Thus, the 2020 will was not revoked by Anatoliy prior to his death. It is generally accepted that a will may be revoked by either a subsequent valid will or an authorized act done to the will. UPC § 2-507 confirms this principle. Accordingly, notwithstanding Anatoliy's expressed intent to revoke the 2020 will and leave his property to Ganna, Anatoliy's intent was not expressed in a writing that met the requirements of a valid will. *See* UPC § 2-502. The e-mail did not meet the statutory requirements of a will. In a non-UPC state, the result is likely to remain the same. *See* McGovern § 5.1.

17. **Answer (B) is correct.** The 2020 will was not revoked by Anatoliy. It is generally accepted that a will may be revoked by either a subsequent valid will or an authorized act done to the will. UPC § 2-507 confirms this principle. Accordingly, notwithstanding Anatoliy's expressed intent to revoke the 2020 will and leave Anatoliy's property to Ganna, Anatoliy's intent was not expressed in a writing that meets the requirements of a valid will. *See* UPC § 2-502. In a non-UPC state the result is likely to be the same. *See* McGovern § 5.1.

    Answer (A) is incorrect. The letter was not a valid will unless the court finds UPC § 2-503 is applicable and Ganna meets the burden of proof required by the statute.

    Answers (C) and (D) are incorrect. These answers are incorrect for the reasons given.

18. **Answer (A) is correct.** UPC § 2-502(b) provides that a will that is not properly witnessed can still be valid if the material provisions of the will are in the testator's handwriting (often referred to as a "holographic" instrument). Accordingly, if the letter manifests "testamentary" or "revocatory" intent (*i.e.*, the letter indicates it was intended to have a dispositive effect and not just a casual expression of what a future will should contain), it is a will that revokes the old will and devises Anatoliy's probate estate to Ganna. Proof of the testator's intent can be made with extrinsic evidence. *See* UPC § 2-502(c). In a significant departure from the generally accepted view, UPC § 3-407 places on the contestants the burden of establishing Anatoliy's lack of testamentary intent. It is worth noting that roughly one-half of the states in the U.S. do not recognize holographic wills. *See* McGovern § 4.4. Some states place the burden of proof on the proponent. *See* Atkinson §§ 100, 101.

     Answers (B), (C), and (D) are incorrect. These answers are incorrect for the reasons given.

19. **Answer (B) is correct.** The 2020 will was not revoked. The document found in the safe deposit box is not a valid will. UPC § 2-502(b) provides that a will that is not properly witnessed must be acknowledged by the testator before a notary public or be in the testator's handwriting. In a non-UPC state, the result is likely to be the same. *See* McGovern § 5.1.

     Answer (A) is incorrect. The document in the safe deposit box is not a valid will unless the court finds UPC § 2-503 is applicable and Ganna meets the burden of establishing Anatoliy intended the document to be his will.

     Answers (C) and (D) are incorrect. Anatoliy was survived by both children but did not die intestate.

20. We know that the 2020 will is valid. The issue, on these facts, is whether the handwritten document is also valid as a testamentary instrument.

     UPC § 2-502(b) provides that a will that is not properly witnessed can still be valid, if the material provisions of the will are in the testator's handwriting (referred to as a "holographic instrument"). Roughly half the states in the United States recognize holographic wills. Delivery is not a prerequisite. Accordingly, the handwritten instrument would be valid as a testamentary instrument and given testamentary effect. If valid, the handwritten instrument revokes the 2020 will to the extent of any inconsistency. The property would go to Ganna. In a state that does not recognize the validity of holographic instruments, this handwritten, unwitnessed instrument would not be given testamentary effect. *See* McGovern § 4.4.

21. **Answer (A) is correct.** UPC § 2-502(b) requires that only the "material portions" of the will be in the testator's handwriting. In states that do not recognize the validity of handwritten (holographic) instruments, the 2020 will will not be revoked because the

new instrument was not properly witnessed. In states that do recognize the validity of holographic instruments, a court may determine that the instrument is invalid because it is not entirely in the testator's handwriting (due to the preprinted blanks for the date). In other states that recognize the validity of holographic instruments, the preprinted language on the stationary will be treated as "mere surplusage" and the instrument will be treated as written entirely in the testator's handwriting (and therefore valid). *See* McGovern § 4.4.

Answers (B), (C), and (D) are incorrect. These answers are incorrect for the reasons given.

22. Since the will was not executed, it cannot be admitted to probate. The comment to UPC § 2-503 seems to indicate that the situation described is not one that could be corrected by the court admitting the unexecuted will to probate. However, Gigi may be successful in requesting the court to impose a constructive trust on Mateo and Emily due to Mateo's wrongdoing in order to prevent unjust enrichment by both Mateo and Emily. Even though only one of the heirs did anything wrong, a court may impose the constructive trust on both the "guilty" and the innocent parties, since the innocent party would not have inherited any part of the estate had it not been for the bad acts of the "guilty" person. *See* McGovern § 6.1.

23. **Answer (D) is correct.** Liam has the burden to prove Olivia's lack of testamentary intent. Upon proof of the circumstances surrounding its execution, the will is not likely to be admitted to probate. Although the document was executed with the requisite testamentary formalities, it did not express Olivia's actual testamentary intent. *See* Atkinson § 55. In some jurisdictions, the proponent has the burden of proof on testamentary intent. *See* Atkinson §§ 100, 101.

    Answers (A), (B), and (C) are incorrect. The will did not reflect Olivia's actual testamentary intent so it should not be admitted to probate.

24. **Answer (C) is correct.** Testamentary intent, in simplest terms, considers whether the testator subjectively intended the contents of a writing to be effective at her death to distribute her property. This writing was nothing more than a class demonstration.

    Answer (A) is incorrect. This is because this instrument is not testamentary in nature.

    Answer (B) is incorrect. This is because present testamentary intent is a requirement to have a valid holographic instrument.

    Answer (D) is incorrect. This is because not every state statute authorizing holographic instruments requires that the instrument be dated.

25. **Answer (D) is correct.** To have a valid holographic will, the testator must be 18 years old, of sound mind, and have present testamentary intent. The instrument must be

signed, with the material provisions in the handwriting of the testator. Many state statutes also require that the holographic instrument be dated. (At least one state requires that the will or codicil be "wholly" in the handwriting of the testator.)

Answer (A) is incorrect. A signature is anything that a testator intends to be his, her, or their signature. Initials may suffice.

Answer (B) is incorrect. In 1948, Cecil George Harris was working on his farm and became trapped under a tractor. He etched 16 famous words on his tractor fender with his pocketknife: "In case I die in this mess I leave all to the wife. Cecil George Harris." Cecil was trapped under the fender for ten hours, and later died from his injuries. The fender was removed from the tractor, presented in court, and found to be a valid holographic instrument. It is unclear if a tractor fender will always be accepted into probate, but this case serves to point out that holographic wills need not always be written on a piece of paper.

Answer (C) is incorrect. No state that permits holographic instruments requires that they be witnessed.

26. **Answer (D) is correct.** The 2008 Uniform Probate Code amendments introduced the concept of the notarized will. A writing that is signed by the testator and notarized is validly executed. In a non-UPC state, a notarized will is often upheld when a court applies a curative doctrine or the harmless error rule. There is little concern that a notarized will represents the wishes of the decedent.

Answer (C) is incorrect. A form will may be probated as a holographic instrument in some states. Holographic instruments are only valid in roughly half the states, however. In some states where they are valid, it is not uncommon for a question to arise as to whether the pre-printed language of the form will may be read as extrinsic evidence to establish testamentary intent, with a lack of consistency as to how this question is decided.

Answers (A) and (B) are incorrect. These answers are incorrect for the reasons explained above.

Will Revocation

1. Testator died intestate because the 2021 will was revoked.

    It is generally accepted that a testator may revoke a will by lining through the testator's signature. Since the 2021 will was found in Xenia's safe deposit box, most courts would presume that Xenia placed the "X" on her signature with an intent to revoke, thereby revoking the will. *See* McGovern § 5.2. UPC § 2-507 adopts this principle. (This answer assumes Xenia had testamentary capacity at all relevant times.)

2. **Answer (A) is correct.** The 2015 will was not revoked. A "proxy" revocation (or the revocation by another of testator's will, at testator's direction) must be done in the "presence" of the testator. UPC § 2-507(a)(2) adopts this principle. It is doubtful that the lawyer's destruction of the 2015 will will be found to have been done in João's presence. To satisfy this presence requirement, some states rely upon a "conscious" presence test while others require "visual presence" or "line of sight." *See* McGovern § 5.2.

    Answers (C) and (D) are incorrect. The will was not destroyed in João's presence. Clara may argue that the proxy revocation was done in João's presence, if the lawyer destroyed it while João was on the phone, and he heard the lawyer destroy it. If Clara is successful, Ana may argue for the application of the "doctrine of dependent relative revocation" to negate the revocation since João's intent to devise his estate to Matilde cannot be carried out. *See* comment to UPC § 2-507.

    Answer (B) is incorrect. There is no writing documenting João's intent to devise the probate estate to Matilde.

3. It appears that João revoked the most current will in favor of Matilde, causing João's probate estate to pass by intestate succession to Ana and Clara. The 2015 will would not likely be revived by the revocation of the later will under these circumstances. *See* UPC § 2-509.

    However, Matilde will likely argue that João did not have the requisite mental capacity to revoke the will. Alternatively, the common law doctrine of "dependent relative revocation" may be applicable, if Matilde can prove that João's mistaken belief of Matilde's death caused João to revoke the will. *See* comment to UPC § 2-507; Andersen § 9(E). If either argument is successful, the new will could be probated notwithstanding its destruction. A will that cannot be produced may be admitted to probate in most jurisdictions upon adequate proof of its contents and the execution. *See* McGovern § 5.2.

Some states, which have not enacted the Uniform Probate Code, have held that the revocation of a revoking document *does* have the effect of reviving the earlier revoked will. *See* McGovern § 5.3.

4. **Answer (B) is correct.** According to UPC § 2-509(a), the 2001 will is likely to have been revived since it is evident from the circumstances and Magdalena's contemporary declarations that Magdalena intended the 2001 will to take effect at her death. The result may be different in a state which has not enacted the Uniform Probate Code. Some courts have held that, because a will is ambulatory, the earlier will is not actually revoked until the testator dies and the later will is admitted to probate. Other courts follow the rule that the earlier will was revoked when the later one was executed. The rule in some states distinguishes between express and implied revocations. *See* Atkinson § 92.

    Answer (A) is incorrect. UPC § 2-509(a) is likely to revive the 2001 will, so Magdalena did not die intestate. However, in some non-UPC states, the 2001 will is not revived and Magdalena died intestate.

    Answer (C) is incorrect. The 2010 will was revoked.

    Answer (D) is incorrect. Even if Magdalena died intestate, the cousins would not be considered heirs despite the estrangement between Magdalena and Chester.

5. **Answer (B) is correct.** The 2001 will was "impliedly" revoked by the execution of the 2010 will due to the wills' inconsistent provisions. *See* UPC § 2-507(c). Since the 2010 will was revoked, UPC § 2-509(a) is likely to revive the 2001 will. In some non-UPC states, the 2001 will was not revoked by the execution of the 2010 will, since the 2010 will was revoked before Magdalena died. In other states, the 2001 will was revoked by the execution of the 2010 will and was not revived when the 2010 will was revoked. The rule in some states distinguishes between express and implied revocations. *See* Atkinson § 92.

    Answers (A), (C), and (D) are incorrect. These answers are incorrect for the reasons given.

6. **Answer (B) is correct.** The 2001 will was revoked by the execution of the 2010 will but is likely to have been revived by Magdalena's destruction of the 2010 will. *See* UPC § 2-509(a). It is irrelevant that the 2010 will was a holographic will. *See* UPC §§ 2-502(b), 2-507. Non-UPC states which recognize holographic wills are likely to adopt the same rule. *See* Atkinson §§ 87, 92. If the state does not recognize holographic wills, the 2001 will was never revoked.

    Answers (A), (C), and (D) are incorrect. These answers are incorrect for the reasons given.

7. Arnold is likely to inherit the entire estate. The 2001 will is likely to have been revived by the revocation of the 2010 will under the circumstances. *See* UPC § 2-509(a). The

fact that the 2001 will was destroyed by the lawyer is not determinative if its contents can otherwise be established. *See* McGovern § 5.2. The lawyer's destruction of the will was not a "proxy revocation." *See* UPC § 2-507(a)(2). The result may be different in a non-UPC state. Some states might hold that the 2001 will was revoked when the 2010 will was executed. Some states might hold that the 2001 will was not revived by the revocation of the 2010 will. *See* Atkinson § 92.

8. **Answer (A) is correct.** It is generally accepted that, if a will was last known to have been in the testator's possession, the will is presumed to have been revoked by the testator destroying the same when it cannot be found after the testator's death. *See* McGovern § 5.2. Without proof of when and why Ruby destroyed the 2015 will, Ruby likely died intestate.

    Answer (B) is incorrect. This answer is incorrect for the reasons given.

    Answers (C) and (D) are incorrect. Even if Ruby died intestate, the siblings would not be considered heirs.

9. **Answer (A) is correct.** The 2015 will was revoked by the nurse at Ruby's direction and in Ruby's presence. UPC § 2-507(a)(2) adopts the generally accepted concept of "proxy revocation." Ruby died intestate.

    Answer (B) is incorrect. This answer for the reasons given.

    Answers (C) and (D) are incorrect. Even if Ruby died intestate, the siblings would not be considered heirs.

10. **Answer (A) is correct.** Although the will was destroyed, it was not revoked since Dural lacked the requisite intent to revoke the will due to C1's coercion. *See* Atkinson § 86. The comments to UPC § 2-507 confirm this principle.

    Answers (B), (C), and (D) are incorrect. Dural lacked the intent to revoke when they destroyed the will.

11. **Answer (C) is correct.** Since the will was not revoked, it can be admitted to probate. However, due to G1's wrongdoing, Bilal may be successful in requesting the court to impose a constructive trust on G1 and G2 to prevent their unjust enrichment. *See* McGovern § 5.2.

    Answers (A) and (B) are incorrect. The will can be admitted to probate, but the court may impose a constructive trust on both G1 and G2.

    Answer (D) is incorrect. The court may impose a constructive trust on both G1 and G2 to prevent their unjust enrichment due to G1's wrongdoing. Why would the constructive trust be imposed *on both* G1 and G2? G1's wrongdoing prevented Aknah's will from being revoked. If the will had been revoked, Aknah would have died intestate and Bilal would be her heir.

Like the law in all states, UPC § 2-507(a)(2) provides that a will may be revoked by the testator performing a revocatory act with the intent and for the purpose of revoking the will. To have the requisite intent, the testator must have testamentary capacity. On these facts, nothing suggests that Emma lacks the requisite capacity to revoke her will. Assuming Emma's will was properly revoked, Charlotte and Drew would be Emma's heirs at law and take through intestacy.

12. What if a copy of the destroyed will was admitted to probate by G1 or G2? UPC § 3-407 places the burden on a will's contestant (here, only Charlotte or Drew) to prove that the testator revoked her will; this rule suggests that the contestant must establish that Emma had the requisite mental capacity to revoke the will. The law in some non-UPC states places the burden on a will's proponent to prove the will was not revoked.

13. **Answer (D) is correct.** Since its material provisions are in the testator's handwriting, the note is a valid will even though it was not signed by any witnesses. *See* UPC § 2-502(b). The earlier will was revoked even though it was signed by two witnesses. *See* UPC § 2-507(a)(1). In a state that does not recognize holographic wills, the earlier will would not have been revoked absent the application of a "harmless error" statute, such as UPC § 2-503. However, in most states that permit holographic wills, a holographic will can revoke an attested one. *See* McGovern § 5.1.

Answer (A) is incorrect. The earlier will has been revoked.

Answer (B) is incorrect. Emma did not die intestate. The note not only revoked the earlier will but also devised Emma's probate estate to Charlotte.

Answer (C) is incorrect. Emma did not die intestate, and even if Emma had died intestate, she was survived by G1 and G2.

14. **Answer (B) is correct.** UPC § 1-201(57) defines the term "will" to include a testamentary instrument that merely revokes another will, and UPC § 2-507 says a will can be revoked by a subsequent will. Because the new will did not contain a new disposition of Emma's estate, her probate estate passes to her heirs at law. The same result is likely to occur in states which have not enacted the Uniform Probate Code.

Answers (A), (C), and (D) are incorrect. The grandchildren of Emma will not be her heirs at law, in any state, if their parents (the child or children of Emma) are living.

15. Aiko's marriage to Stephen after the execution of the will did not revoke the will. *See* UPC § 2-508. However, Stephen is generally entitled to what he would have received had Aiko died intestate. *See* UPC § 2-301. The amount is deducted from the augmented estate to determine Stephen's elective share amount as defined in UPC § 2-202. In addition, Stephen will be entitled to assert any rights he might have under local law in or to the homestead, homestead allowance, exempt property, and family allowance.

In a community property state, the surviving spouse already owns one-half of the community property. The rights of the forgotten or "pretermitted" spouse in the other half of the community property will vary from state to state. Additionally, in some states, any will executed prior to marriage may be revoked. *See* Atkinson § 85.

16. **Answer (C) is correct.** Aiko generally has the right to devise her estate to whomever she chooses, subject to Stephen's elective share percentage amount. *See* UPC § 2-202. In addition, Stephen will be entitled to assert any rights he might have under local law in or to the homestead, homestead allowance, exempt property, and family allowance.

     In a community property state, a surviving spouse generally retains half of any community probate property. In non-UPC states that are also not community property states (other than Georgia), surviving spouses have a right to some share of the estate. *See* McGovern § 3.7.

     Answer (A) is incorrect. Stephen will be entitled to an elective share amount as described above. In addition, Stephen will be entitled to assert any rights he might have under local law in or to the homestead, homestead allowance, exempt property, and family allowance.

     Answers (B) and (D) are incorrect. The will is valid; Aiko did not die intestate.

17. According to UPC § 2-804(b), the divorce revoked any dispositive provision of Sebastián's will in favor of Jerome. Since the will devised all of Sebastián's probate estate to Jerome, the probate estate passes by intestate succession to Sebastián's heirs. If Jerome is named as the executor of Sebastián's estate, the divorce also revoked the nomination of Jerome as executor.

     Statutes in most non-UPC states would produce the same result, although state statutes may be nuanced and vary as to the scope of the revocation. In some states, the executor designation may not be revoked by operation of law. Also, even without a statute, case law may work a revocation by operation of law due to the change of circumstances. In a few states, a divorce revokes the entire will and not just the provisions in favor of the former spouse. *See* McGovern § 5.4.

Will Interpretation & Construction

1. The term "will interpretation" is frequently used to refer to the evidentiary process of attempting to determine a testator's actual intent by examining the language of the will, as well as any other admissible extrinsic evidence. "Will construction" is used to describe the process to determine the deemed intent of the testator when the testator's actual intent may be uncertain or cannot be ascertained. Will construction is a legal concept; will interpretation is factual in nature. *See* Atkinson § 146.

2. **Answer (A) is correct.** Oskar's probate estate passes to his devisee subject to the rights of Oskar's creditors, as well as any expenses incurred in the administration of his estate. *See* UPC § 3-101.

   In states that have not enacted the Uniform Probate Code, a personal representative typically discharges the decedent's debts out of the probate estate. *See* McGovern § 13.5.

   Answers (B), (C), and (D) are incorrect. Oskar's creditors will be paid first, prior to any distribution to beneficiaries. It does not matter if the debt arises out of tort or contract.

3. **Answer (D) is correct.** Ella may have a right to an amount payable out of Oskar's probate estate equal to $50,000 as a homestead allowance. *See* UPC § 2-402. In addition, Ella may be entitled to $15,000 in household furnishings, furniture, automobiles, and personal effects. *See* UPC § 2-403. In addition, if Oskar had an obligation to support Ella prior to Oskar's death, Ella may also be entitled to a reasonable allowance for maintenance for a period not to exceed one year. *See* UPC §§ 2-404, 2-405. The balance of the estate will be used to satisfy the debts and expenses

   A minor child's right to these types of allowances will vary considerably from state to state, regardless of whether or not a state has enacted the Uniform Probate Code. *See* McGovern § 3.4.

   Answers (A), (B), and (C) are incorrect. These answers are incorrect for the reasons explained above.

4. **Answer (A) is correct.** Absent a provision in relevant state law (*e.g.*, the state constitution) that either (i) grants a decedent's surviving spouse a right to occupy the home owned by the deceased spouse regardless of the solvency of the estate or who actually inherits the home and/or (ii) exempts the family home from the claims of unsecured

creditors and estate administration expenses, if the owner is survived by a spouse, the home will likely be sold to raise cash to pay allowances and the obligations. *See* UPC §§ 2-401, 2-402.

The availability of the homestead to satisfy a decedent's general obligations will vary from state to state. *See* McGovern § 3.4.

Answers (B), (C), and (D) are incorrect. Unless relevant state law creates a homestead right in Willa as described above, the home will be sold to pay expenses and debts.

5. **Answer (A) is correct.** UPC § 2-607 provides that a specific devise passes subject to any indebtedness secured by the property unless the will provides otherwise. In those states that have not enacted the Uniform Probate Code, or a statute similar to UPC § 2-607, the common law rule of exoneration creates a presumption that a testator intends a devisee to inherit a specific devise free of indebtedness. In those states, half of the stock would be sold to raise the cash to pay the note. See McGovern § 8.4.

    Answers (B) and (C) are incorrect. The Uniform Probate Code creates a presumption of "nonexoneration." Jurisdictions that still follow the common law rule of "exoneration of liens" grant Shelly the right to receive the home free of debt.

    Answer (D) is incorrect. In some jurisdictions, the secured creditor can elect either to have the debt paid in due course of administration or pursuant to the terms of the creditor's contract with the decedent. This decision should not affect whether Shelly or Drew bears the burden of the debt.

6. **Answer (A) is correct.** Because the will does not direct the order of "abatement," the debt should be paid out of the residuary devise. *See* UPC § 3-902. Many non-UPC states have abatement statutes that are similar to UPC § 3-902; other states follow common law abatement which would produce the same result under these circumstances. *See* McGovern § 8.4.

    Answers (B) and (C) are incorrect. The debts paid by the executor should be paid out of the residuary devise.

    Answer (D) is incorrect. The source of the debt payment depends on the relevant abatement rule.

7. Abatement is the process by which gifts under a will are reduced when the funds or assets available in the estate are insufficient to pay all beneficiaries. An executor will typically use the most liquid non-exempt asset of the estate which has not been specifically devised by the testator in the will.

    $500,000 would normally be distributed through the residuary clause to Child3. This $500,000 will be applied to the $1 million debt, and Child3 will receive nothing. The executor must also sell the $1 million of stocks and bonds to satisfy the pecuniary gift to Child2. One-half of the $1 million will be used to pay the remainder of the debt.

The debt will be paid, and then Child2 will receive $500,000. *See* UPC § 3-902 and § 3-906.

States that have not enacted the Uniform Probate Code are likely to have statutes or common law rules that reach a similar result. However, some states' laws will require the executor to satisfy the pecuniary bequest in cash unless the devisee agrees to a distribution "in kind." *See* McGovern § 12.3 (p. 585).

8. **Answer (A) is correct.** In this question, the house (and its contents) is being distributed through the residuary clause. The order of abatement in UPC § 3-902 (absent a provision in the will that provides otherwise) is (1) property not disposed of through the will, (2) residuary gifts, (3) general gifts, (4) specific gifts.

    States that have not enacted the Uniform Probate Code will typically have a similar statute or a common law rule that reaches a similar result. *See* McGovern § 8.4.

    Answer (B) is incorrect. If the executor uses the cash to pay the debts, the home and its contents may have to be sold to raise the $1 million to satisfy the bequest to Child2.

    Answer (C) is incorrect. Child3 was specifically devised all of the stocks and bonds.

    Answer (D) is incorrect. UPC § 3-902 prescribes how the probate estate abates in order to satisfy the decedent's debts.

9. **Answer (A) is correct.** The executor will typically use the most readily available liquid non-exempt asset available to pay the creditors. Pursuant to UPC § 3-906(a)(2), the executor may need to sell other assets, like the stocks and bonds, to raise the cash necessary to satisfy Child2's pecuniary bequest. *See* McGovern § 8.4.

    States that have not enacted the Uniform Probate Code will typically have a similar statute or common law rule that reaches a similar result. *See* McGovern § 8.4.

    Answers (B), (C), and (D) are incorrect. These answers are incorrect for the reasons given.

10. **Answer (B) is correct.** UPC § 2-605 directs that Child1 is entitled to the Disney stock. UPC § 2-606(a)(5) directs that Whiteacre passes to Child2.

    The results may differ in states that have not enacted some version of UPC § 2-605. Under the common law, the rule of "ademption by extinction" may cause the entire probate estate, including the stock and land, to pass to Child3. *See* McGovern § 8.2.

    Answer (A) is incorrect. UPC § 2-606(a)(5) directs that Child2 is entitled to Whiteacre since Loujain acquired it as a replacement for Blackacre. Many non-UPC states have enacted statutes similar to UPC § 2-605, but not statutes like UPC § 2-606. In those states, Answer (A) would be correct.

    Answers (C) and (D) are incorrect. The Uniform Probate Code has replaced the common law's strict "identity" test with a more liberal "change in form" rule.

11. UPC § 3-902 directs that the debts are to be paid from the residuary devise, and if it is not sufficient, from the general devises. After the debts and expenses are paid, specific devises are distributed, general devises are paid to the extent assets are available, and if there is anything remaining, it is delivered to the residuary devisee. Accordingly, after the home and the stocks and bonds are sold to pay the debts, Child1 will receive the proceeds paid by the insurance company for the damage to the car. *See* UPC § 2-606(a)(3). Child2 will receive the balance. Child3 will receive nothing.

In states that have not enacted the UPC or similar statutes, the common law rule of "ademption by extinction" may limit Child1 to only $1,000, the value of the car at the time of Grover's death, and the balance would pass to Child2. *See* Atkinson § 134.

12. **Answer (B) is correct.** An inter vivos gift to a person named as a devisee in the donor's will is not treated as the "satisfaction" of the testamentary devise unless the will provides for a deduction of the gift or there is a written document in which the donor or donee indicates that the gift is to be taken into account at the time of the donor's death. *See* UPC § 2-609.

In states that have not enacted the UPC or similar statutes, the states may still follow the common law rule which presumes a gift to a general or residuary devisee is either a partial or total "satisfaction" of a testamentary devise. *See* Atkinson § 133.

Answers (A) and (C) are incorrect. Where applicable, the doctrine of satisfaction generally applies to both general and residuary devises.

Answer (D) is incorrect. Absent written evidence to the contrary in the will or another written document, the gifts are not to be taken into account when Lily dies.

13. **Answer (C) is correct.** An executor has a duty to expend reasonable efforts to collect any valid debts due and owing to the decedent, including one owed by a devisee, particularly if the estate is insolvent. *See* Atkinson § 117.

Answer (A) is incorrect. Lily's death does not extinguish the debt.

Answer (B) is incorrect. Since the estate is insolvent, Child2 is obligated to repay the entire $10,000.

Answer (D) is incorrect. Since the estate is insolvent, Child1, Child2, and Child3 do not receive any part of Lily's estate.

14. **Answer (D) is correct.** Since the estate's assets exceed the debts by more than $10,000, the executor has enough non-exempt liquid assets on hand to pay the creditors what they are owed and to pay Child1 the pecuniary bequest of $10,000. From a practical perspective, there is no reason for the executor to collect the $10,000 from Child2 since he, in effect, owes half of that amount to himself or herself as a residuary devisee. *See* UPC § 3-903.

The result is likely to be the same in a non-UPC state pursuant to the common law concept of "retainer." *See* Atkinson § 141.

Answers (A), (B), and (C) are incorrect. These answers are incorrect for the reasons given.

15. **Answer (A) is correct.** The statute of limitations for collecting a debt varies by state. When there is a promissory note, the statute of limitations ranges from as short as three years to as long as fifteen years. This debt cannot be collected by the executor because it is almost certainly barred by the statute of limitations. *See* Atkinson § 117.

    Answers (B) and (C) are incorrect. These answers are incorrect for the reasons given.

    Answer (D) is incorrect. Since the estate is insolvent, Child2 does not have a residuary share to reduce by the amount of the debt.

16. **Answer (A) is correct.** UPC § 3-903 provides that, while a debt of a devisee is to be off-set against the devisee's share of the estate, the devisee has the benefit of "any defense" that would be available in a proceeding for recovery of the debt, including the statute of limitations. In states that have not enacted the UPC or similar statutes, the result may be different. *See* Atkinson § 141.

    Answers (B) and (C) are incorrect. The debt is not collectible due to the statute of limitations.

    Answer (D) is incorrect. UPC § 3-903 grants Child2 "any defense," including the statute of limitations. It is important to note, however, that in some non-UPC states, Child2's share of the residuary may be reduced by half of the debt.

17. Since a will is a disposition of property that becomes effective at the testator's death, the common law required a devisee to survive the testator by an "instant" of time. Most states have enacted statutes that require devisees to survive testators by 120 hours unless the will provides otherwise. The Uniform Probate Code has adopted this rule. *See* UPC § 2-702. UPC § 2-604 adopts the common law rule that a lapsed specific devise becomes part of the residuary devise. *See* Atkinson § 140. Accordingly, only Child3 survived Brigitta by 120 hours, and the entire estate, including the two tracts of land, passed (subject to formal administration of Child3's estate) to Child3's spouse.

18. **Answer (D) is correct.** UPC § 2-604 does not address what happens if the residuary beneficiary does not survive the testator. Because all three children died before Brigitta, their devises lapsed, and Brigitta's probate estate probably passes by intestate succession to Brigitta's intestate heirs under the "no residue of the residue" rule. Brigitta's closest relatives that survived her were the cousins. *See* McGovern § 8.5 (p. 404).

    Answers (A), (B), and (C) are incorrect. The devisees named in Brigitta's will died before her; their gifts lapsed. UPC § 2-603, or a similar statute in a non-UPC state, is not applicable because the children did not have descendants.

19. **Answer (D) is correct.** UPC § 2-702 requires that a devisee survive the testator by 120 hours unless the will provides otherwise. Because Child1 and Child2 did not survive Brigitta by 120 hours, their devises "lapsed." However, UPC § 2-604 is not applicable, and the two tracts do not become part of the residuary devise. UPC § 2-603 directs that the two tracts pass to the children of Child1 and Child2.

Most states that have not enacted the UPC have similar "anti-lapse" statutes. *See* McGovern § 8.5.

Answers (A), (B), and (C) are incorrect. They fail to take into consideration both UPC §§ 2-702 and 2-603.

20. The devise to Aaron, Beula, and Chase lapsed because they died before Ibrahim. The anti-lapse provisions of UPC § 2-603 apply only to certain categories of devisees. No part of his estate passes to the spouses or children of Aaron, Beula, and Chase. Ibrahim's probate estate passes by intestate succession to Delilah.

In a state that has not enacted the UPC, the result may differ depending on the terms of the applicable anti-lapse statute. However, most states have statutes which create the same result as UPC § 2-603 on these facts. *See* McGovern § 8.5.

21. **Answer (C) is correct.** S1 died before Amelia; S2 is deemed to have died before Amelia because of the 120-hours rule. *See* UPC § 2-702. Their gifts lapsed, but the "anti-lapse" provisions of UPC § 2-603 direct that the two-thirds of the estate they would have received pass equally to their children.

Most states that have not enacted the Uniform Probate Code have enacted similar statutes. *See* McGovern § 8.5.

Answers (A), (B), and (D) are incorrect. The testamentary gifts to S1 and S2 "lapsed," but their children succeed to what they would have been entitled had they survived Amelia by 120 hours.

22. **Answer (A) is correct.** Because S1 and S2 did not survive Amelia by 120 hours, their gifts lapsed. *See* UPC § 2-702. According to UPC § 2-604(b), the interests in Amelia's probate estate S1 and S2 would have received pass to S3. In non-UPC states, the result may be different. The common law typically applied the "lapsed fractional gift" rule to this type of situation, and the two-thirds of the estate devised to S1 and S2 would pass by intestate succession to Amelia's heirs. *See* Atkinson § 140.

Answers (B) and (C) are incorrect. The gifts to S1 and S2 lapsed.

Answer (D) is incorrect. The gifts to S1 and S2 lapsed, and the two-thirds of Amelia's probate estate they would have received pass to S3. The common law rule typically resulted in the two-thirds passing to Amelia's heirs, S3 and Drew.

23. **Answer (A) is correct.** Amelia's will devised her probate estate to three individuals, not including S4. Only "omitted children," not omitted grandchildren, have rights under UPC § 2-302. "Pretermission" statutes in some non-UPC states may afford rights to descendants of omitted children. *See* McGovern § 3.5.

    Answers (B), (C), and (D) are incorrect. S4 is not entitled to any portion of Amelia's probate estate.

24. **Answer (A) is correct.** A testator may devise property to a "class" of beneficiaries rather than to several named individuals. According to UPC § 2-603(b)(2), the "anti-lapse" provisions apply to certain class gifts. So, Zenia and Yelania succeed to the interests G1 and G2. G2 and not Yelania would take had G2 survived Grace by 120 hours. In states which have not enacted the UPC or similar statutes, the result may differ. *See* McGovern § 8.5.

    Answers (B), (C), and (D) are incorrect. These answers are incorrect for the reasons given.

25. **Answer (D) is correct.** The "class" of devisees opened at Grace's death and included G3 and G4, as well as the substituted takers, Zenia and Yelania. *See* UPC § 2-603(b)(2). The same result would occur in states that have not enacted the Uniform Probate Code but have a similar "anti-lapse" statute that applies to "class" gifts. *See* McGovern § 8.5.

    Answers (A), (B), and (C) are incorrect. These answers do not take into account both the nature of "class gifts" and the applicable "anti-lapse" statute. In a state that does not extend anti-lapse provisions to class gifts, G3 and G4 would share the estate equally. McGovern § 8.5.

26. The "anti-lapse" provisions of UPC § 2-603 prescribe a rule of construction to apply in the absence of a contrary intention expressed in the testator's will. However, UPC § 2-603(b)(3) also provides that words of survivorship like "my surviving children" are not, in the absence of additional evidence, a sufficient indication of "contrary intention." Accordingly, Zenia and Yelania may take the two-thirds of what their parents would have received had they survived Grace by 120 hours, and G3 takes the balance.

    The view in many states that have enacted the UPC, or a statute similar to UPC § 2-603(b)(3), is that words of survivorship attached to a devise, like "who survive me," are sufficient to negate the applicable "anti-lapse" statute. In those states, G3 would inherit the entire estate. *See* McGovern § 8.5 (p. 394).

27. **Answer (D) is correct.** At the time of Grigori's death the "class" of devisees "opened" and "closed." G3 was the only member of the class that survived Grigori. *See* McGovern § 10.2.

    Answers (A) and (B) are incorrect. These answers are incorrect for the reasons given.

    Answer (C) is incorrect. G1 and G2 did not survive Grigori by 120 hours.

28. **Answer (D) is correct.** A died before Ophelia; B is deemed to have died before Ophelia because of the 120-hours rule. *See* UPC § 2-702. Their gifts lapsed, and according to UPC § 2-603, stepchildren of the testator's children are not included among the devisees whose gifts can be saved by the anti-lapse statute. UPC § 2-604(b) directs that C succeed to the entire residuary estate.

States that have not enacted the Uniform Probate Code typically do not extend their "anti-lapse" provisions to stepchildren. However, in some non-UPC states, the two-thirds of the estate that A and B would have received will pass to Ophelia's heir, Dalia, pursuant to the common law's "lapsed fractional gift" rule. *See* Atkinson § 140.

Answers (A), (B), and (C) are incorrect. The testamentary gifts to A and B "lapsed," and their children do not succeed to what they would have been entitled had they survived Ophelia by 120 hours.

29. The initial question is who were the intended beneficiaries of Ophelia's estate? Absent evidence of contrary intent in the will, stepchildren of a child would normally be excluded from the class of defined beneficiaries in the will — testator's grandchildren (unless they were adopted by the child). The Uniform Probate Code appears to have adopted this prevailing view. *See* UPC § 2-705. However, UPC § 2-705(c) creates an exception for relatives by marriage. It is arguable that A, B, and C are to be considered Ophelia's grandchildren under the will. *See* comment to UPC § 2-705. The result may differ in a state that has not adopted UPC § 2-705 or a similar statute. *See* Atkinson § 60.

30. Modern statutes, such as UPC § 2-1105, authorize heirs and devisees to disclaim their interests in decedents' estates. However, the law varies from state to state on the effect a disclaimer has on the rights of the disclaimant's creditors. Federal law will control if the disclaimant is in bankruptcy. *See* McGovern § 2.8. In any event, Blackacre passes (subject to any rights Mari's creditors may retain) as if Mari had predeceased Testator to the charity under the residuary clause pursuant to UPC § 2-604.

31. **Answer (B) is correct.** A will may dispose of property by incorporation by reference or reference to facts that have significance independent from their effect on the disposition made by the will. Accordingly, the stock passes to A, and the jewelry passes to B. UPC §§ 2-510, 2-512 codify these generally accepted concepts. *See* McGovern § 6.2. The described items of other tangible personal property will pass to C even though the memo was not executed with testamentary formalities because the will refers to it. *See* UPC § 2-513. Results may differ in non-UPC states. Some states, including New York, Connecticut, and Louisiana, do not recognize incorporation by reference. Absent a statute similar to UPC § 2-513, such items may pass to the residuary devisee, Elliott. *See* McGovern § 6.2.

Answers (A), (C), and (D) are not correct. These answers are incorrect for the reasons given.

32. At issue in this question is the fact that there appears to be an oral trust of real property (Blackacre) that violates the Statute of Frauds. Because the will makes no reference to the intended trust, a testamentary trust was not created. *See* RESTATEMENT (THIRD) of Trusts § 17. If Freddie does not volunteer to perform as agreed, the court may admit evidence of the oral agreement to prevent Freddie from being unjustly enriched. On these facts, the parties may seek a constructive trust to be imposed on Freddie, in favor of Carol and Gigi. If successful, Freddie would be ordered to transfer the property to another person who will carry out the intended purposes of the oral agreement. *See* RESTATEMENT (THIRD) of Trusts § 18.

33. **Answer (D) is correct.** An express inter vivos trust was not created when the agreement was signed or during Zephyr's lifetime because a valid trust requires a trust res. On these facts, no property had been transferred to Freddie. *See* RESTATEMENT (THIRD) of Trusts §§ 2, 3, 10. Because the will makes no reference to the intended trust, a testamentary trust was not created. *See* RESTATEMENT (THIRD) of Trusts § 17. However, the court would likely impose a constructive trust on Freddie in favor of Carol and Gigi. *See* RESTATEMENT (THIRD) of Trusts § 18. Also, see the answer to the immediately preceding question.

Answer (A) is incorrect. An express inter vivos trust was not created when the agreement was signed because property had not been transferred to Freddie during Zephyr's lifetime. Because the will makes no reference to the intended trust, a testamentary trust was not created. The comment to UTC § 401 notes that a trust instrument signed during the settlor's lifetime is not invalid because the trust was not funded until after the settlor's death. Accordingly, it is arguable that an express trust was created when Zephyr devised Blackacre to Freddie. However, the Restatement takes the position that an express trust is not created if the settlor fails during life to complete the contemplated transfer. *See* RESTATEMENT (THIRD) of Trusts § 16.

Answer (B) is incorrect. Equity will not allow Freddie to be unjustly enriched.

Answer (C) is incorrect. The situation does not fit the limited circumstances that justify the imposition of a resulting trust.

34. **Answer (D) is correct.** Although Zephyr's will manifests an intent to create an express trust, other elements essential to the creation of a testamentary trust are not in the will. Accordingly, a testamentary trust was not created. *See* RESTATEMENT (THIRD) OF TRUSTS § 17. The Restatement takes the position that the court should impose a constructive trust on Freddie in favor of Carol and Gigi if Freddie does not agree to perform as agreed. *See* RESTATEMENT (THIRD) of Trusts § 18. However, some courts may impose a resulting trust on Freddie in favor of the charity notwithstanding the modern trend adopted by the Restatement. *See* comment c to RESTATEMENT (THIRD) of Trusts § 18.

Answer (A) is incorrect. Because the will failed to identify the beneficiaries, an express trust was not created.

Answer (B) is incorrect. The modern trend appears to impose a constructive trust in favor of Carol and Gigi.

Answer (C) is incorrect. The situation does not fit the circumstances that justify the imposition of a resulting trust in favor of Zephyr's heirs.

35.   **Answer (B) is correct.** Obviously, Zephyr did not intend for Freddie to inherit fee simple title. The problem, however, is that the will does not create an express trust because no terms for a trust are included in the will. A constructive trust is unavailable because there is no evidence of the intended beneficiaries or the purpose of the trust. When a settlor's attempt to create an express trust fails, the courts will typically impose a resulting trust on the intended trustee in favor of the settlor or the settlor's successor in interest. In this case, the charity will likely succeed to Blackacre. *See* Restatement (Third) of Trusts §§ 8, 18.

Answer (A) is incorrect. An express trust was not created because the will did not name the beneficiaries or describe the terms of the intended trust. Further, there is no evidence of any pre-existing agreement between Zephyr and Freddie.

Answer (C) is incorrect. Obviously, Zephyr did not intend for Freddie to acquire fee simple title.

Answer (D) is incorrect. The charity, not Zephyr's heir, is Zephyr's successor in interest and has standing to seek the imposition of the resulting trust.

36.   Although Jagger's will manifests the intent to create an express trust, other elements essential to the creation of a testamentary trust, such as the purposes of the trust, are not in the will. Further, the purposes of the trust cannot be inferred from the will. Consequently, an express testamentary trust was not created. *See* Restatement (Third) of Trusts § 17.

However, if Ziggy does not perform as agreed, evidence of the oral agreement may be admissible to impose a constructive trust on Ziggy in favor of Cecilia and Gloria to carry out Jagger's intent. *See* Restatement (Third) of Trusts § 18. If evidence of the oral agreement is not admissible, or if the oral agreement is not proven, even if admissible, the trust is "passive," and the intended beneficiaries, Cecilia and Gloria, are entitled to the property. The statute of uses, or a similar statute, may merge legal and equitable titles in Cecilia and Gloria. *See* Restatement (Third) of Trusts § 6.

37.   **Answer (D) is correct.** The trust is "passive," and the legal and equitable titles merge in Cecilia and Gloria. UTC § 402 has codified this common law concept that a trustee must have duties to perform in order to have a valid, express trust. *See* Restatement (Third) of Trusts § 6. In a state that does not have a statute of uses (or its equivalent), the intended beneficiary is entitled to possession upon demand to the person in possession. *See* McGovern § 9.3.

Answer (A) is incorrect. An express trust was not created since the will did not impose on Ziggy any affirmative duties.

Answer (B) is incorrect. The charity, as the residuary beneficiary, inherits only those probate assets which have not been specifically or generally devised.

Answer (C) is incorrect. Jagger did not die intestate.

38. **Answer (D) is correct.** Because Xander's sister-in-law died before Xander, only Gregor has standing to seek the imposition of a constructive trust if Fiona does not behave as (orally) agreed and convey Blackacre to Gregor. *See* RESTATEMENT (THIRD) OF TRUSTS § 18.

Answer (A) is incorrect. Because the will makes no reference to the intended trust, a testamentary trust was not created. *See* RESTATEMENT (THIRD) of Trusts § 17.

Answer (B) is incorrect. Equity will not allow Fiona to retain the property upon proof of the oral agreement between Xander and Fiona.

Answer (C) is incorrect. In view of the oral agreement between Xander and Fiona, a constructive trust in favor of Gregor is the appropriate remedy.

39. **Answer (C) is correct.** Because (i) Xander's attempt to create an express trust failed, and (ii) the trust intention does not appear in the will, Xander's successor in interest, the charity, will have the court impose a constructive trust on Fiona to prevent her from being unjustly enriched. *See* RESTATEMENT (THIRD) OF TRUSTS § 18.

Answers (A) and (B) are incorrect. Since Gregor did not survive Xander, neither GS nor GG has standing to impose a constructive trust.

Answer (D) is incorrect. Although it appears from the will that Fiona has inherited Blackacre, equity will not allow Fiona to retain the property once satisfactory evidence of the oral agreement is produced.

40. **Answer (D) is correct.** Fiona died before Xander devised Blackacre to her; neither Fiona's spouse nor child acquired an interest in Blackacre. The gift to Fiona lapsed, and Blackacre passed to the charity upon Xander's death. *See* UPC § 2-604.

Xander's sister-in-law and Gregor will argue that the court should impose a constructive trust in their favor on the charity to avoid the charity from being unjustly enriched. A constructive trust typically arises out of an intended express trust that is unenforceable because of the failure to satisfy the applicable wills act. *See* RESTATEMENT (THIRD) of Trusts § 18. The imposition of a resulting trust is not appropriate since Xander's successor in interest, the charity, already has acquired title.

Answers (A) and (B) are incorrect. Because Fiona died before Xander, neither Fiona's spouse nor child acquired an interest in Blackacre.

Answer (C) is incorrect. Xander's sister-in-law is not his successor in interest and does not have standing to seek a resulting trust.

41. **Answer (C) is correct.** Fiona should be able to accept the specific devise of Blackacre and convey the property to Xander's sister-in-law and Gregor, provided that both are competent adults. After accepting the deed, Xander's sister-in-law and Gregor, as the intended beneficiaries, can decide the ultimate disposition of the property. Because an express trust was not created, UPC §2-707 should not be applicable. If UPC §2-707 is applicable, Gregor's remainder interest is contingent on Gregor surviving Xander's sister-in-law, and the charity may have inherited Xander's reversionary interest. If Xander's sister-in-law and Gregor do not agree to the proposed conveyance, or if either is not a competent adult, Fiona should consider asking for court authority to convey the property to another party who would agree in writing to carry out the purposes of the original oral agreement. Alternatively, Fiona may want to consider disclaiming the property.

    Answer (A) is incorrect. Fiona can refuse to accept Blackacre by filing a qualified disclaimer. If Fiona disclaims, Blackacre would vest in the charity, and Xander's sister-in-law and Gregor will have to deal with the charity concerning the oral agreement. They may have to incur expenses in convincing a court to impose a constructive trust on the charity to avoid its unjust enrichment. *See* RESTATEMENT (THIRD) of Trusts §18.

    Answer (B) is incorrect. If Fiona disclaims, Blackacre passes to the charity. *See* UPC §2-1106.

    Answer (D) is incorrect. An express trust was not created. *See* RESTATEMENT (THIRD) of Trusts §17.

42. The will makes no reference to the intended trust, and so a testamentary trust was not created. *See* RESTATEMENT (THIRD) of Trusts §17. If Fiona accepts the stock under the will, equity will not allow her to retain it for her own use. Extrinsic evidence will be admissible to establish the existence of an oral agreement. Xander's sister-in-law and Gregor will likely seek to impose a constructive trust if Fiona attempts to keep and manage the stock for herself. *See* RESTATEMENT (THIRD) of Trusts §18.

Limitations on Testamentary Power

1. Generally, an adult individual with the requisite mental capacity has the right and power to direct how the individual wishes his or her property to be distributed after the individual's death. However, there are limits on the individual's testamentary power. *See* McGovern Ch. 3.

2. **Answer (A) is correct.** Suki appears to have died intestate. Since the letter was typewritten by Suki and not signed by the friends, the document does not meet the requirements for a valid will. *See* UPC § 2-502. However, UPC § 2-503 allows a probate court to "excuse a harmless error" and probate a defectively executed document if there is "clear and convincing evidence" that the otherwise defective document represents the decedent's testamentary intent. Ann will likely argue that the letter manifests testamentary intent and for the application of UPC § 2-503.

   Most states do not have a statute similar to UPC § 2-503. *See* Andersen § 7(B)(4). Eleven states have adopted some version of the harmless error doctrine: California (CAL PROB. CODE § 6110(c)(2)), Colorado (Colo. Rev. Stat. § 15-11-503), Hawaii (Haw. Rev. Stat. Ann. § 560:2-503), Michigan (Mich. Comp. Laws. Ann. § 700.2503), Montana (Mont. Code. Ann. § 72-2-523), New Jersey (N.J. Stat. Ann. § 3B:3-3), Ohio (Ohio Rev. Code. Ann. § 2107.24(A)), Oregon (Or. Rev. Stat. § 112.238), South Dakota (S.D. Codified Laws § 29A-2-503), Utah (Utah Code Ann. § 75-2-503) and Virginia (Va. Code. Ann. § 64.2-404). *See* Dukeminier, at 177.

   Answers (B), (C), and (D) are incorrect. Unless Ann meets the burden of proof required in UPC § 2-503, the letter cannot be admitted to probate. *See* UPC § 2-502.

3. **Answer (A) is correct.** Suki still appears to have died intestate. Unless the material provisions of the will are in Suki's handwriting, a testamentary writing that is not acknowledged by the testator before a notary public or does not include the signatures of two witnesses cannot be admitted to probate. *See* UPC § 2-502. Delivery is not a prerequisite to a will. However, UPC § 2-503 allows the probate of a defectively executed will if there is "clear and convincing evidence" that the otherwise defective document represents the decedent's testamentary intent.

   Most states do not have a statute similar to UPC § 2-503. *See* Andersen § 7(B)(4). Eleven states have adopted some version of the harmless error doctrine: California (Cal Prob.

Code § 6110(c)(2)), Colorado (Colo. Rev. Stat. § 15-11-503), Hawaii (Haw. Rev. Stat. Ann. § 560:2-503), Michigan (Mich. Comp. Laws. Ann. § 700.2503), Montana (Mont. Code. Ann. § 72-2-523), New Jersey (N.J. Stat. Ann. § 3B:3-3), Ohio (Ohio Rev. Code. Ann. § 2107.24(A)), Oregon (Or. Rev. Stat. § 112.238), South Dakota (S.D. Codified Laws § 29A-2-503), Utah (Utah Code Ann. § 75-2-503) and Virginia (Va. Code. Ann. § 64.2-404). *See* Dukeminier, at 177.

Answers (B), (C), and (D) are incorrect. Ann may argue that Bob had agreed with Suki that Ann was to receive the house and its contents and that the court should impose a constructive trust on Bob to prevent Bob from being unjustly enriched. *See* Restatement (Third) of Trusts § 18.

4. **Answer (B) is correct.** UPC § 2-502(b) recognizes "holographic" wills. Accordingly, assuming the letter properly manifested Suki's intent to make a disposition effective at Suki's death, the holographic will can be admitted to probate. If so, the house and its contents will pass to Ann. If the letter is not considered to be a valid will, Suki's estate will pass vis-à-vis intestacy. See answers to the preceding questions.

   Some states which have not enacted the Uniform Probate Code have similar statutes. *See* McGovern § 4.4. "In a little more than half of the states, holographic wills are permitted. A *holographic will* is written by the testator's hand and is signed by the testator; it need not be attested by witnesses." Dukeminier, at 199. In states that do not recognize holographic wills, a handwritten will may nonetheless be effective if it is properly witnessed.

   Answer (A) is incorrect. UPC § 2-502(b) recognizes holographic wills. However, answer (A) would be the correct answer in a number of states.

   Answers (C) and (D) are incorrect. In a state which recognizes holographic wills, a properly executed holographic will can devise both real and personal property.

5. **Answer (C) is correct.** Wills are revocable dispositions of property that take effect upon the testator's death. The execution of a joint will does not create a presumption of a contract not to revoke the will. *See* UPC § 2-514. Accordingly, absent written evidence of a contract, Les had the power and the right to revoke the 2000 will, which Les did by the execution of the 2010 will. *See* UPC §§ 2-507(c), 2-514.

   Many non-UPC states have similar statutes. Absent a statute, the common law of a state may create a presumption that the parties intend to have a contractual will when they execute a joint will. *See* McGovern § 4.9.

   Answer (A) is incorrect. The 2000 document was intended by Les and Moe to be a will. In order for it to be effective, the 2000 will must be admitted to probate. However, it was apparently revoked by Les when he executed the 2010 will.

   Answer (B) is incorrect. The 2000 will was revoked. Further, there is no evidence that Les ever revoked the 2010 will.

Answer (D) is incorrect. UPC § 2-514 creates a presumption that the 2000 will was not executed pursuant to a contract not to revoke it. Accordingly, unless Moe can establish that a contract existed pursuant to UPC § 2-514, he is without a cause of action. If a contract could be established, Les revoked the 2000 will, and Moe's remedy would typically be limited to a breach of contract action. *See* McGovern § 4.9, at 279.

6. The provision in the will stating the material provision of the parties' agreement allows Moe to enforce the terms of the contract. *See* UPC § 2-514. However, the prevailing view is that Les did have the power to revoke the 2000 will, and the 2010 will can be admitted to probate. Les's interest in Blackacre passes to Fran. Consequently, Moe is typically limited to bringing a breach of contract action against Les's estate and/or Fran and seeking specific performance, the imposition of a constructive trust, or money damages. *See* McGovern § 4.9, at 279.

   The same result would occur in most states. However, in some jurisdictions, a contract may not have existed because Les did not comply with the terms of the agreement (*i.e.,* Les revoked the will and devised the property to Fran). Under this approach, the agreement was an offer by Moe to be accepted by Les, and Les did not accept Moe's offer. Consequently, Moe would have no cause of action.

7. **Answer (A) is correct.** Assuming that the intent expressed in the 2000 document is not testamentary in nature (but, rather, a valid agreement to create a right of survivorship), Les and Moe converted their tenancy in common into a joint tenancy with rights of survivorship. Andersen § 18(A). Consequently, upon the death of Les, his interest passed nonprobate to Moe. Les's will only controls the disposition of his probate estate (*i.e.,* property which would otherwise pass by intestate succession). *See* UPC § 1-201(57). The same result would also follow in non-UPC states. *See* Andersen Ch. 5.

   Answer (B) is incorrect. The 2000 document was not intended to be a will. If testamentary intent had been evident, UPC § 2-502(a)(3)(B) allows for the testator to acknowledge it before a notary public.

   Answers (C) and (D) are incorrect. While the 2010 will devises Les's probate estate to Fran, Blackacre passed nonprobate to Moe.

8. **Answer (A) is correct.** UPC § 2-514 creates the presumption that the mutual 2015 wills were not contractual. Spouse 1's estate passed to Spouse 2 when the 2015 will was probated. Absent another written document establishing a contract, Spouse 2 has the power and the right to devise his entire estate to anyone, and Chelsea would not have a valid cause of action against Spouse 1 or Spouse 2's estate.

   Many non-UPC states have statutes that produce the same result. The result may be different in states that have not enacted the Uniform Probate Code or a similar statute. In these states, the execution of mutual wills may raise a presumption that a contract does exist. *See* McGovern § 4.9.

   Answers (B), (C), and (D) are incorrect. These answers are incorrect for the reasons given.

9.   **Answer (C) is correct.** UPC § 2-514 will allow Chelsea to enforce the terms of the contract as the third-party beneficiary of the contract of Spouse 1 and Spouse 2. However, in most jurisdictions, Chelsea cannot stop Spouse 2 from executing a new will. *See* McGovern § 4.9. At Spouse 2's death, his new will can be admitted to probate, and Chelsea's remedy typically will be limited to a breach of contract action against Spouse 2's estate. Chelsea may seek specific performance, a constructive trust, or money damages. A few cases have allowed a suit by the third-party beneficiary of the contract during the promisor's lifetime. *See* McGovern § 4.9.

     Answer (A) is incorrect. The provisions of UPC § 2-514 have been met.

     Answer (B) is incorrect. A will by its nature is a revocable disposition to take effect at death. Accordingly, a will can be revoked. Chelsea's cause of action will not accrue until Spouse 2's death.

     Answer (D) is incorrect. The terms of the 2015 will did not devise to Chelsea a remainder interest.

10. **Answer (A) is correct.** Spouse 2's contract with Spouse 1 required Spouse 2 to devise all property to Chelsea when Spouse 2 dies. Since a will does not become effective until the testator dies, Chelsea's rights under the contract were dependent on Chelsea surviving Spouse 2. *See* McGovern § 4.9.

     Answers (B) and (C) are incorrect. Chelsea would have had to survive Spouse 2 in order for Harvey to enforce the terms of the contract.

     Answer (D) is incorrect. The terms of Spouse 1's 2015 will did not devise to Chelsea a remainder interest.

11. **Answer (D) is correct.** Spouse 1 and Spouse 2 agreed not to revoke the 2015 wills, and their contract can be established pursuant to UPC § 2-514. Had Chelsea not died, she would likely have been in a position to bring a breach of contract cause of action against Spouse 2's estate if he revokes his 2015 will. *See* McGovern § 4.9. If Spouse 2 does not revoke the 2015 will, at Spouse 2's death, Chelsea's child CC may be able to probate Spouse 2's 2015 will, and the entire estate would pass to CC pursuant to the "anti-lapse" provisions of UPC § 2-603. Accordingly, if Spouse 2 revokes his 2015 will and devises the estate to his new boyfriend, CC may have a breach of contract action against Spouse 2's estate. The new boyfriend will argue that CC was not the intended third-party beneficiary of the contract. This supports Andersen's theory that "these contracts are notorious litigation breeders." *See* Andersen § 10, at 75. Most non-UPC states have statutes similar to UPC § 2-603. *See* McGovern § 8.5.

     Answer (A) is incorrect. UPC § 2-603 may give CC a breach of contract action.

     Answer (B) is incorrect. The terms of Spouse 1's 2015 will did not devise to Chelsea a remainder interest.

Answer (C) is incorrect. Any cause of action CC may have will generally not accrue until Spouse 2's death. A few cases have allowed a suit during the promisor's lifetime. *See* McGovern § 4.9.

12. Although a contract not to revoke a will can be established if the provisions of UPC § 2-514 are met, Fernando or the personal representative of Emma's estate can argue "failure of consideration" as a defense to any breach of contract action brought by Charles. Because Emma and Nadia owned Blackacre as joint tenants with rights of survivorship, Nadia acquired Emma's interest in Blackacre by reason of the form of ownership, not pursuant to Emma's will. Arguably, Nadia's promise to devise Blackacre to Charles was not supported by consideration. Charles will likely argue there was, in fact, consideration, if relevant law permits joint tenants to unilaterally sever the joint tenancy. *See* McGovern §§ 4.8, 4.9.

13. **Answer (C) is correct.** Although Blackacre passed nonprobate to Nadia due to the survivorship rights associated with the joint tenancy, Nadia is put to an "equitable election," and Nadia cannot accept any benefits under Emma's will without agreeing, in effect, to convey Blackacre to Fernando. If Nadia accepts any benefits under the will, Fernando will be entitled to Blackacre. Charles' rights as a third-party beneficiary under the original contract would likely be revoked by the original parties' subsequent modification of the original agreement. *See* Atkinson §§ 40, 138.

Answers (A), (B), and (D) are incorrect. These answers are incorrect for the reasons given.

14. **Answer (B) is correct.** Due to the joint tenancy, Emma acquired fee simple title to Blackacre by reason of Nadia's death. *See* Andersen § 18. At Emma's death, Blackacre passes to Fernando, and the residuary estate is divided between Fernando and C1, who takes as a substituted taker for Nadia pursuant to UPC § 2-603(b)(1). Assuming Emma's promise to Nadia to devise Blackacre to Charles was not supported by consideration, Charles appears to be without a legitimate cause of action. If consideration is found, Charles may have a breach of contract cause of action against Emma's estate. *See* McGovern § 4.9. Most non-UPC states have statutes similar to UPC § 2-603. *See* McGovern § 8.3.

Answers (A) and (C) are incorrect. These answers are incorrect for the reasons given.

Answer (D) is incorrect. It is arguable that Emma's promise to Nadia not to revoke the 2015 will was not supported by any consideration. However, Charles will likely argue that Emma's promise was supported by consideration, if relevant law permits a joint tenant to unilaterally sever a joint tenancy.

15. Although a testator has the power in a will to declare how the individual wishes his or her property to be distributed after the individual's death, that authority is effectively limited to the individual's probate estate. Nonprobate assets pass to their designated beneficiaries. Thus, Blackacre will pass to Adam, and the insurance will be payable to Bob. *See* McGovern § 5.5, at 303–04.

16. No, for the same reason discussed in the immediately preceding question. *See* Dukeminier 469–74. If the will had included a specific devise of the insurance policy or proceeds, the Restatement takes the position the proceeds should be paid to the devisee. *See* Restatement (Third) of Property: Wills & Donative Transfers § 7.2 cmt.

17. **Answer (D) is correct.** Since Sunny did not survive Olive, and there was no alternative beneficiary designated on the policy, the proceeds become part of the probate estate and pass pursuant to the provisions of the will. *See* Restatement (Third) Property § 7.1.

    Answers (A), (B), and (C) are incorrect. These answers are incorrect for the reasons given.

18. C2 would have an election. C2 could retain the $1 million as the designated beneficiary of the policy. However, if C2 accepts any benefits under the will, C2 will be required to assign the $1 million to C1. *See* Atkinson § 138.

19. **Answer (C) is correct.** In community property states, the first spouse to die has testamentary power over that spouse's separate property and one-half of the community property. The surviving spouse retains his or her separate property and half of the community property. *See* Andersen § 28(A).

    Answers (A), (B), and (D). These answers are incorrect for the reasons given.

20. Spouse 2 would have an election to make. Spouse 2 can retain Greenacre and a one-half interest in Whiteacre by disclaiming the residuary estate (*e.g.*, Blackacre). However, if Spouse 2 elects to "accept" under the will in order to receive the residuary estate, including Blackacre, Spouse 2 will need to convey Spouse 2's half of Whiteacre to Cobb. *See* Atkinson § 138; McGovern § 3.8, at 196.

Surviving Spouses, Former Spouses & Omitted Children

1. The answer depends on the marital property law of the state where the couple resided, since marital property laws vary considerably from state to state. If they resided in a community property state, or a state which has enacted the Uniform Marital Property Act (1983) (thereby enacting the "partnership theory" of marriage), Shawna may have a half ownership interest in all or a part of the property titled in Gregor's name; Gregor may have owned half of the assets held in Shawna's name. Only Gregor's separate property and half interest in the community property passes to Chelsea in a community property state. Andersen § 28(A). In most other states, it appears that the property in question would have been owned by Gregor prior to his death. While these states have abolished the common law concepts of dower and curtesy, Shawna may be entitled to an elective share amount or percentage payable out of the probate estate and other non-probate transfers. *See* Andersen §§ 28(B), 28(C). In community and non-community property states, the surviving spouse may also have other rights in and to the deceased spouse's estate, such as homestead, exempt property, or family allowance, depending on state law. *See* UPC §§ 2-401–2-405; McGovern § 3.4.

2. **Answer (D) is correct.** Because the couple was married for four years, Shawna's "elective share" is an amount out of the marital property portion of the "augmented estate" of Gregor and Shawna. *See* UPC §§ 2-202, 2-203. Generally, if the value of the property Shawna owned prior to Gregor's death — when added to the value of Greenacre (plus most other assets passing to Shawna by reason of Gregor's death) — exceeds that amount, Shawna will not receive anything else. If not, the difference is paid out of Gregor's probate estate and other nonprobate transfers. *See* UPC § 2-209.

    While the results may vary in both UPC and non-UPC states, the surviving spouse may have to elect between what is devised in the will and the elective share amount. *See* McGovern § 3.7 at 179. In a community property state, the residuary estate is typically limited to the decedent's separate property and half of any community property. In those states, the surviving spouse retains the surviving spouse's half of the community property and also inherits what the deceased spouse devised to the surviving spouse. *See* McGovern § 3.8.

    Answers (A), (B), and (C) are incorrect. These answers are incorrect for the reasons given.

189

3. **Answer (A) is the correct answer.** Chelsea, an adult child, is not entitled to any share of Gregor's probate estate. Assuming Gregor's will was executed after Chelsea's birth, she is not "omitted" or "pretermitted" as that term is defined in UPC § 2-302. Note that statutes in some non-UPC states may afford Chelsea the status of pretermitted heir. *See* Andersen § 29.

    Answer (B) is incorrect. Chelsea would be entitled to an intestate share of Gregor's probate estate only if Gregor died intestate. Gregor died testate and can devise Gregor's estate to Shawna, thereby disinheriting Chelsea.

    A decedent may intentionally disinherit a child in all but one state. Louisiana still retains the civil law concept of "legitime" or "forced heirship" under some circumstances. The preterttmitted child statute in some non-UPC states may protect Chelsea from an unintentional disinheritance if Gregor's will does not expressly disinherit her.

    Answers (C) and (D) are incorrect. Because Chelsea is an adult, neither Gregor nor his estate following his death have a legal obligation to support Chelsea — absent a contract which would have created a debt of the estate.

    Note that if Chelsea is an adult with special needs, the family law of some states may impose some form of legal obligation on the estate of Gregor to support Chelsea following his death.

4. If Gregor had a legal obligation to support Chelsea — and was in fact supporting Chelsea at the time of his death — she would have been entitled to a reasonable allowance for her maintenance during the period of administration. *See* UPC § 2-404. Absent a contractual obligation to the contrary, a general rule of family law is that a parent's legal obligation of support ends at the parent's death. *See* McGovern § 3.3.

    States that have not enacted the Uniform Probate Code typically provide for some type of support for minor or dependent children during formal administration. *See* McGovern § 3.4. Regarding Louisiana's forced heirship rules, see the answer to Question 3.

5. **Answer (A) is correct.** Because Jane and Matt were married for one year, Matt may be entitled to an elective share percentage of the augmented estate. However, since Jane's will devised the residuary estate to Matt, the value of the residuary, when added to the value of other property received by Matt by reason of Jane's death, as well as Matt's own property, will likely exceed the elective share amount. *See* UPC §§ 2-202–2-203; Andersen § 28(C)(3).

    In a community property state, Matt would not likely retain his half of Greenacre and also inherit Jane's residuary estate. Matt would be put to an election: (i) retain Matt's half of the community property assets and disclaim his rights under Jane's will, or (ii) accept Matt's rights under Jane's will and allow Matt's half of Greenacre to pass to Charlie. *See* McGovern § 3.8; Atkinson § 138.

Answer (B) is incorrect. Matt did not own an interest in Greenacre at Jane's death, and it is likely that Greenacre will not be needed to satisfy Matt's elective share percentage.

Answer (C) is incorrect. In some non-UPC states, the surviving spouse may have to elect between what is devised to the spouse in the will or the elective share amount.

Answer (D) is incorrect. An adult child of a prior marriage is not entitled to any share of the probate estate. Since Jane's will was presumably executed after Charlie's birth, Charlie is not omitted or pretermitted.

6. **Answer (C) is correct.** Because Blake failed to designate a third-party beneficiary of the life insurance, the proceeds are payable to his personal representative and become part of the probate estate. Like group life insurance, most pensions are subject to ERISA, a federal law which may require all or a portion of the death benefit of the pension plan to be paid to the employee's spouse. Employment Retirement Income Security Act (ERISA) of 1974, 88 Stat. 829 (codified as amended at 29 U.S.C.A. §§ 1001–1461 (West 2009 & Supp. 2013); *see also* McGovern § 3.7 at 179. Both death benefits are taken into consideration in determining the augmented estate in order to compute Ruby's elective share amount. *See* UPC §§ 2-203–2-207; Andersen § 28(C).

In a community property state, the surviving spouse may be entitled to one-half of the proceeds of the community property life insurance policy. *See* McGovern § 3.8.

Answer (A) and (B) are incorrect. ERISA preempts state law as it would otherwise apply to the pension plan, but ERISA does not require the proceeds of a group life insurance policy to be made payable to the employee's spouse.

Answer (D) is incorrect. This answer is incorrect for the reasons given.

Since the couple resided in a non-community property state, Ruby's death does not affect Blake's pension plan. If they resided in a community property state, it is likely that Ruby had acquired a community property interest in Blake's pension plan. However, the United States Supreme Court in *Boggs v. Boggs*, 520 U.S. 833 (1997), ruled that ERISA preempts state law and prohibits Ruby from devising her interest in the plan to Ruby's heirs and/or devisees. *See* McGovern § 3.8.

7. **Answer (C) is the correct answer.** Chevy is entitled to an amount equal to the value of Chevy's elective share percentage of the augmented estate, less the value of Chevy's property included in the augmented estate — and Paul will inherit the balance. *See* UPC §§ 2-202–2-212.

In a community property state, a spouse's testamentary power of disposition is typically limited to the spouse's separate property and half the community property (because the surviving spouse retains the other half of the community property). *See* McGovern § 3.8.

8. **Answer (A) is incorrect.** UPC §§ 2-202–2-212 prevent Paul from succeeding to the entire probate estate notwithstanding the terms of Will 2 unless the value of Chevy's property included in the augmented estate exceeds the percentage share amount.

    In a non-community property state that has neither adopted the augmented estate concept followed in the Uniform Probate Code nor adopted an elective share system, answer (A) would be correct.

    Answers (B) and (D) are incorrect. Max, as Judith's heir, is entitled to an intestate share of the probate estate only if Judith died intestate. Since there is a valid will, Max does not receive anything.

9. **Answer (D) is correct.** The change of beneficiary is likely to be invalid. ERISA requires the participant's spouse to agree to a change of beneficiary. It does not matter if the participant resides in a non-community property state or a community property state. Chevy is still likely to receive some death benefit, such as a qualified pre-retirement survivor's annuity under ERISA. *See* McGovern §§ 3.7 at 179, 3.9.

    Answers (A), (B), and (C) are incorrect. These answers are incorrect for the reasons given.

10. Teddy's marriage to Sybil after the execution of the will did not revoke the will. *See* UPC §§ 2-508, 2-804. However, Sybil may be entitled to what she would have received had Teddy died intestate. *See* UPC § 2-301. The amount is a factor in determining Sybil's elective share amount as defined in UPC § 2-202.

    In a community property state, the surviving spouse is generally entitled to one-half of any community property. *See* McGovern § 3.8. The rights of the forgotten or omitted spouse, if any, in non-UPC states will vary. In some states, the will may have been revoked by operation of law on the date of marriage. *See* McGovern § 3.6, 5.1.

11. **Answer (C) is correct.** Teddy generally has the right to devise their estate to whomever they choose, subject to Sybil's elective share rights. *See* UPC § 2-202.

    In a community property state, the surviving spouse generally retains one-half of any community property. *See* McGovern § 3.8. In non-UPC states that are also not community property states, surviving spouses may have a right to some share of the estate. *See* McGovern § 3.7.

    Answer (A) is incorrect. Sybil will be entitled to an elective share amount as described above.

    Answers (B) and (D) are incorrect. The will is valid; Teddy did not die intestate.

12. **Answer (A) is correct.** Because Andromeda's will devised all of her estate to their surviving parent, C1 and C2 will not receive an interest in her probate estate even though

they were omitted from the will. *See* UPC § 2-302(a)(1). The birth of C1 and C2 did not revoke the will. *See* UPC § 2-508. Why? It is a common estate plan—for parents with shared minor children—for the surviving parent to receive the entire estate, thereby avoiding management of property issues that arise for minors. It is assumed that the surviving parent will serve as a conduit and use the inheritance to care for the minor children of the decedent.

In almost every state that has not enacted the Uniform Probate Code, statutes grant omitted or pretermitted children rights in their parents' estates under some circumstances. The details vary from state to state. *See* McGovern § 3.5.

Answers (B), (C), and (D) are incorrect. These answers are incorrect for the reasons given.

13. **Answer (A) is correct.** The "omitted children" provisions of the Uniform Probate Code provide protection from unintended disinheritance under certain circumstances only for children born or adopted after the execution of the will. *See* UPC § 2-302. The pretermitted child statutes in non-UPC states vary considerably. *See* McGovern § 3.5.

Answers (B), (C), and (D) are incorrect. These answers are incorrect for the reasons given.

14. **Answer (D) is correct.** C2 will receive an intestate share of Sarah's estate, since C2 was omitted from the will. *See* UPC § 2-302(a)(1).

In almost every state that has not enacted the Uniform Probate Code, statutes grant marital and non-marital omitted or pretermitted children certain rights in their parents' estates under some circumstances. The details vary greatly from state to state. *See* McGovern § 3.5.

Answer (A) is incorrect. C2 is an "omitted child" and entitled to the share C2 would have received had Sarah died intestate.

Answer (B) is incorrect. The birth of the children after the execution of the will did not revoke the will.

Answer (C) is incorrect. Since Tom is the surviving parent of C1, C1 is not entitled to an interest in Sarah's estate.

15. According to UPC § 2-804(b), the divorce revoked any dispositive provision of Trevor's will in favor of Shelly. Since the will devised all of Trevor's probate estate to Shelly, the probate estate passes by intestate succession to Trevor's heirs. If Shelly is named as the executor of his estate, the divorce also revoked Trevor's nomination of Shelly as executor. The estate passes intestate to Mom and Dad.

Statutes in most non-UPC states would produce the same result. In some states, even without a statute, case law may work a revocation by operation of law due to the change of circumstances. In a few states, a divorce revokes the entire will and not just the provisions in favor of the former spouse. *See* McGovern § 5.4.

16. **Answer (D) is correct.** The Uniform Probate Code revokes a pre-divorce beneficiary designation of a transfer-on-death account. As a result, the accounts pass to Mom and Dad. *See* UPC § 2-804.

    In a state that has not enacted the Uniform Probate Code, or a statute similar to UPC § 2-804, the result may differ. Absent a statute, some courts have allowed the former spouse to enforce the terms of the contract. *See* McGovern § 5.5.

    Answers (A), (B), and (C) are incorrect. These answers are incorrect for the reasons given.

17. If the policy was not part of Olivia's employee benefit package, the designation of Steph as beneficiary of the policy was revoked by the divorce. *See* UPC § 2-804. However, notwithstanding state law to the contrary, the designation of Steph as the beneficiary of a group life policy provided by Olivia's employer or the pension plan may still be enforceable by Steph despite the divorce. ERISA's preemption clause has been invoked to override state statutes similar to UPC § 2-804 where the death benefit was provided by the employer as part of an employee benefit plan. *Egelhoff v. Egelhoff ex rel. Breiner*, 532 U.S. 141 (2001). *See* comment to UPC § 2-804; McGovern §§ 3.8, 5.5.

    Many non-UPC states have statutes similar to UPC § 2-804. Absent a statute, courts have allowed the former spouse to enforce the terms of the contract. *See* comment to UPC § 2-804.

Trusts as Will Substitutes

1. No, the following issues, factors, and considerations should be discussed with Client:

Comparing Costs. Going through probate with a will may be more expensive than avoiding probate with a revocable trust. The fees of executors and their attorneys may be based on the size of the "probate" estate in some states, and thus the fees can be reduced by nonprobate transfers. There is, however, a growing trend against basing fees simply on the value of the probate estate. Costs are state law specific. The preparation and funding of a revocable trust may be costlier than the preparation of a will in that a revocable trust often requires additional work, such as transferring title of assets to the trustee, and these additional expenses could offset some of the contemplated savings in probate costs. Since revocable trusts tend to be more complicated than wills, the legal fees for preparing the revocable trust and administering the trust during the settlor's lifetime are often greater than the fees for simply preparing a comparable will. Thus, whether or not avoiding probate reduces costs depends on each client's situation and can vary from state to state. *See* McGovern § 9.4.

Delays. While the typical delay associated with probate administration is a source of popular dissatisfaction, its significance should not be exaggerated. The needs of the beneficiaries of the estate during probate administration can sometimes be met by family allowances and by partial distributions. Again, the real issue depends on state law. For example, in some states, testamentary trusts are subject to close court supervision, which can create costs and delays, but the number of states in which court supervision of testamentary trusts is required is declining. In most states, trusts, whether revocable or irrevocable, are generally not subject to continuing court supervision. *See* McGovern § 9.4.

Creditors' Rights. While creditors of the settlor of a revocable trust in some states may not have a right to reach the assets of the revocable trust once the settlor dies, this possible benefit of revocable trusts is no longer true in most jurisdictions. *See* McGovern § 9.4.

Estate Tax Issues. Revocable trusts have no real tax advantages. If the settlor retains the power to revoke the trust, the trust income continues to be taxed to the settlor, and the trust property is included in the settlor's gross estate at death. *See* McGovern § 9.4, at 423. Further, in 2023, the first $25.84 million of a U.S. married couple's estate can pass through gift or bequest without incurring the estate or gift tax. Under post-2017 tax rules, very few taxpayers worry about paying estate tax (fewer than 600 estate tax returns were filed in 2020).

Pour-Over Will. There is still a need for a will that "pours over" into the trust any probate assets not in the trust when the settlor dies. Most individuals using a revocable trust will still need a will to coordinate the various parts of the estate plan. Pour-over wills are used for this purpose. *See* McGovern § 9.4, at 423.

Miscellaneous Issues. Homestead exempt property and family allowance rights may be affected by placing the estate in a revocable trust prior to the settlor's death. Depending on the jurisdiction, there may be restrictions on testamentary power that do not apply to revocable trusts (*e.g.*, pretermitted child statutes or reduced complications for trustees of inter vivos trusts compared to testamentary trusts). *See* Dukeminier 461–65.

2. **Answer (D) is correct.** Shelby's trust instrument does not need to be executed in compliance with the statutory formalities required for wills because the trust is not a will. The property subject to Shelby's trust is not probate property at death because it is then no longer owned by Shelby, individually, but rather by the trustee and the beneficiary. An inter vivos trust (unlike a will) is a means to presently transfer ownership during the settlor's lifetime. Shelby transferred legal title to Trustee and a nonpossessory future equitable interest to Bob when the trust *was created*, not when Shelby died. The fact that Bob's interest was subject to Shelby's power to revoke or amend the trust, and is also subject to a condition of surviving Shelby, does not make the trust a will (*i.e.*, the trust instrument need not comply with the statutory formalities for wills). *See* Andersen ch. 4.

Answers (A), (B), and (C) are incorrect. These answers are incorrect for the reasons explained.

3. No, Shelby's declaration of trust is a present transfer of an equitable nonpossessory future interest to Bob the same way it would have been had Shelby entered into an agreement of trust with a third party. The identity of the trustee does not affect whether or not the trust must comply with the statutory formalities for wills in order for beneficial interests to pass as a result of the settlor's death. *See* Andersen § 2(B).

4. Because the express trust was irrevocable, the divorce did not affect Wilhamina's income interest. *See* UPC § 2-804. However, G1's death terminated G1's interest, and a substituted gift was created in Gigi. *See* UPC § 2-707. Gigi will have to survive Wilhamina to take; if not, Gigi's contingent remainder interest may fail, and Oliver's reversionary interest in Blackacre may pass to Oliver's successor in interest, presumably the devisee under Oliver's will, G2. *See* Andersen § 45(B)(2)(b).

The result may differ in a state that has not adopted the UPC approach as it relates to the substituted gift in favor of Gigi. G1's interest is likely to have been a vested remainder which passed to S when G1 died. *See* Andersen § 45(B)(2)(c).

5. Answer (D) is correct. The divorce had the effect of revoking Wilhamina's income interest because the trust was revocable. *See* UPC § 2-804(b). Since G1 died before Oliver, G1's contingent remainder failed, and Gigi is the substituted taker pursuant to UPC § 2-707(b). See the answer to the immediately preceding question.

In a state that has not adopted the UPC approach, Wilhamina may still retain her income interest, and G1's vested remainder may have passed to S. *See* Andersen § 45(B)(1).

Answers (A), (B), and (C) are incorrect. The substituted taker, Gigi, survived until the distribution date, Oliver's death. In a non-UPC state, S may have succeeded to G1's vested remainder. *See* Andersen § 45(B)(2)(c).

6. Because the stocks and Blackacre are probate assets, the executor of Olivia's estate can use them to satisfy her debts. According to UPC § 3-902, shares of distributees abate without any preference between real or personal property. The stocks and real property should be abated proportionately. After the debts are paid by the personal representative of the estate, what is left should be delivered to the bank to be distributed pursuant to the terms of the trust.

States that have not adopted the Uniform Probate Code approach may provide that personal property should be abated prior to real property within the same classification of devises. *See* McGovern § 8.4. Accordingly, in a non-UPC state, the stock may need to be sold to pay the debts, and the real property will pass to G1 assuming the state allows testamentary additions to inter vivos trusts. Most states have statutes similar to UPC § 2-511, which does allow probate assets to "pour over" into the trust. If testamentary additions to inter vivos trusts are not allowed, C1 and C2 would succeed to the estate remaining after debts are paid. *See* McGovern § 6.2.

7. Answer (B) is correct. Sam is entitled to an elective share amount out of the decedent's net probate estate augmented by the $100,000 in the revocable trust. *See* UPC §§ 2-202, 2-203, 2-205.

The answer may differ in a state that has not adopted the UPC approach. *See* Andersen § 28(C). For example, in a community property state, the surviving spouse will likely be entitled to half of the community's probate assets and be compensated for half of what the decedent contributed to the trust. *See* McGovern § 3.7- 3.8.

Answer (A) is incorrect. The trust is valid.

Answers (C) and (D) are incorrect. The augmented estate consists of the net probate estate and certain nonprobate dispositions.

8. Answer (D) is correct. It appears as if a valid, enforceable express trust was created during Squiggy's lifetime even though title remained in her name until the time of her death. *See* UTC §§ 401–402. At Squiggy's death, Tom's equitable remainder interest became possessory. *See* Andersen § 12.

Answers (A) and (B) are incorrect. An express inter vivos trust does not need to be executed with testamentary formalities. The family farm passes pursuant to the terms of the trust, not by the will or by intestate succession.

Answer (C) is incorrect. Since Squiggy did not change the title to the family farm when the trust was created, the family farm still appears to be a probate asset, and Tom will need to take steps to establish the existence of the trust and his ownership under the trust.

9. **Answer (D) is correct.** The fact that there was no transfer of title before Squiggy's death and that she retained the power to revoke the trust does not affect the trust's validity. *See* UTC §§ 401- 402; Andersen § 12. Since Squiggy did not revoke the apparently valid, enforceable express trust prior to her death, the terms of the trust control the disposition of the family farm. Since the trust was created by Squiggy's declaration of trust, at her death, Tom's equitable remainder interest became possessory.

Answers (A) and (B) are incorrect. An express trust does not need to be executed with testamentary formalities.

Answer (C) is incorrect. Since Squiggy did not change the title to the family farm when the trust was created, the family farm still appears to be a probate asset, and Tom will need to take steps to establish the existence of the trust and Tom's ownership under the trust.

10. **Answer (D) is correct.** If the creation and funding of the trust were a transfer in fraud on River's creditors, the creditors can pursue their claims against the trust estate pursuant to state law on fraudulent transfers. The transfer may also constitute a voidable preference in bankruptcy. *See* UTC § 505, cmt. to (a)(2). If River did not become insolvent because of the creation of the trust, the trust estate probably is not reachable to satisfy her debts. UTC § 505 adopts this generally accepted principle. *See* McGovern § 9.8.

Answers (A) and (B) are incorrect. These answers are incorrect for the reasons given.

Answer (C) is incorrect. As long as there is no fraudulent transfer involved, it is worth noting that these assets placed in an irrevocable trust by River no longer belong to her. Assets in the trust would only be reachable to the extent that River retained an interest in the trust.

11. **Answer (D) is correct.** During the lifetime of the settlor, the trust estate of a revocable trust is subject to claims of the settlor's creditors whether or not the original creation and funding of the trust were fraudulent. *See* UTC § 505(a)(1). The result is likely to be the same in a state that has not adopted the Uniform Trust Code. *See* Andersen § 12(E).

Answers (A), (B), and (C) are incorrect. These answers are incorrect for the reasons given.

12. **Answer (D) is correct.** Following the settlor's death, the trust estate of a revocable trust continues to be subject to claims of the settlor's creditors. UTC § 505 adopts this widely accepted principle. *See* Andersen § 12(E), n. 79. The result may differ in some non-UTC states. *See* Bogert § 148.

    Answers (A), (B), and (C) are incorrect. These answers are incorrect for the reasons given.

13. **Answer (A) is correct.** A donor does not make a gift for federal tax purposes until the donor has relinquished all dominion and control. The power to revoke is an explicit reservation of dominion and control to determine what, if anything, Eliana is to receive. *See* 26 CFR § 25.2511-2.

    Answer (B) is incorrect because the gift to Eliana through the revocable trust will not be complete until the death of Chucky.

    Answers (C) and (D) are incorrect. Eliana has no enforceable (present or future) interest in the house. If an enforceable interest had been transferred to her, not in exchange for consideration in money or money's worth, it would give rise to tax consequences.

14. No, it is the settlor's retained power of revocation that prevents the transfer from being a completed gift for gift tax purposes. *See* 26 CFR § 25.2511-2.

15. **Answer (B) is correct.** The trust estate of a revocable trust is included in the settlor's gross estate. *See* I.R.C. § 2038.

    Answers (A), (C), and (D) are incorrect. These answers are incorrect for the reasons given.

16. **Answer (C) is correct.** There is no gift for tax purposes when the trust is created because Miley did not part with dominion and control over the trust estate since she had retained the power to revoke the trust. *See* 26 CFR § 25.2511-2. However, whenever a legitimate distribution is made to Cal pursuant to the trust terms, a gift is made by the settlor to the beneficiary.

    Answers (A), (B), and (D) are incorrect. These answers are incorrect for the reasons given.

17. **Answer (A) is correct.** Under I.R.C. § 676, the $5,000 is taxable to Miley because she retained the power to revoke the trust. This is a result of the "grantor trust" income tax rules.

    Answer (B) is incorrect. This answer sounds credible if one is not versed in tax law. The problem, however, is that the federal income tax does not allow one to take a deduction for gifts.

Answer (C) is incorrect. Under the grantor trust rules, the settlor (*i.e.*, the "grantor") is taxable on the trust's income, not the trustee (*i.e.*, not the trust).

Answer (D) is incorrect. The $5,000 distribution to Cal was a gift to him, and gifts (gratuitous transfers motivated by detached and disinterested generosity) are generally not taxable to donees. *See* I.R.C. § 102(a).

18. Absent specific language to the contrary, trustees of express trusts are held to strict fiduciary standards and can be held personally liable to the trust's beneficiaries for the breach of those fiduciary duties. *See* UTC § 802(a); Andersen § 12.1. However, if Miley commits an act of omission or commission in her role as trustee that otherwise would be a breach of trust, there is nothing Cal can do while the trust is revocable; the duties of the trustee are owed exclusively to the settlor of the trust. *See* UTC § 603.

19. The same test of mental capacity applies for wills and revocable trusts. *See* UTC § 601. Some states require the mental capacity needed to create and fund any inter vivos trust (*e.g.*, contract capacity). *See* Bogert § 9.

20. The answer depends on the applicable state law. In every state, if the trust instrument is silent, there is a default rule governing revocability. In some states, inter vivos trusts are deemed to be irrevocable unless the settlor expressly retained the right to revoke the trust. In other states, inter vivos trusts are deemed to be revocable unless expressly made irrevocable. UTC § 602(a) adopts the latter view. *See* McGovern § 9.4.

Express Trusts

1. False. An express trust is a fiduciary relationship with respect to property that subjects the person who has legal title to legally enforceable duties to deal with the property for the benefit of another. *See* Restatement (Third) of Trusts § 2.

2. **Answer (B) is correct.** If the only proof of the oral trust is Ginger's testimony of what Oskar told Ginger about the conveyance after the alleged transaction took place, it is likely that Freddie will retain the fee simple title. Ginger's testimony may not even be admissible under relevant rules of evidence. *See* Restatement (Third) of Trusts § 18.

    Answers (A), (C), and (D) are not incorrect. These answers are incorrect because there may (likely be) no admissible evidence of the actual transaction that took place between Oskar and Freddie.

3. The Uniform Trust Code permits the creation of an express oral trust if its terms can be established by clear and convincing evidence. However, the relevant statute of frauds may require a writing for the creation of an inter vivos trust of real property. If so, the oral express trust may not be enforceable if Freddie is not willing to perform as agreed, notwithstanding the willingness of the friends to testify as to the oral agreement. *See* Restatement (Third) of Trusts §§ 22, 24. Traditionally, Freddie would be allowed to retain Blackacre unless Ginger was able to prove that he acquired Blackacre by fraud, undue influence, or duress, or that Freddie, at the time of the transfer, was in a confidential relationship with Oskar. In which event, the imposition of a constructive trust for Ginger was the appropriate remedy. There appears, however, to be a modern trend developing toward the use of a resulting trust or a constructive trust to prevent Freddie's unjust enrichment under these circumstances. Some cases favor the intended beneficiaries; others favor the settlor, or his or her successor in interest. *See* Restatement (Third) of Trusts § 24 cmt. h.

4. **Answer (B) is correct.** The relevant statute of frauds may require a writing for the inter vivos creation of enforceable express trusts of interests in real property. *See* Restatement (Third) of Trusts §§ 22, 24. Since there is no writing evidencing the trust, Freddie may be able to retain Blackacre, notwithstanding his acknowledgment of the oral agreement, unless Ginger can prove that Freddie procured the transfer by fraud, duress, or undue influence, or that Oskar and Freddie were in a confidential relationship at the time of the transfer. *See* answer to previous question.

Answers (A), (C), and (D) are incorrect. Assuming there is no other evidence of Freddie's intent at the time of the conveyance or of a special relationship existing between Oskar and Freddie at the time of the conveyance, a constructive trust may not be appropriate. The traditional view is that a constructive trust can be imposed on a grantee of a deed only if the grantee did not intend to perform as agreed when the promise was made. *See* McGovern § 6.4. There are, however, cases in some jurisdictions suggesting the use of a constructive trust is appropriate to prevent the unjust enrichment of a grantee who orally agrees but later refuses to act in accordance with the agreement. *See* Restatement (Third) of Trusts § 24 cmt. h.

5. **Answer (C) is correct.** Because of the pre-existing fiduciary relationship that existed between Oskar and Freddie, a court is likely to impose a constructive trust on Freddie in favor of Ginger to avoid unjust enrichment by Freddie. *See* Restatement (Third) of Trusts § 24.

   Answers (A) and (B) are incorrect. Because of the pre-existing fiduciary relationship between Oskar and Freddie, equity will not likely permit Freddie to retain Blackacre.

   Answers (D) is incorrect. A resulting trust arises by operation of law when an express trust fails or less than a fee simple has been transferred. In this example, there is no express trust and the property has been transferred to Freddie in fee simple.

6. **Answer (B) is correct.** The testimony of the friends is likely to be the evidence needed to prove the creation of the oral express trust and its terms. Most states do not require a writing to create or enforce an inter vivos express trust of personal property under these circumstances. *See* Restatement (Third) of Trusts §§ 20, 21. However, UTC § 407 does require "clear and convincing evidence" of the creation of the oral trust and its terms. Some states that have not enacted the Uniform Trust Code may require only a "preponderance of the evidence." *See* Bogert § 21.

   Answer (A) is incorrect. Assuming Ginger has "clear and convincing" evidence of the oral agreement, she can simply bring an action to enforce the express trust.

   Answer (C) is incorrect. Lakshmi's attempt to create the express trust did not fail for lack of a beneficiary or for failure of the trust's purpose.

   Answer (D) is incorrect. Sufficient evidence is available to prevent Freddie from retaining the stock for his own use.

7. **Answer (C) is correct.** The oral trust agreement does not satisfy a statute of frauds that requires a writing for inter vivos trusts of real property. Thus, Ginger cannot enforce the express trust. *See* Restatement (Third) of Trusts §§ 22, 24. However, it is apparent by the grant to "Freddie, as trustee" that Star did not intend Freddie to take Blackacre for his own use, thereby leading to the imposition of a resulting trust in favor of Cici, as Star's successor in interest. Other cases suggest a constructive trust for Ginger is the appropriate remedy. *See* Restatement (Third) of Trusts § 24 cmt. i.

Answer (A) is incorrect. To satisfy the requirements of the statute of frauds, the writing must not only manifest trust intention, but also identify the trust property, the beneficiaries, and the purposes of the trust.

Answer (B) is incorrect. In some states, Cici, as Star's successor in interest, has standing to require Freddie to return the property. *See* Restatement (Third) of Trusts § 24. Some states may allow Ginger to impose the constructive trust to avoid Freddie's unjust enrichment. *See* Restatement (Third) of Trusts § 24 cmt, i.

Answer (D) is incorrect. Equity will not allow Freddie to retain the property.

8. **Answer (B) is correct.** Freddie can carry out the terms of the oral express trust if the creation and the terms of an oral trust can be proven by clear and convincing evidence. Only Freddie can assert the statute of frauds as a defense and take advantage of the oral express trust being unenforceable. *See* Restatement (Third) of Trusts § 24. If he elects to take advantage of the statute of frauds or the existence of the oral agreement cannot be proven, the trust is "passive," and Ginger can demand the transfer of the property back to her. If the statute of uses, or a similar statute, is applicable, Freddie's legal title merges with Ginger's equitable interest, and Ginger already owns fee simple title. *See* Restatement (Third) of Trusts § 6. While UTC § 407 requires clear and convincing evidence to prove an oral trust, many non-UTC states require proof by only a preponderance of the evidence.

    Answers (A), (C), and (D) are incorrect. These answers are incorrect for the reasons given.

9. If a valid, enforceable trust has been created, Blackacre is not subject to the personal obligations of Freddie. *See* Restatement (Third) of Trusts § 42. UTC § 507 has codified this generally accepted principle. However, because there is not a written evidence of the trust, UTC § 407 requires that the creation of the trust and its terms be proven by "clear and convincing evidence." Will the court accept Freddie's acknowledgment of the trust as sufficient proof of the existence of the trust and its terms? If Freddie and Ginger fail to meet the burden of proof, the creditors can attach the property. In states that have not enacted the Uniform Trust Code, the creation of the trust and its terms may have to be proven by only a preponderance of the evidence.

10. Even if the terms of the trust agreement can be established by Ginger, Freddie could plead the statute of frauds as an affirmative defense, thereby making the trust unenforceable and allowing the creditor to attach Blackacre — unless Ginger can intervene and meet the burden of proof to have a constructive trust imposed on Freddie in favor of Ginger. *See* Restatement (Third) of Trusts § 24. Alternatively, Freddie can acknowledge the oral trust, not plead the statute of frauds, and prevent Blackacre from being attached, if there is clear and convincing evidence of the oral trust. *See* UTC § 407. In states that have not enacted the Uniform Trust Code, the creation of the trust and its terms may have to be proven by only a preponderance of the evidence.

11. **Answer (A) is correct.** If you allow the creditor to attach Blackacre, you will breach your fiduciary duties to Ginger. *See* McGovern § 12.1. A valid, enforceable express trust exists. Since an express trust exists, Blackacre is not subject to the personal obligations of Freddie. *See* Restatement (Third) of Trusts § 42. UTC § 507 codifies this generally accepted principle.

    Answer B is incorrect. Because a valid, enforceable express trust has been established, the trust property is not subject to the personal obligations of Freddie.

    Answers (C) and (D) are incorrect. Since an express trust exists, Blackacre is not subject to the personal obligations of Freddie.

12. **Answer (A) is correct.** An enforceable express trust was created; the death of Ginger did not terminate the trust. At common law, conditions of survivorship were not implied with respect to future interests. *See* comment to UPC § 2-707. However, UPC § 2-707 provides that a future interest under the terms of a trust is contingent on the beneficiary surviving the distribution date. Since Ginger was not survived by any lineal descendants, the property passed to Octavia's heir, Cici, at Octavia's death. *See* UPC § 2-707.

    Answers (B) and (C) are incorrect. Because Ginger predeceased Octavia, neither Cici nor Doug inherited Ginger's interest in the trust. In a state that has not enacted UPC § 2-707, or a similar statute, the result is likely to differ. Ginger's interest would likely be inherited by her heirs, Cici and Doug, unless the express trust failed. *See* Restatement (Third) of Trusts §§ 8, 55.

    Answer (D) is incorrect. In any event, Freddie does not retain the property for his personal use.

13. **Answer (B) is correct.** Absent additional evidence of Octavia's intentions, UPC § 2-707 directs that the trustee deliver the property to Cici as Octavia's heir. In states that have not enacted the Uniform Probate Code, Ginger's contingent remainder failed, and Octavia's reversionary interest passed to Cici, as Octavia's heir. *See* Restatement (Third) of Trusts §§ 8, 55. However, if Ginger would have been survived by a child, the child would have acquired Ginger's interest notwithstanding the "survivorship" language. According to UPC § 2-707, words of survivorship are not, in the absence of additional evidence, a sufficient indication of contrary intent to negate the "substitute gift" rule of UPC § 2-707. *See* comment to UPC § 2-707. In a state that has not enacted the Uniform Probate Code, the result will likely differ. *See* Restatement (Third) of Trusts § 55 cmt. a.

    Answer (A) is incorrect. The death of the surviving trust beneficiary does not generally pass fee simple ownership to the trustee.

    Answers (C) and (D) are incorrect. Ginger's contingent remainder interest failed; the purpose of the trust has become frustrated.

14. Answer (D) is correct. An express trust is created in a will only if the testator manifests the intent to impose on the devisee legally enforceable duties to manage the property for another. However, only such manifestations of intent which are admissible as proof in a judicial proceeding may be considered. *See* Restatement (Third) of Trusts § 13. The Uniform Trust Code has codified these generally accepted common law principles. *See* UTC § 402 and commentary. Accordingly, without additional proof of Mai's intent, the language in her will is likely to be found to be "precatory" rather than "mandatory."

Answer (A) is incorrect. The use of the words "with the request" by Mai generally is considered to be "precatory" rather than "mandatory."

Answer (B) is incorrect. Either Lenore has fee simple title, or an express trust was created for the benefit of Rolf.

Answer (C) is incorrect. Either an express trust was created for the benefit of Rolf or Lenore owns the stock.

15. Answer (A) is correct. It is evident that Mai did not intend Lenore to acquire the stock for Lenore's personal use and benefit. All the elements of an express trust are present. *See* Restatement (Third) of Trusts § 17. The Uniform Trust Code has codified these generally accepted common law principles. *See* UTC §§ 401, 402.

Answer (B) is incorrect. An express trust has been created. Rolf will seek to enforce the terms of the express trust.

Answer (C) is incorrect. All the elements of an express trust are present.

Answer (D) is incorrect. Lenore inherited the legal title only; Rolf inherited an equitable interest in the stock.

16. Answer (B) is correct. Because Rolf died before Mai, an express trust was not created. *See* RESTATEMENT (THIRD) OF TRUSTS § 17. The devise to Lenore fails, and Mai's executor should deliver the stock to Mai's residuary beneficiary, the charity. *See* Restatement (Third) of Trusts § 8. The Uniform Probate Code has codified this generally accepted common law principle. *See* UPC § 2-604.

Answer (A) is incorrect. Mai's attempt to create an express trust for the benefit of Rolf failed because he died before the trust was created. Rolf's heirs did not acquire any interest in the stock.

Answer (C) is incorrect. The executor should not deliver the stock to Lenore. If she already has the stock, the charity may need to seek the imposition of a resulting trust to acquire the stock as Mai's successor in interest.

Answer (D) is incorrect. It is evident that Mai did not intend Lenore to acquire the stock for her own personal use and benefit.

17. An express trust can be created by the settlor's declaration that the settlor holds identifiable property for another. *See* Restatement (Third) of Trusts § 10. The Uniform Trust Code has codified this generally accepted common law principle. *See* UTC § 401. The fact that Hector's declaration of trust was oral is problematic. However, the Uniform Trust Code has adopted the view that, absent a statute to the contrary, an express trust does not need to be evidenced by a trust instrument, if the creation of the oral trust and its terms can be established by clear and convincing evidence. *See* UTC § 407. Assuming there is no such statute and that the friends' testimony will be accepted by the court as "clear and convincing" evidence of the creation of the express trust, an express trust was created, and the court should appoint a successor trustee to manage Blackacre until Ed attains age 21.

The result will differ in a state where the statute of frauds requires a signed writing in order for trusts of real property to be enforceable. The statute of frauds in many jurisdictions requires oral declarations of trust to be in writing. In those states, Jan, as Hector's heir, would likely retain Blackacre. *See* Restatement (Third) of Trusts § 22. However, a possible exception exists that may permit Ed to seek a constructive trust on Jan to prevent her unjust enrichment. *See* Restatement (Third) of Trusts § 24 cmt. j.

18. **Answer (A) is correct.** An express trust can be created by the settlor's declaration that the settlor holds identifiable property for another. *See* Restatement (Third) of Trusts § 10. The Uniform Trust Code has codified this generally accepted common law principle. *See* UTC § 401. The fact that Hector's declaration of trust was oral is problematic. However, the Uniform Trust Code has adopted the view that, absent a statute to the contrary, an express oral trust does not need to be evidenced by a trust instrument if its creation and terms can be established by clear and convincing evidence. *See* UTC § 407.

The result will differ in a state where the statute of frauds requires a signed writing for declarations of trusts of personal property. *See* Restatement (Third) of Trusts § 22.

Answer (B) is incorrect. Assuming that the friends' testimony will be accepted by the court as "clear and convincing" evidence of the creation of the trust, an express trust was created.

The statute of frauds in some jurisdictions requires oral declarations of trusts to be in writing. In those states, Jan, as Hector's heir, would likely retain the stock.

Answer (C) is incorrect. The traditional view is that a constructive trust is an appropriate remedy when a transferee committed a fraud, exerted undue influence, or breached a confidential relationship. Neither Hector nor Jan committed any of those acts. However, a possible exception exists that may permit Ed to seek a constructive trust on Jan to prevent her unjust enrichment. *See* Restatement (Third) of Trusts § 24 cmt. j.

Answer (D) is incorrect. It is not the role of a personal representative to manage the settlor's inter vivos trust.

19. **Answer (A) is correct.** An express trust can be created by the settlor's declaration that the settlor was holding identifiable property for the benefit of another. *See* Restatement (Third) of Trusts § 10. The Uniform Trust Code has codified this generally accepted common law principle. *See* UTC § 401.

    The same result is likely in a non-UPC state since the writing requirement would satisfy the statute of frauds. *See* Restatement (Third) of Trusts § 23.

    Answer (B) is incorrect. All of the elements of a valid, enforceable express trust are present.

    Answer (C) is incorrect. If Jan had possession and refused to cooperate when Ed seeks to enforce the express trust, the court might need to impose a constructive trust.

    Answer (D) is incorrect. It is not the role of a personal representative to manage the settlor's inter vivos trust.

20. **Answer (A) is correct.** Assuming the Uniform Trust Code was in effect at the time the express trust was created, the settlor may revoke the trust unless the terms of the trust provide the trust is irrevocable. *See* UTC § 602. The Uniform Trust Code has reversed the generally accepted common law rule that trusts are presumed to be irrevocable. *See* Restatement (Third) of Trusts § 63. Presumably, a court would likely find that Hector's conveyance to George was evidence of Hector's intent to revoke the trust.

    The result is likely to be different in a state that does not presume inter vivos trusts are revocable.

    Answers (B) and (C) are incorrect. Hector retained the power to revoke the trust. In a state that has not adopted the Uniform Trust Code approach, or if the trust was created before the state adopted that approach, Ed can file suit for breach of fiduciary duty by Hector. If successful, the court may be able to impose a constructive trust on George since he was not a good-faith purchaser.

    Answer (D) is incorrect. While a court may impose a constructive trust on a third party who participates in a trustee's breach of trust, the third party is generally not personally liable to the beneficiary, if the third party is not aware of the trust. *See* UTC § 1012.

21. **Answer (D) is correct.** It appears as if a valid, enforceable express trust was created during Maricella's lifetime, even though title remained in her name until she died. *See* UTC §§ 401, 402. At Maricella's death, Blackacre is a nonprobate asset, and Freddie's equitable remainder interest became possessory.

    The result is likely to be the same in states that have not enacted the Uniform Trust Code. *See* Restatement (Third) of Trusts § 10.

    Answers (A) and (B) are incorrect. An express inter vivos trust does not need to be executed with testamentary formalities. Blackacre passes pursuant to the terms of the trust, not by the will or by intestate succession.

Answer (C) is incorrect. Because Maricella did not change the title to Blackacre when the trust was created, Blackacre still appears to be a probate asset, and Freddie will need to take steps to establish the existence of the trust and his ownership under the trust.

22. **Answer (D) is correct.** The fact that there was no transfer of title before Maricella's death and that she retained the power to revoke the trust does not affect the trust's validity. *See* UTC §§ 401, 402. *See* Restatement (Third) of Trusts § 10. Since Maricella did not revoke the apparently valid, enforceable express trust prior to her death, the terms of the trust control the disposition of Blackacre. Since the trust was created by Maricella's declaration of trust, at her death, Blackacre is a nonprobate asset, and Freddie's equitable remainder interest becomes possessory. The result is likely to be the same in states that have not enacted the Uniform Trust Code. *See* comment to the UTC § 401.

    Answers (A) and (B) are incorrect. An express inter vivos trust does not need to be executed with testamentary formalities.

    Answer (C) is incorrect. Since Maricella did not change the title to Blackacre when the trust was created, Blackacre still appears to be a probate asset, and Freddie will need to take steps to establish the existence of the trust and his ownership under the trust.

23. **Answer (A) is correct.** As a general rule, a court may authorize an assignee of a beneficiary's interest to reach the beneficiary's interest by attachment of present or future distributions. *See* Restatement (Third) of Trusts § 51. The Uniform Trust Code has codified this generally accepted common law principle. *See* UTC § 501; Bogert § 38.

    Answers (B), (C) and (D) are incorrect. As a general rule, to the extent a beneficiary's interest is not subject to a "spendthrift" provision or a "forfeiture" provision, or a statute limiting the beneficiary's power of alienation, the interest is assignable.

24. **Answer (D) is correct.** Absent a "spendthrift" or "forfeiture" provision, or a state statute limiting the beneficiary's power of alienation, a court may authorize an assignee to reach the beneficiary's interest by attachment of present or future distributions to or for the benefit of a beneficiary. *See* UTC § 501. In other words, the assignee is generally entitled to receive any distributions the trustee makes, or is required to make, after the trustee has knowledge of the transfer. However, an assignee cannot acquire an interest greater than the one owned by the beneficiary prior to the assignment, and the court should limit the award to such relief as is appropriate under the circumstances. *See* UTC § 501. Gary is entitled to whatever is not properly distributed to or for the benefit of Uma's health, support, education or maintenance. *See* Bogert § 48.

    Answers (A) and (B) are incorrect. An assignee cannot acquire an interest greater than the one the assignor owned prior to the assignment. Restatement (Third) of Trusts takes the position that "support" trusts are discretionary trusts and that the assignee is entitled to "judicial protection from abuse of discretion by the trustee." However, it also acknowledges that the trustee's refusal to make a distribution under these circumstances may not be an abuse of discretion, suggesting that the balancing process typical of discretionary issues is weighted against assignees. Restatement (Third) of Trusts § 60 cmt. e.

Answer (C) is incorrect. The answer is incorrect for the reasons given. However, the law in some states may prohibit assignments of support interests unless they were made for the purpose of acquiring goods or services for Uma's support, assuming that the interests were not limited by a "spendthrift" or "forfeiture" provision, or a statute limiting the beneficiaries' powers of alienation. *See* Bogert §§ 38, 42.

25. Absent a "spendthrift" or "forfeiture" provision, or a state statute that limits the beneficiary's power of alienation, a beneficiary's assignee has a right to receive discretionary distributions to which the beneficiary would otherwise be entitled. *See* RESTATEMENT (THIRD) OF TRUSTS § 60. However, the assignee cannot compel the trustee to make a distribution, if the beneficiary could not do so. In a discretionary trust, the assignee would have to prove the trustee abused its discretion after consideration of the beneficiary's circumstances and the effect the decision will have on Gary in light of the purposes of the trust. *See* Restatement (Third) of Trusts § 60 cmt. e. Traditionally, the assignment is only effective if and when the trustee elects to make a distribution. *See* Bogert § 41.

26. **Answer (C) is correct.** Assuming the trust agreement did not contain a "spendthrift" or "forfeiture" provision, and state law does not limit the beneficiary's power of alienation, the assignment of a beneficiary's future interest is valid. *See* Restatement (Third) of Trusts § 51. UTC § 501 has codified this generally accepted common law principle. At Uma's death, the trust estate should be delivered to Quinn, if Gary survives Uma. *See* UPC § 2-707; Bogert § 38.

Answer (A) is incorrect. A beneficiary of a trust owns an interest in property which, as a general rule, is assignable.

Answer (B) is incorrect. The assignee cannot acquire an interest greater than that owned by the beneficiary.

Answer (D) is incorrect. As a general rule, the assignment is enforceable against the trustee.

27. **Answer (A) is correct.** The terms of the trust include a "spendthrift" provision. Accordingly, Gary cannot assign his interest in the trust estate to Quinn. *See* Restatement (Third) of Trusts § 58. UTC § 502 codifies this widely accepted principle of trust law. However, the comment to UTC § 502 notes that the trustee may choose to honor the assignment unless Gary revokes the assignment. *See* Bogert § 40.

Answer (B) is incorrect. In most jurisdictions, a beneficiary may not transfer an interest in a trust in violation of a valid "spendthrift" provision.

Answer (C) is incorrect. Whether the assignee paid consideration for the assignment is irrelevant.

Answer (D) is incorrect. The spendthrift provision made it impossible for Gary to make a legally binding transfer. However, Gary may be estopped to deny the assignment once the property is delivered to him.

28. **Answer (D) is correct.** As a general rule, the beneficiaries of an express trust can assign their interests to assignees, including the person serving as the trustee. *See* RESTATEMENT (THIRD) OF TRUSTS § 51. However, this particular assignment is problematic even in the absence of a "spendthrift" or "forfeiture" provision, or a statute limiting the beneficiary's power of alienation. Because of the fiduciary relationship existing between Uma, Gary, and Tomás, the transaction is suspect, and if there was improper conduct by Tomás, or if Uma and Gary were not aware of all of the material facts, the assignment may be set aside. *See* Restatement (Third) of Trusts § 51 cmt. b.

    Answer (A) is incorrect. In most states, Orin is a "stranger" to the trust because the trust is irrevocable and Orin did not retain any interest in, or power over, the trust estate. However, in a state that has adopted UPC § 2-707, Gary's remainder interest is a contingent interest, and if Gary does not survive Uma, Gary's descendants, or Orin, may have an interest in the property. Orin's interest may or may not be too remote to have standing to challenge the transaction.

    Answer (B) is incorrect. If the assignment is valid, legal title and equitable title merged, and the trust no longer exists, subject to the possible interests of Gary's descendants and Orin.

    Answer (C) is incorrect. Answer (C) would be correct if the assignment is valid.

29. A trustee has the fiduciary duty to act impartially, giving due regard to interests of all the beneficiaries. In addition, Ylfa has a fiduciary duty to exercise a discretionary power in good faith and in accordance with the terms and purposes of the trust and the interests of the beneficiaries. Accordingly, either beneficiary has standing to bring a cause of action to remedy a breach of trust. *See* Bogert §§ 153, 157. The Uniform Trust Code has codified these generally accepted principles of trust law. *See* UTC §§ 803, 814, 1001.

30. **Answer (D) is correct.** Because Ylfa is still a fiduciary, the terms of the trust are not interpreted literally and the burden of proof is typically on the beneficiary to plead and prove that the trustee "abused" the trustee's exercise or non-exercise of the discretionary power by not acting in good faith or in accordance with the purposes of the trust. *See* UTC § 814(a); Bogert § 89.

    Answers (A), (B), and (C) are incorrect. The determinative issue is whether Ylfa "abused" the discretion granted by the settlor. The trier of fact is not to substitute its judgment, or even the judgment of a reasonably prudent trustee, for the decision of the trustee.

31. **Answer (D) is correct.** The Restatement treats "support" trusts as a category of discretionary trusts. Accordingly, the issue is whether the trustee abused its discretion. *See* RESTATEMENT (THIRD) OF TRUSTS § 50. The burden of proof may differ in states that have not adopted the Restatement view. *See* Bogert §§ 89, 109.

Answers (A), (B), and (C) are incorrect. In states that have not adopted the Restatement view, the burden may be on the beneficiary to prove what amount was actually necessary for Carrie's health, support, education, or maintenance.

Creditor Rights

1. **Answer (C) is correct.** If the creation and funding of the trust were in fraud of Jeremiah's creditors, the creditors can pursue their claims against the trust estate pursuant to the relevant state's law on fraudulent transfers. The transfer may also constitute a voidable preference in bankruptcy. *See* comment to UTC § 505. If Jeremiah did not become insolvent by reason of the creation and funding of the trust, the trust estate is not reachable to satisfy Jeremiah's debts. UTC § 505 adopts this generally accepted principle. *See* Bogert § 48.

   Answers (A) and (B) are incorrect. If the creation and funding of the trust were in fraud of the creditors, they can still reach the trust estate.

   Answer (D) is incorrect. The trust assets are not reachable by the creditors unless the creation and funding of the trust were in fraud of the creditors.

2. **Answer (D) is correct.** During the lifetime of the settlor, the trust estate of a revocable trust is subject to claims of the settlor's creditors. *See* UTC § 505(a)(1). The result is likely to be the same in a state that has not adopted the Uniform Trust Code. *See* Restatement (Third) of Trusts § 25 cmt. e.

   Answers (A), (B) and (C) are incorrect. These answers are incorrect for the reasons given.

3. **Answer (D) is correct.** Following the settlor's death, the trust estate of a revocable trust continues to be subject to claims of the settlor's creditors. UTC § 505(a)(3) adopts this widely accepted principle. The result may differ in a non-UTC state. *See* Bogert §§ 39, 48, 148.

   Answers (A), (B), and (C) are incorrect. These answers are incorrect for the reasons given.

4. **Answer (C) is correct.** Assuming the terms of the trust, including its irrevocability, can be established by clear and convincing evidence, the fact that the express trust was created pursuant to an oral agreement should not be determinative of the issue. *See* UTC § 407. If the transfer to Ted had been in fraud of Jeremiah's creditors, the creditors can pursue their claims against the property transferred. If not, the property is not reachable to satisfy Jeremiah's debts. *See* UTC § 505. The same result is likely to occur in a non-UTC state. *See* Bogert §§ 39, 48.

Answers (A), (B), and (D) are incorrect. These answers are incorrect for the reasons given.

5. **Answer (A) is correct.** The trust property is not subject to the personal obligations of the trustee. UTC § 507 has codified this generally accepted principle. *See* Restatement (Third) of Trusts § 42. If you use the trust estate to satisfy your creditors, you will breach your duty of loyalty to the trust's beneficiaries. *See* McGovern § 12.1.

    Answers (B), (C), and (D) are incorrect. Trust property is not subject to the trustee's personal debts.

6. As long as the creation of the oral trust and its terms can be established, the trust property cannot be reached by the trustee's personal creditors. *See* RESTATEMENT (THIRD) OF TRUSTS § 42. Since the trust is oral, the UTC requires "clear and convincing evidence" of the terms of the trust. *See* UTC § 407. If the trustee of an oral trust performs and conveys the trust income or principal to the beneficiary, the creditors of the trustee may not seek to attack the transfer on the grounds that the oral trust is unenforceable, and the trustee is the legal owner of the property. Courts have almost universally denied the creditors of the trustee any ability to attach trust assets in an oral trust where the trustee is performing. *See* RESTATEMENT (THIRD) OF TRUSTS § 24. In a state that has not adopted the UTC approach, the existence of the trust may need to be proven by only a "preponderance of the evidence."

7. **Answer (B) is correct.** Absent a "spendthrift" or "forfeiture" provision in the trust agreement, the court may authorize a creditor to reach a beneficiary's interest in the trust by attachment of either present or future distributions. UTC §§ 501, 502 has codified this generally accepted common law principle. *See* McGovern § 9.8.

    Answer (A) is incorrect. Bran's interest is limited to the income the trust generates during his lifetime.

    Answer (C) is incorrect. It does not matter whether the debt is tortious or contractual in nature.

    Answer (D) is incorrect. To the extent a beneficiary's interest is not subject to a "spendthrift" or "forfeiture" provision, it is generally available to satisfy the beneficiary's creditors. *See* Bogert §§ 39–40.

8. **Answer (D) is correct.** Generally, the interest of a beneficiary is liable to be taken by a beneficiary's creditors. The process varies from state to state. *See* Bogert §§ 39–41. Regardless of whether the trust agreement contains a "spendthrift" or "forfeiture" provision, a creditor of a beneficiary generally does not have standing to compel a trustee to make a discretionary distribution from the trust to the creditor or the beneficiary. *See* UTC § 504; McGovern § 9.8. However, the creditor may be able to attach the ben-

eficiary's interest, and although the interest is not subject to execution sale, the trustee may be held personally liable to the creditor for any amount paid by the trustee to the beneficiary if the trustee has been served with notice of the attachment. *See* Restatement (Third) of Trusts § 60 cmt. c.

Answer (A) is incorrect. Bran's interest is effectively limited to whatever income, if any, is distributed to Bran in Vanna's discretion. The Restatement takes the position that the creditor is entitled to "judicial protection from abuse of discretion by the trustee." However, it also acknowledges that the trustee's refusal to make a distribution under these circumstances may not be an abuse of discretion. *See* Restatement (Third) of Trusts § 60 cmt. e.

Answer (B) is incorrect. Bran does not have a mandatory right to the income.

Answer (C) is incorrect. Generally, the only creditor that may be excepted from the general rule is a child, spouse, or former spouse of the beneficiary with a judgment or order against Bran for support. *See* UTC § 504(c)(2).

9. **Answer (D) is correct.** See the answer to the previous question. UTC § 504 applies to distributions defined by an ascertainable standard. *See* Restatement (Third) of Trusts § 60 cmt. c. The result may differ in a state that has not adopted the UTC or the Restatement's approach since Bran's interest in the trust estate is limited to whatever income is necessary for his health, education, maintenance, or support, and when Bran dies, Caitlin is entitled to the income not properly distributed to Bran. *See* McGovern § 9.8.

Answers (A), (B), and (C) are incorrect. The only creditor that may be excepted from the general rule is a child, spouse, or former spouse of a beneficiary with a judgment or order against Bran for support. *See* UTC § 504(c)(2).

10. **Answer (D) is correct.** See the answer to the previous question. A creditor of a beneficiary cannot compel a discretionary distribution from a trust, even if the trustee has failed to comply with a standard of distribution. *See* comment to UTC § 504.

The result may differ in a state that has not adopted the Uniform Trust Code approach. Here, Bran's interest is limited to whatever income is distributed to Bran pursuant to the described standard of distribution. Because the hospital rendered medical services, it is arguable that it should be able to garnish Bran's interest in the trust. *See* McGovern § 9.8.

Answers (A), (B), and (C) are incorrect. These answers are incorrect for the reasons given.

While UTC § 504 appears to prohibit the creditor from compelling a distribution, states that have not adopted the Uniform Trust Code approach may allow the hospital to collect from the trustee out of the trust's income if the trust agreement does not contain a "spendthrift" or "forfeiture" provision. *See* McGovern § 9.8.

11. **Answer (B) is correct.** Absent a "spendthrift" or "forfeiture" provision in the trust agreement, the court may authorize a creditor to attach a beneficiary's future interest in the trust estate. The Uniform Trust Code codifies this generally accepted common law principle. *See* UTC § 501. The court may even order a sale of the beneficiary's future interest. *See* McGovern § 9.8. However, the value of Caitlin's remainder interest is diminished by it being contingent on Caitlin surviving Bran. *See* UPC § 2-707.

Answer (A) is incorrect. The creditor cannot divest Bran's interest in the trust.

Answer (C) is incorrect. While a creditor, in theory, may force a judicial sale of a beneficiary's interest, such a sale cannot adversely affect the interests of other beneficiaries.

Answer (D) is incorrect. Only Caitlin's future interest can be attached.

12. In most jurisdictions, a settlor has the power to include as part of the terms of the trust a provision that prevents a creditor from reaching a beneficiary's interest in the trust or a distribution by the trustee before its actual receipt by the beneficiary. *See* Bogert §§ 39–40. This so-called "spendthrift" provision is generally valid in most states so long as it prohibits both voluntary and involuntary transfers of beneficial interests. *See* McGovern § 9.8. These generally accepted principles have been codified in UTC § 502. Accordingly, if the agreement prohibits both voluntary and involuntary alienation, the creditor cannot attach the beneficiaries' interests in the trust, and the creditor must wait until there are actual distributions to the beneficiaries. *See* McGovern § 9.8. If valid under state law, the spendthrift provision will be effective in bankruptcy. *See* Restatement (Third) of Trusts § 58 cmt. a.

Note that there are a few states that still do not recognize the effectiveness of "spendthrift" provisions. *See* McGovern § 9.8; RESTATEMENT (THIRD) OF TRUSTS § 58 cmt. a.

New Hampshire, Ohio, and Rhode Island do not recognize the validity of spendthrift provisions, and states such as Alaska, Idaho, New Mexico and Wyoming have no authority as to the validity of spendthrift trusts. *See* Bogert § 222 at 406.

13. **Answer (C) is correct.** Caitlin's interest will pass to the charity. Even in jurisdictions that do not accept the effectiveness of "spendthrift" provisions, a settlor can generally place a "condition subsequent" on a beneficiary's interest, causing the beneficiary's interest to terminate or change if there is an attempted involuntary or voluntary alienation. Sometimes the condition subsequent converts the beneficiary's interest into a discretionary interest. *See* Bogert § 44; McGovern § 9.8.

Answer (A) is incorrect. Bran's interest is not affected by the termination of Caitlin's interest. Only Caitlin's interest will pass to the charity.

Answer (B) is incorrect. The trust instrument does not provide that Caitlin's terminated interest pass to Bran.

Answer (D) is incorrect. The provision is likely valid. Most jurisdictions accept the effectiveness of these so-called "forfeiture" provisions.

14. **Answer (B) is correct.** It is not uncommon for successful business owners and professionals to be concerned about uninsurable risk or liability that exceeds insurance coverage limits. Kermit is engaging in asset protection by establishing a trust. If creation and funding of the trust were in fraud of Kermit's creditors, the creditors can pursue their claims against the trust estate pursuant to the relevant state's law on fraudulent transfers. However, this is not the scenario presented in this question. As of the day that the trust is established, Kermit is aware of no potential lawsuits. When the $10 million is placed into a trust for Kermit's children, Kermit ceases to be the owner of the $10 million and it is likely protected from his creditors.

15. **Answer (A) is incorrect.** Kermit's judgment creditors can likely reach the assets in the trust to the extent of Kermit's interest in the trust. A possible workaround for Kermit is to create a self-settled asset protection trust (or domestic asset protection trust), which would potentially protect Kermit's assets even if he holds a life income interest in the trust. As of the date of this publication, only seventeen states recognize the validity of the self-settled asset protection trust.

16. **Answer (C) is incorrect.** During the lifetime of the settlor, the trust estate of a revocable trust is subject to claims of the settlor's creditors. *See* UTC § 505(a)(1). The result is likely to be the same in a state that has not adopted the Uniform Trust Code. *See* Restatement (Third) of Trusts § 25 cmt. e.

17. **Answer (D) is incorrect.** A will is an ambulatory document that does not take effect until the death of Kermit. It will not protect Kermit's money from creditors.

Powers of Appointment

1. A donee with a general power of appointment has the authority to appoint the appointive property to (i) the donee or the donee's estate or (ii) the creditors of the donee or the donee's estate. The donee of a non-general power of appointment does not have such authority. *See* Andersen § 37(C)(1); Restatement (Third) of Property § 17.3.

2. **Answer (C) is correct.** Arnold owns the equitable life estate and is the donee of a non-general power of appointment. The charity owns an equitable remainder interest that is subject to divestment, if Arnold validly exercises the testamentary power. The children, as permissible appointees, are not beneficiaries of the trust. It will not be known until Arnold dies if the power is exercised and the charity is divested. *See* UTC § 103(3); Restatement (Third) of Property § 19.7, comment c.

   Answer (A) is not correct. Arnold owns an equitable life estate and is the donee of a testamentary non-general power of appointment. Arnold is a beneficiary of the trust in both capacities according to the Uniform Trust Code. As discussed above, the charity is also a beneficiary.

   Answers (B) and (D) are incorrect. Arnold's exercise of the power will not be effective until his death. Until the power is exercised, the objects of the power have expectancies and are not beneficiaries.

3. **Answer (B) is correct.** Arnold was the donee of a non-general testamentary power of appointment. Since such a power is presumed to be "exclusionary" or "exclusive," Arnold can appoint to any one or more of the objects of the power or permissible appointees. *See* Andersen § 39(B). When the will is admitted to probate, the charity is divested.

   Answers (A) and (C) are incorrect. The charity's remainder interest has been divested.

   Answer (D) is incorrect. C3 does not acquire an interest in the trust estate.

4. **Answer (A) is correct.** It is widely accepted that a general disposition of a testator's property in a will does not exercise a non-general power of appointment. *See* Andersen § 39(A). The Uniform Probate Code has codified this principle. *See* UPC § 2-608.

   Answers (B), (C), and (D) are incorrect. These answers are incorrect for the reasons given.

5. In order for the charity's remainder interest to be divested, Arnold, as the donee of the power, must validly exercise the power. A testamentary power can only be exercised in a document which is formally sufficient to be admitted to probate. *See* Andersen § 37(C). Thus, the charity was not divested. UPC § 2-503 (*or a similar statute in a non-UPC state*) may provide the opportunity to probate the defective will if there is clear and convincing evidence that Arnold intended the document to be his will.

6. The charity is not divested because Arnold's attempt to exercise the non-general power was invalid in that S was not a permissible appointee. *See* Andersen § 37(C). C1 and C2 may argue for the application of the doctrine of dependent relative revocation. If successful, the earlier will may still be valid to exercise the power. *See* Andersen § 9(E).

7. **Answer (A) is correct.** Arnold failed to exercise the power. Consequently, the charity was not divested.

   Answers (B), (C), and (D) are incorrect. Arnold was not under any legal obligation to exercise the power. The permissible appointees have no standing to complain about his inaction.

8. **Answer (B) is correct.** Bette expressly exercised the general testamentary power in her will. *See* Andersen § 39.

   Answer (A) is incorrect. The charity was divested.

   Answers (C) and (D) are incorrect. Because Bette was not the donor of the power, the value of Bette's augmented estate in order to determine Sam's elective share amount does not include property over which Bette had a testamentary general power of appointment. *See* RESTATEMENT (THIRD) of Property § 23.1. The UPC adopts this position. *See* UPC § 2-205(1)(A).

   Note that the result may differ in a non-UPC state. *See* McGovern § 10.5 (p. 513).

9. **Answer (C) is correct.** Because Abraxas' will contained a "gift over" in the event the power was not exercised, the charity's remainder interest was not divested. *See* UPC § 2-608. Bette did not expressly or impliedly exercise the testamentary general power of appointment. *See* McGovern § 10.5 (p. 515); RESTATEMENT (THIRD) of Property § 19.4.

   Answer (A) is incorrect. Bette did not have a legal obligation to exercise the power and did not manifest an intent to exercise the power. It is widely accepted that a general disposition of a testator's property in a will does not exercise a non-general power of appointment. *See* Andersen § 39(A). The Uniform Probate Code has codified this principle. *See* UPC § 2-608.

   Answers (B) and (D) are incorrect. Because Bette did not hold an inter vivos general power, Blackacre is not included in Bete's augmented estate for Sam's elective share determination. *See* UPC § 2-205(1)(A). Note that the result may differ in a non-UPC state.

10. Because Bette did not effectively exercise the power, as Chuck was deceased, Blackacre passes to the taker in default, the charity. *See* Andersen § 39(C).

11. **Answer (A) is correct.** Bette attempted to exercise the power in favor of a permissible appointee who predeceased Bette. However, the anti-lapse provisions of UPC § 2-603(b)(5) create a substitute gift in favor of CC. Note that the result may differ in states that have not enacted the UPC or similar legislation.

    Answer (B) is incorrect. Chuck died before Bette and could not devise Blackacre to CS.

    Answer (C) is incorrect. Sam did not acquire any interest in Blackacre.

    Answer (D) is incorrect. The charity has been divested.

12. RESTATEMENT (THIRD) of Property § 22.3 takes the position that the property subject to a general testamentary power is subject to the claims of the donee's creditors to the extent the donee's probate estate is insufficient to satisfy the donee's creditors. The states seem to be divided on this issue, but absent a specific statute on point, the majority view reaches a similar result. Since the general testamentary power was exercised, the donee's creditors can reach the property subject to the power. Courts in some states, however, have held the creditors of the donee cannot reach the property, even if the power was exercised. *See* McGovern § 10.5.

13. **Answer (D) is correct.** It is generally accepted that, during the settlor's lifetime, the settlor's creditors may reach the maximum amount that can be distributed to, or for the benefit of, the settlor even if the initial creation and funding of the trust did not amount to a fraudulent transfer. The Uniform Trust Code has codified these principles. *See* UTC § 505(a)(2). *See also* comment e to RESTATEMENT (THIRD) of Trusts § 58.

    Answers (A), (B), and (C) are incorrect. A settlor who is also a beneficiary cannot use a trust as a shield against the settlor's creditors under these circumstances.

14. RESTATEMENT (THIRD) of Trusts § 60, comment g, takes the position that the creditors of a donee of a power who has the authority to distribute or appoint to the donee can reach the property over which the donee has the power, even if the power is exercised in a fiduciary capacity and whether or not it is limited by an ascertainable standard. The Uniform Trust Code has been amended to negate the possible application of the Restatement position if the beneficiary/trustee's power is limited by an ascertainable standard as defined in the Internal Revenue Code. *See* UTC § 504(e). Spendthrift statutes in some states also maintain the "spendthrift" protection if the donee's power is limited to the donee's health, education, maintenance, and support. However, the result may differ in other jurisdictions.

15. **Answer (D) is correct.** If, under applicable state law, Anurak's power to distribute to himself was limited to the ascertainable standard of health, education, maintenance or support, the trust estate described in Question 14 would not be included in his gross estate. *See* I.R.C. § 2041. The trust estate of the trust described in Question 13 will be included in Anurak's gross estate because he was the settlor of the trust. *See* I.R.C. §§ 2036, 2037.

16. **Answers (A), (B), and (C) are incorrect.** These answers are incorrect for the reasons given.

Death & Taxes

1. The use of the term "death tax" is misleading, but it is a label that has been used to fuel political fires in favor of repeal of taxes. *See* Victoria J. Haneman, *Intergenerational Equity, Student Loan Debt, and Taxing Rich Dead People*, 39 Va. Tax Rev. 179 (2019).

   An estate may be subject not only to federal transfer tax but also state tax. A longstanding issue is whether and how the federal tax system should accommodate state taxes imposed at time of death. *See* Joseph M. Dodge, Wendy C. Gerzog, Bridget J. Crawford, Jennifer Bird-Pollan & Victoria Haneman, Federal Taxes on Gratuitous Transfers: Law and Planning (Aspen, 2d ed. 2023).

   An inheritance tax is a tax imposed when a beneficiary receives any type of inheritance, and it is generally imposed on the heirs of the decedent. There is no federal inheritance tax. Only six states impose an inheritance tax in 2023 (Iowa, Kentucky, Maryland, Nebraska, New Jersey, Pennsylvania), and the tax in Iowa will be repealed as of January 1, 2025. Maryland is the only state to impose both an inheritance and an estate tax.

   An estate tax is an excise tax on a decedent's privilege of transferring property at death. It is imposed on the estate of the decedent. Approximately twelve states and also the federal government impose an estate tax. *See* Andersen § 59.

2. **Answer (D) is correct.** Any property over which the decedent possessed a general power of appointment (*i.e.*, the authority to appoint to the donee, the donee's estate, the donee's creditors, or the creditors of the donee's estate), either immediately prior to or at the time of death, is included in the decedent's gross estate. *See* I.R.C. § 2041. Amira only had a non-general power over Blackacre, so it is not included in her gross estate. However, Amira did possess a general testamentary power over the trust estate.

   Answers (A), (B), and (C) are incorrect. Amira did not have the power to appoint Blackacre to her estate or creditors, so Blackacre is not included in her gross estate. Because Amira had the power to appoint the trust estate to her probate estate, the power is a general power, and the trust estate is included in Amira's gross estate.

3. **Answer (D) is correct.** Any property over which the decedent possessed a general power of appointment, either immediately prior to or at the time of death, is included in the decedent's gross estate, even if the decedent does not exercise the power. *See* I.R.C. § 2041.

Answers (A), (B), and (C) are incorrect. A did not have the power to appoint Blackacre to Amira's estate or creditors, so Blackacre is not included in Amira's gross estate. Because she had the power to appoint the trust estate to her probate estate, the power is a general power, and the trust estate is included in Amira's gross estate.

4. No, even though the trust estate is included in A's gross estate. Because Amira did not exercise the general testamentary power over the trust estate, the trust estate passes to the taker in default, Big State University, and qualifies for the charitable deduction. *See* I.R.C. § 2055.

5. **Answer (A) is correct.** A decedent's gross estate includes the decedent's entire probate estate (*i.e.*, any assets passing by will or intestate succession). *See* I.R.C. § 2033.

    Answers (B) and (C) are incorrect. These answers are incorrect for the reasons explained.

    Answer (D) is incorrect. Whether or not a probate asset is subject to administration under state law is irrelevant.

6. My answer would not change. The identity of the heirs or devisees is irrelevant for determining the value of the gross estate. *See* I.R.C. § 2033. The devise to the surviving spouse will qualify for the marital deduction and reduce the value of the taxable estate by the value of what was devised to Sarah. *See* I.R.C. § 2056.

7. **Answer (D) is correct.** If a decedent had the power immediately prior to the decedent's death to appoint the property to the decedent, the power would be classified as a general power, and the value of the appointive property would be included in the decedent's gross estate unless the power was limited by an "ascertainable" standard. *See* Treas. Reg. § 20.2041-1(c)(2). Beatrice's power over trust one was limited by an ascertainable standard, and the trust estate is excluded. However, Beatrice's power over trust two was not limited by an ascertainable standard. The value of trust two is included in Beatrice's gross estate.

    Answers (A), (B), and (C) are incorrect. An "ascertainable" standard is one that limits distributions for the purposes of the health, education, maintenance, or support of the donee. A standard defined by the words "comfort or welfare" may not be considered to be "ascertainable" and is likely to cause inclusion of trust two in Beatrice's gross estate.

8. **Answer (B) is correct.** Beneficiary's interests in both trusts terminated at his death, and Beneficiary did not possess any power (directly or indirectly) over either trust estate. The federal estate tax is an excise tax on a decedent's privilege to transfer property at death. *See* I.R.C. § 2033.

    Answers (A), (C), and (D) are incorrect. Since Beneficiary was not the settlor, did not possess a power of appointment, and did not have the right to transfer any part of the trust estates when Beneficiary died, neither trust estate is included in Beneficiary's gross estate.

9. No federal estate tax is due. All probate assets, whether real, personal, tangible or intangible, are included in the decedent's gross estate. Accordingly, the fair market value of any property of Taxpayer's passing by will or intestate succession by reason of her death is included in Taxpayer's gross estate. *See* I.R.C. § 2033. If any of the described assets were community property according to relevant state law, only the decedent's half interest would be included in Taxpayer's gross estate. The fact that a spouse may have a right to an elective share does not affect the makeup of the decedent's gross estate. *See* I.R.C. § 2034. The fact that the assets were devised to Spouse does not affect the makeup of the gross estate, provided Spouse is a U.S. citizen, but the net value of the assets devised to Spouse will qualify for the marital deduction and be deducted from the value of the gross estate to determine the value of the taxable estate. *See* I.R.C. § 2056.

Accordingly, since $6,000,000 is the value of the gross estate and it was devised to Spouse, it qualifies for the marital deduction, and there is no estate tax liability.

What if Taxpayer left her property to someone other than Spouse? There would still be no estate tax liability. The lifetime exemption in 2023 is $12.92 million or $25.84 million per married couple because of portability rules, which allow any credit unused at the death of spouse 1 to be used on the death of spouse 2. *See* I.R.C. § 2010(c). The lifetime exemption amount will reduce by roughly half at the end of 2025 (to $6.2 million per individual taxpayer) unless action is taken by Congress after the date of publication of this book.

10. Assuming Taxpayer's executor elected "portability" in Taxpayer's federal estate tax return, when Spouse died, Spouse's estate of $17,000,000 (Spouse's $11,000,000, plus Taxpayer's $6,000,000) will not generate any estate tax liability because of Spouse's 2023 exemption equivalence of $12.92 million and Taxpayer's unused 2023 exemption (exclusion) amount of $6,920,000.

11. Answer (A) is correct. The gross estate includes the value of all property transferred by the decedent during life if the decedent retained for life the possession or enjoyment of, or the right to receive the income from, the property transferred. *See* I.R.C. §§ 2036, 2037.

Answers (B), (C), and (D) are incorrect. It does not matter whether Owen's retained interest is a life estate or a fee simple interest subject to an executory interest.

12. Answer (A) is correct. Nonprobate assets are also included in the decedent's gross estate. *See* I.R.C. §§ 2033, 2036, 2038.

Answers (B) and (C) are incorrect. One cannot avoid inclusion in the gross estate by making this type of nonprobate disposition of the property.

Answer (D) is incorrect. Even though the checking account is in the names of both Owen and C2, 100% of the account is included in Owen's gross estate because Owen created and funded the account.

13. **Answer (A) is correct.** An insurance policy on the decedent's life is included in the decedent's gross estate if (i) the policy is payable to the decedent's probate estate or (ii) the decedent owned the policy immediately prior to death. *See* I.R.C. § 2033, 2042.

   Answers (B), (C), and (D) are incorrect. Owen owned both policies at the time of death. Accordingly, the proceeds of each policy are included in the gross estate.

14. Owen did not own either policy at the time of death, and neither policy was payable to Owen's estate. Accordingly, neither policy is included in the gross estate under I.R.C. § 2042. However, the whole-life policy is included in the gross estate under I.R.C. § 2035(a)(2) because Owen transferred the policy to C1 within three years of Owen's death. The proceeds of the term policy are excluded from the gross estate, but the value of the policy on the date of the assignment (in excess of any available annual exclusion for gift tax purposes) will be added to Owen's taxable estate to determine the tax base. *See* I.R.C. § 2001.

15. **Answer (B) is correct.** Since Owen did not own the stock at the time of death, the stock is not included in the gross estate. The estate tax is an excise tax on the transfer of property at death. *See* I.R.C. § 2033.

   Answers (A), (C) and (D) are incorrect. Owen did not own the stock at the time of death. However, the value of the stock on the dates of the gifts (in excess of any available annual exclusion for gift tax purposes) will be added to Owen's taxable estate to determine the tax base as an adjusted taxable gift. *See* I.R.C. § 2001.

16. **Answer (A) is correct.** The amount of any debt legally owed by Omre and payable out of the assets included in his gross estate is properly deducted from the gross estate to determine the taxable estate. *See* I.R.C. § 2053.

   Answers (B), (C), and (D) are incorrect. It does not matter whether the debts are secured or unsecured. However, if Omre is not personally liable for a secured debt, the debt is subtracted from the fair market value of the asset securing the debt to determine the amount to include in the gross estate. *See* Treas. Reg. § 20.2053-1(a)(1)(iv).

17. Omre's estate has been valued at $6 million. In addition to the $700,000 debts owed by Omre prior to his death, expenses of last illness, funeral expenses, and administration expenses are also deductible. *See* I.R.C. § 2053. These expenses total $50,000, creating deductions of $750,000. In 2023, the lifetime estate and gift tax exemption (also known as the unified credit) is $12.92 million. *See* I.R.C. § 2010. If Omre is married, the credit amount doubles to $25.84 million because of credit portability available to U.S. citizen spouses — the availability of the credit changes for non-citizen spouses. For more infor-

mation, see Chapter 10 of JOSEPH M. DODGE, WENDY C. GERZOG, BRIDGET J. CRAW-FORD, JENNIFER BIRD-POLLAN & VICTORIA HANEMAN, FEDERAL TAXES ON GRATUI-TOUS TRANSFERS: LAW AND PLANNING (Aspen, 2d ed. 2023).

Omre's $6 million estate, less applicable deductions, is fully sheltered by the 2023 lifetime estate and gift tax exemption.

It is worth noting that the lifetime estate and gift tax exemption is adjusted for inflation every year and will increase slightly for tax years 2024 and 2025, until it returns (or "sunsets") to pre-2018 levels on December 31, 2025. Unless Congress acts to extend the post-2018 increased credit amount, the lifetime estate and gift tax exemption will return to $5.49 million indexed for inflation — probably ending up around $6 million.

18. **Answer (C) is correct.** The amount devised to Taxpayer's child is not deductible. The devise to Spouse likely qualifies for the "marital deduction," and the devise to Big State University qualifies for the "charitable deduction." *See* I.R.C. §§ 2055, 2056.

     Answers (A), (B), and (D) are incorrect. Congress, for public policy reasons, encourages testamentary gifts to decedents' spouses and to qualified charities.

19. **Answer (B) is correct.** A "qualified terminable interest property" trust (or "QTIP" trust) allows a taxpayer (or the grantor) to leave assets in a trust, to be used by the surviving spouse during his or her lifetime *only*, with the trust controlling how the unused portion of those assets (if any) passes after the death of the surviving spouse.

     The $1,000,000 devised to the first described trust would not qualify for the marital deduction because Spouse was given a "non-deductible terminable" interest in the trust. *See* I.R.C. § 2056(b)(1). The $10,000,000 devised to the second trust appears to meet the requirements of a QTIP trust in that Spouse is entitled to all of the trust's income for the remainder of Spouse's lifetime. *See* I.R.C. § 2056(b)(7).

     Answer (A) is incorrect. The first trust does not qualify for the marital deduction.

     Answer (C) is incorrect. The first trust does not qualify for the marital deduction, but the second trust is, because $10 million passes through a QTIP trust.

     Answer (D) is incorrect. However, if the second trust does not meet the requirements of a QTIP trust, or if Taxpayer's executor does not make the "QTIP election," this answer would be correct.

20. The trust estate of the first trust will not be included in Spouse's gross estate when he or she dies. At Spouse's death, their life estate simply terminates, and the child's remainder interest becomes possessory. Whether the trust estate of the second trust will be included in Spouse's gross estate depends on two factors. First, did the trust meet the requirements of a "QTIP" trust? Second, did Taxpayer's executor make the "QTIP election"? *See* I.R.C. § 2056(b)(7). If the answer is yes to both questions, the trust estate of the second trust is included in Spouse's gross estate. *See* I.R.C. § 2044.

Jurisdiction, Practice, Procedure

1. The probate exception to federal jurisdiction is a long-standing principle that reserves to state probate courts the probate and contests of wills, the determination of heirship and the administration of decedents' estates. Federal courts do have jurisdiction to hear certain estate-related matters. *See* McGovern §§ 12.8, 13.3.

2. **Answer (D) is correct.** According to general principles of conflict of laws, the substantive law of a decedent's domicile normally governs rights of succession to the decedent's personal property. *See* McGovern § 1.2 (p. 33). Because all of the described assets are personal property, the law of the State of X will determine whether these assets will pass (i) by intestate succession to Sarah's heirs determined under the law of X or (ii) to devisees described in a will of Sarah that is admitted to probate in accordance with the law of the State of X. *See* UPC §§ 1-301, 1-302.

    Answer (A) is incorrect. Even though the heirs may reside in different states and certain assets of Sarah are located in different states, these facts do not trigger the application of any federal statutes to determine who owns what.

    Answer (B) is incorrect. While federal banking laws govern many of the practices of the bank, the succession of the checking account is a matter of state law. While (i) the State of Y may have jurisdiction over the shares of stock due to the corporation being a Y corporation and (ii) the State of Z has jurisdiction over the tangible personal property located in Z, the succession of those assets is a matter of the law of the state where Sarah was domiciled, the State of X.

    Answer (C) is incorrect. While (i) the State of Y may have jurisdiction over the shares of stock due to the corporation being a Y corporation and (ii) the State of Z has jurisdiction over the tangible personal property located in Z, the succession of those assets is still a matter of the law of X.

3. **Answer (B) is correct.** UPC § 1-201(38) defines the term "property" to include both real and personal property, and UPC §§ 1-301 and 1-302 appear to give the State of X the authority to determine the rights of succession to the real property in Y and Z. However, conflict of laws principles provide that the substantive law of the decedent's domicile normally governs the rights of succession to the decedent's personal property, but the law of the situs of real property usually governs the rights of succession to the real property. *See* McGovern § 1.2 (p. 31).

Answer (A) is incorrect. Conflict of laws principles generally provide that the law of the decedent's domicile governs the succession to the decedent's personal property, but the law of the situs of real property governs the succession of the real property. A state statute may permit the probate of a will that is valid under another state's law even if the will was not executed in accordance with the formalities of the state's applicable wills act. *See* UPC § 2-506.

Answers (C) and (D) are incorrect. These answers are incorrect for the reasons given.

4. **Answer (C) is correct.** A proceeding to settle a decedent's estate is an in rem action. Accordingly, any state has territorial jurisdiction over the property of a decedent physically located in the state even though the decedent was domiciled in another jurisdiction. In addition, the state where the decedent was domiciled at the time of death also has jurisdiction over the personal property of the decedent located in another jurisdiction. *See* McGovern §§ 1.2, 13.4.

    Answers (A), (B), and (D) are incorrect. Conflict of laws principles dictate that the situs state has jurisdiction over property, both real and personal, located in that state. The domiciliary state also has jurisdiction over the decedent's personal property wherever located.

5. **Answer (C) is correct.** Conflict of laws principles dictate that the situs state has territorial jurisdiction over property, both real and personal, located in that state. The domiciliary state also has jurisdiction over the decedent's personal property wherever located. Conflict of laws principles presume that the law of the decedent's domicile governs the rights of succession to the decedent's personal property, but the law of the situs of real property governs the rights of succession to the real property. *See* McGovern § 1.2.

    Answers (A), (B), and (D) are incorrect. Conflict of laws principles generally provide that the law of the decedent's domicile governs the succession of the decedent's personal property, but the law of the situs of real property governs the succession of the real property.

6. **Answer (D) is correct.** In general, a lawyer's duty of confidentiality continues after the death of a client. Accordingly, a lawyer ordinarily should not disclose confidential information following a client's death. However, if consent is given by the client's personal representative, or if the deceased client had expressly or impliedly authorized disclosure, the lawyer who represented the deceased client may provide an interested party with information regarding a deceased client's estate plan and intentions. *See* AMERICAN COLLEGE OF TRUST AND ESTATE COUNSEL, COMMENTARIES ON THE MODEL RULES OF PROFESSIONAL CONDUCT Section 1.6 (4th ed. 2006) (hereinafter "ACTEC Commentary ___"). In this situation, the client did not authorize the disclosure. Thus, consent by the bank would be required.

Answer (A) is incorrect. Upon the client's death, the personal representative has the legal rights of the client, which include the rights to any confidential information held by the deceased client's lawyer.

Answer (B) is incorrect. Sonny has no right to authorize the disclosure of the information held by the client's lawyer, even if he is the "object" of such information. Only the client and the client's personal representative have this right.

Answer (C) is incorrect. Spouses have no greater rights than any other third party to any confidential information held by the deceased client's lawyer.

7. **Answer (C) is correct.** A lawyer is impliedly authorized to disclose otherwise confidential information to the courts, administrative agencies and other individuals and organizations as the lawyer believes is reasonably required by the representation. This authority includes making arrangements, in case of the lawyer's death or disability, for another lawyer to review the files of his or her clients. It is assumed that reasonable clients would likely not object to, but rather approve of, efforts to ensure that their interests are safeguarded. *See* ACTEC Commentary 1.6.

Answer (A) is incorrect. It is not necessary that clients expressly authorize disclosure of information since there are situations in which they do so by implication. As explained above, this is one of those situations.

Answer (B) is incorrect. While a lawyer does have implied authorization to share confidential information with partners, associates and employees to the extent reasonably necessary to the representation, as explained above, the lawyer also has implied authorization to make arrangements with lawyers who are not partners or associates in case of the lawyer's death or disability.

Answer (D) is incorrect. The authorization from the client is implied, so it is not necessary for it to be express. Further, there is no requirement that a lawyer seek court approval for the arrangement.

8. **Answer (A) is correct.** When a lawyer reasonably believes that a client is at risk of substantial harm unless action is taken and that a normal client-lawyer relationship cannot be maintained because the client lacks sufficient capacity to make decisions, the lawyer can take protective measures deemed necessary and disclose information to the extent necessary. These measures include seeking a court-appointed guardian or similar representative or consulting with family members, support groups, adult-protective agencies or others who have the ability to protect the client. *See* MODEL RULES OF PR. CONDUCT r. 1.14 (Am. Bar Ass'n 1980); ACTEC Commentary 1.6. In this situation, because Lawyer reasonably believes that Chuck is going to suffer substantial harm if no one else intervenes, Lawyer may take the steps Lawyer believes reasonably necessary to protect Chuck.

Answer (B) is incorrect. This answer is incorrect for the reasons explained above.

Answer (C) is incorrect. A lawyer does not need approval by a court prior to taking the protective steps discussed above.

Answer (D) is incorrect. The protective alternatives available to the lawyer are not limited to court actions. The lawyer may take less formal alternatives, such as contacting family members or adult-protective agencies.

9. **Answer (C) is correct.** A client may wish to have family members or other persons participate in discussions with the lawyer. When necessary to assist in the representation, the presence of such persons generally does not affect the applicability of the attorney-client evidentiary privilege. Cassandra's participation was necessary for Attorney to understand Mother's directions, so the privilege should not be affected. *See* comment 3 to Model Rule 1.14.

   Answers (A), (B), and (D) are incorrect. The attorney-client relationship between Attorney and Mother is independent of Attorney's relationship with Cassandra. Cassandra's participation in the discussions did not affect the formation of the relationship between Mother and Attorney, nor does a pre-existing relationship with Cassandra and Attorney affect the applicability of the attorney-client privilege for information Mother provides.

10. Due to (i) the obvious confidential relationship that exists between Cassandra and Mother and (ii) Attorney's pre-existing relationship with Cassandra, Attorney should not proceed any further in the matter. Because of Cassandra's participation in the meeting, she will be presumed to have exerted undue influence on Mother in any future will contest. *See* McGovern § 7.3 (p. 359). Attorney should advise Mother to seek independent legal counsel. *See* ACTEC Commentary 1.6.

11. **Answer (A) is correct.** Absent an agreement otherwise, when multiple parties consult with a lawyer on a matter, the presumption is that the lawyer represents the clients jointly rather than separately. *See* ACTEC Commentary 1.6. The best practice, of course, is to detail the terms of representation in writing.

   Answer (B) is incorrect. The presumption is that the representation is joint.

   Answer (C) is incorrect. Representation is either joint or separate, never both.

   Answer (D) is incorrect. There is probably no option more wrong than D. It does not matter who made the appointment.

12. Joint representation means the lawyer represents both clients. What one client discusses may be disclosed to the other if the discussion is legally relevant to the representation. The lawyer cannot withhold legally relevant information from either client. The lawyer cannot give legal advice or take any actions without the clients' mutual knowledge and consent. If a conflict arises between the clients, all the lawyer can do is point out the "pros" and "cons" of the positions, opinions and alternatives. If a conflict arises that

makes it impossible for the lawyer to perform impartially, it would be necessary for the lawyer to withdraw from being either client's lawyer. *See* ACTEC Commentary 1.6.

13. **Answer (C) is correct.** In deciding how to respond to a private communication with one spouse when a lawyer represents the spouses jointly, the lawyer must consider the relevance and significance of the information. If the information is irrelevant to the legal representation, then it need not be communicated to the other. A disclosure of prior adultery may be considered irrelevant under the circumstances. Merely knowing one spouse's secret does not mean the attorney must inform the other spouse. The attorney's obligation is only with respect to relevant and significant information. Unless Husband's prior romantic relationship seems likely to affect their joint estate planning, Lawyer need not disclose it. *See* ACTEC Commentary 1.6.

    Answers (A) and (B) are incorrect. These answers are incorrect for the reasons given.

    Answer (D) is incorrect. One of the consequences of joint representation is that matters disclosed by one of the joint clients may be disclosed by the attorney to the other client. ACTEC Commentary 1.6.

14. **Answer (B) is correct.** Since the information is inherently relevant and significant, Lawyer should explain to Husband that Lawyer has ethical duties to both clients. Lawyer may encourage Husband to tell Wife or to consent to Lawyer telling Wife. If Husband refuses, Lawyer likely will have to withdraw from representation. Before withdrawing, Lawyer should use professional judgment as how best to limit the negative consequences to both clients.

    Answer (A) is incorrect. One of the consequences of joint representation is that matters disclosed by one of the joint clients may be disclosed by the attorney to the other client. *See* ACTEC Commentary 1.6.

    Answers (C) and (D) are incorrect. In deciding how to respond to a private communication with one spouse when a lawyer represents the spouses jointly, the lawyer must consider the relevance and significance of the information. *See* ACTEC Commentary 1.6. Since the estate plan involves coordinating the nonprobate and probate assets, the information about the beneficiaries of the nonprobate assets is inherently relevant and significant even though the lawyer was not retained to review the nonprobate designations.

15. **Answer (C) is correct.** A lawyer may accept a gift from a client. However, a substantial gift may be voidable by the client under the doctrine of undue influence, which treats client gifts as presumptively fraudulent. *See* McGovern § 7.3. In no event should a lawyer suggest a gift. *See* ACTEC Commentary 1.8.

    Answers (A), (B), and (D) are incorrect. These answers are incorrect for the reasons given.

16. Lawyer should explain that it is not professional for a lawyer to prepare a will including a substantial gift to the lawyer. *See* ACTEC Commentary 1.8. In some states, a gratuitous transfer to the drafting lawyer is presumptively fraud or undue influence. *See e.g.,* CAL. PROBATE CODE § 21380.

17. A lawyer is not prohibited from serving as a fiduciary for the client so long as the client is properly informed of the consequences of naming the lawyer, including the apparent conflict of interest for the lawyer to draft the document. The discussion should be memorialized in a writing signed by the client. *See* ACTEC Commentary 1.7.

18. **Answer (A) is correct.** The general rule is that the personal representative is the lawyer's client. What duties, if any, are owed by the lawyer to the beneficiaries of the estate vary among jurisdictions, but the fiduciary is the client in most jurisdictions. *See* ACTEC Commentary 1.13.

   Answer (B) is incorrect. A minority of cases and ethics opinions have adopted the so-called "entity approach" under which the estate is characterized as the lawyer's client. Generally, however, an estate (unlike a corporation or partnership) is not considered an entity.

   Answers (C) and (D) are incorrect. While a lawyer may owe certain duties to those interested in an estate (beneficiaries), the general rule is that the executor (or other fiduciary) is the lawyer's client, unless the lawyer, expressly or impliedly, agrees to some sort of joint representation.

19. An executor is a fiduciary who has a duty to administer the estate solely in the interests of the estate's beneficiaries. Placing the interests of anyone else above the interests of the beneficiaries is a breach of that duty. Attorney should refuse to accept the work absent the informed consent of the beneficiaries. *See* McGovern § 12.1.

20. While an executor is generally free to retain the services of a lawyer of his or her own choice, Elizabeth still has a conflict of interest: divided loyalties between the estate beneficiaries and Elizabeth's law partners. The testator may have expressly or impliedly authorized the retention of Elizabeth's law partners in the will. Absent such authorization, Attorney should advise Elizabeth to obtain the consent of the estate's beneficiaries. *See* McGovern § 12.1.

21. **Answer (B) is correct.** The rules do not prohibit the drafting lawyer from being named as a fiduciary in a will. Generally, it is best for the lawyer not to suggest being named and to provide written information to the client explaining his or her options and how executor's fees and other compensation are determined. The objective is to make it clear (and preserve as evidence) that the client understood the advantages and disadvantages, and the costs and benefits before making a decision. *See* ACTEC Commentary 1.7.

Answers (A), (C), and (D) are incorrect. These answers are incorrect for the reasons given.

22. No, unless Attorney establishes that the clause was fair and that its existence and consequences were adequately communicated to Chelsea. In determining whether the clause was fair, the court will consider: (1) the extent of the prior relationship between Attorney and Chelsea; (2) whether Chelsea received independent advice; (3) Chelsea's sophistication with respect to business and fiduciary matters; (4) Attorney's reasons for inserting the clause; and (5) the scope of the particular provision inserted. *See* comment to UTC § 1008(b).

23. Lawyer may retain the will subject to Cian's later instructions. Lawyer should provide Cian with a letter or other writing confirming that Lawyer is holding the document for safekeeping subject to Cian's future instructions. Cian should also be encouraged to share with his loved ones or interested parties that his will is on file at his attorney's office. And, of course, Lawyer must properly identify and appropriately safeguard Cian's will while it is in Lawyer's possession. *See* ACTEC Commentary 1.8.

Practice Final Exam

1. UPC § 2-804(b) revokes any disposition to a relative of the divorced individual's former spouse. In a non-UPC state, a careful review of the relevant statute is necessary to determine if the terms of the statute revoke only the disposition as to the former spouse or to the former spouse and the former spouse's relatives.

2. **Answer (D) is correct.** As Esmerelda's joint tenant, Frodo succeeded to complete ownership of the real estate when Esmerelda died. *See* Andersen § 18(A). Furthermore, in some states, Esmerelda's creditors may not be able to attach the interest Esmerelda owned in the real estate during her lifetime because her interest terminated at death. The general rule in those states is that a creditor must attach a joint tenant's interest during the tenant's lifetime. Thus, Frodo is now the sole owner of the real estate, free and clear of any of claims of Esmerelda's creditors. In other states, Esmerelda's interest may pass nonprobate subject to her debts. *See* McGovern § 13.6.

   Answers (A), (B), and (C) are incorrect. The joint tenants had rights of survivorship. A joint tenant in real estate cannot devise his or her share by will. When Esmerelda died, she had no interest in the real estate that could be devised by her will. If Esmerelda wanted to devise the property in her will, she would have had to sever the joint tenancy with Frodo, converting it into a tenancy in common. However, she had no power to sever the joint tenancy at her death in her will. *See* McGovern § 5.5 (p. 304–06).

3. **Answer (D) is correct.** The deed does not need to have been executed in compliance with the statutory formalities required for wills because the deed created an inter vivos trust, not a will. The property subject to Atticus' trust is not probate property at death because it was no longer owned by Atticus, individually, but rather by the successor trustee and the beneficiary. An inter vivos trust (unlike a will) is a means to presently transfer ownership during the settlor's lifetime. The fact that Vivi's interest was subject to Atticus' power to revoke or amend the trust did not make the trust a will (*i.e.*, the trust instrument need not comply with the statutory formalities for wills). *See* Andersen § 2(B).

   Answers (A), (B), and (C) are incorrect. These answers are incorrect for the reasons explained.

4. **Answer (C) is correct.** Wills are revocable dispositions of property that take effect upon the testator's death. The execution of a joint will does not create a presumption of a contract not to revoke the will. *See* UPC § 2-514. Accordingly, absent written evidence of a

contract, Azra had the power and the right to revoke the 2020 will, which she did by the execution of the 2022 will. *See* UPC §§ 2-507(c), 2-514.

Many non-UPC states have similar statutes. Absent a statute, the common law of a state may create a presumption that the parties intended to have a contractual will when they executed the joint will. *See* McGovern § 4.9.

Answer (A) is incorrect. The 2020 document was intended by Azra and Bobbi to be a will, but was apparently revoked by Azra when she executed the 2022 will. The 2022 will passes the interest to Fred.

Answer (B) is incorrect. The 2020 will was revoked. Further, there is no evidence that Azra ever revoked the 2022 will.

Answer (D) is not correct. UPC § 2-514 creates a presumption that the 2020 will was not executed pursuant to a contract not to revoke it. Accordingly, unless Bobbi can establish that a contract existed pursuant to UPC § 2-514, Bobbi is without a cause of action. If a contract can be established, however, Azra revoked the 2020 will, and Bobbi's remedy would typically be limited to a breach of contract action. *See* McGovern § 4.9 (p. 279).

5. **Answer (A) is correct.** Since Gigi's will devised all of her estate to surviving her spouse, Spouse, who is also the common parent of both children, Romeo and Juliet will not receive an interest in Gigi's probate estate even though they were omitted from the will. *See* UPC § 2-302(a)(1). Their births did not revoke the will. *See* UPC § 2-508.

In almost every state that has not enacted the Uniform Probate Code, statutes grant "omitted" or "pretermitted" children certain rights in their parents' estates under some circumstances; the details vary from state to state. *See* McGovern § 3.5.

Answers (B), (C), and (D) are incorrect. These answers are incorrect for the reasons given.

6. **Answer (B) is correct.** When a devisee disclaims, the property disclaimed passes as if the disclaimant had predeceased the testator. *See* UPC § 2-1106(b)(3). The "anti-lapse" provisions of UPC § 2-603 create a "substitute gift" in favor of the disclaimant's descendants, if any. Gidget was correct — it is not deemed to be a gift by her for tax purposes. *See* I.R.C. § 2518.

The same result is likely to occur in a state that has not enacted the Uniform Probate Code. *See* McGovern §§ 2.8, 8.5, 15.4.

Answers (A), (C), and (D) are incorrect. These answers are incorrect for the reasons given.

7. **Answer (A) is correct.** When a devisee disclaims, the property disclaimed passes as if the disclaimant had predeceased the testator. *See* UPC § 2-1106(b)(3). The "anti-lapse"

provisions of UPC § 2-603 provide a "substitute gift" in favor of the disclaimant's descendants. However, a stepchild of the testator's child does not qualify as a devisee whose death before the testator qualifies for "anti-lapse" treatment. The entire estate passes to Hector's only heir, Doug.

The same result may occur in a state that has not enacted the Uniform Probate Code. Anti-lapse statutes vary considerably from state to state. *See* McGovern §§ 2.8, 8.5.

Answers (B), (C), and (D) are incorrect. These answers are incorrect for the reasons given.

8. **Answer (D) is correct.** Octavio died intestate. The Uniform Probate Code requires wills to be in writing. Octavio's oral statements as to his testamentary wishes do not control the disposition of any of Octavio's probate estate. *See* UPC § 2-502. The home and its contents are part of Octavio's probate estate and pass subject to formal administration equally to his heirs, Clover and Emery.

The same result is likely in states that have not enacted the Uniform Probate Code. However, there are limited situations in some states which may give rise to a valid oral will of personal property. *See* Atkinson § 76; McGovern § 4.4 (p. 239).

Answers (A), (B), and (C) are incorrect. Whether real or personal property, testamentary dispositions require a writing executed pursuant to the requisite testamentary formalities.

9. **Answer (A) is correct.** Octavio died intestate. UPC § 2-502 requires that testamentary wishes be reduced to a writing executed with the requisite testamentary formalities. It is irrelevant how many witnesses heard Octavio's oral statements and when they heard the statements.

The same result is likely in states that have not enacted the Uniform Probate Code. There are limited situations in some states which may give rise to a valid oral will of personal property. *See* Atkinson § 76; McGovern § 4.4 (p. 239).

Answers (B), (C), and (D) are incorrect. A testamentary disposition requires a writing executed with testamentary formalities.

10. Because there is no writing signed by Octavio evidencing the contract, UPC § 2-514 would appear to prevent Clover from enforcing the terms of the oral agreement assuming the contract was agreed to after the effective date of the Uniform Probate Code. Thus, since Octavio died intestate, the probate estate, including the home and its contents, passed to Clover and Emery. However, because Clover rendered good and valuable consideration to Octavio during his lifetime, Clover may seek recovery against Octavio's estate in quantum meruit for the value of the services rendered. *See* comment to UPC § 2-514.

The result may differ in states that have not adopted UPC § 2-514 or a similar statute. *See* McGovern § 4.9. For example, Clover's partial performance of the agreement may excuse any writing requirement and allow Clover to enforce the terms of the agreement against Octavio's estate.

11. **Answer (D) is correct.** Octavio still died intestate. However, because of Clover's performance, she appears to have a valid, enforceable contract claim to enforce against Octavio's estate. *See* UPC § 2-514; McGovern § 4.9. Accordingly, Clover can possibly seek to recover from Octavio's estate through specific performance or the imposition of a constructive trust, or a recovery in quantum meruit. *See* Atkinson § 48.

    Answers (A), (B), and (C) are incorrect. Even though Octavio died intestate, Clover may wind up with the home and its contents, as provided in the contract.

12. **Answer (C) is correct.** At common law, conditions of survivorship were not implied with respect to future interests. *See* comment to UPC § 2-707. However, UPC § 2-707 provides that a future interest under the terms of an express trust is contingent on the beneficiary surviving the distribution date. Since Greg predeceased Oliwier, Greg Junior is the substituted taker of Greg's interest pursuant to UPC § 2-707.

    In a state that has not enacted the Uniform Probate Code, or a similar statute, the result is likely to differ. *See* Restatement (Third) of Trusts § 55.

    Answers (A) and (D) are not correct. An express trust was created; the death of the beneficiary does not generally extinguish the trust. Chucky may ask for the imposition of a resulting trust if he can convince the court that the trust was fully performed or failed upon the deaths of Oliwier and Greg. *See* Restatement (Third) of Trusts §§ 7, 8. If Greg had not been survived by any lineal descendants in a UPC state, the property would have passed to Oliwier's heir, Chucky. *See* UPC § 2-707.

    Answer (B) is incorrect. UPC § 2-707 provides that Greg Junior acquires Greg's interest. However, in some non-UPC states, Spouse would have succeeded to Greg's vested remainder interest in the trust estate.

13. **Answer (A) is correct.** Oliwier retained a reversionary interest in Blackacre when the trust was created because the remainder interest was not assigned to Greg. Why? Because Greg predeceased the creation of the trust. Chucky inherited Oliwier's reversionary interest when Oliwier died and has standing to seek the imposition of a resulting trust since the trust now lacks a beneficiary. *See* Restatement (Third) of Trusts §§ 7, 8.

    Answer (B) is incorrect. The traditional remedy when a settlor attempts but fails to create an express trust is the resulting trust.

    Answers (C) and (D) are incorrect. Since Greg was not alive when the trust was created, Greg owned no interest that could have passed to Greg Junior pursuant to UPC § 2-707, or that Spouse could have inherited in a non-UPC state.

14. Answer (A) is correct. A valid, enforceable express trust has been created. UTC § 401 and § 402 codify the generally accepted principles for the creation of an express trust. *See* RESTATEMENT (THIRD) OF TRUSTS § 22.

Answers (B), (C), and (D) are incorrect. Assuming Oliwier had the mental capacity, he transferred the property to Tom and indicated an intent for Tom to hold and manage the trust property on behalf of Greg.

15. Assuming the trust document did not address the issue of whether Oliwier could revoke the trust, the answer depends on several factors. Most important is the law of the state that governs the administration of the trust. In some states, trusts are presumed revocable unless the terms of the trust expressly provide that the trust is irrevocable. The Uniform Trust Code adopts this position. *See* UTC § 602(a). Some states have retained the common law rule that a trust is presumed irrevocable unless the terms of the trust expressly provide that the trust is revocable. *See* Bogert § 148. The second factor is the effective date of the statute, if any, which reversed the common law rule. The third factor is the date the trust was created. Why? The law in effect at that time will control whether Oliwier retained the right to revoke the trust, thereby requiring the trustee to deliver the property as the settlor directs. If Oliwier retained the right to revoke, neither Tom, Oliwier's estate, nor GFP is liable to Greg. If not, Tom breached his fiduciary duties owed to Greg. Oliwier's estate may also be liable since Oliwier conspired with Tom to breach the terms of the trust agreement. GFP will probably be treated as a good-faith purchaser and held harmless.

16. Answer (A) is correct. The donor's intent controls. Alice was the donee of an exclusive non-general testamentary power of appointment. Alice can only appoint to any one or more of the objects of the power or permissible appointees. *See* Andersen § 39(B). Alice's stepchildren were not part of the class of permissible appointees. As the taker in default, the charity is not divested.

Answers (B), (C), and (D) are incorrect. These answers are incorrect for the reasons given.

17. Answer (C) is correct. The amount devised to Cora is not deductible. The devise to Blake does not qualify for the "marital deduction" because Adam and Blake were not married. The devise to Starfleet University, a qualified charity, may be deducted (as a "charitable deduction"). *See* I.R.C. §§ 2055, 2056.

Answers (A), (B), and (D) are incorrect. Congress, for public policy reasons, encourages testamentary gifts to decedents' spouses and to qualified charities. There is no deduction on the federal level for amounts transferred to one's children.

18. Answer (D) is correct. On June 26, 2015, in *Obergefell v. Hodges,* the U.S. Supreme Court ruled that a state ban on same-sex marriage is unconstitutional in violation of the Equal Protection Clause of the Fourteenth Amendment. By virtue of this ruling, state bans on same-sex marriage are unconstitutional. The government in the State of Y does not have the power to unilaterally overrule Supreme Court decisions or federal law such as the Respect for Marriage Act (RFMA), signed into law in 2022. The RFMA requires states to recognize same-sex marriage if it was performed in another state where same-sex marriage was legal. A law attacking same-sex marriage passed in the State of Y will have no effect on the calculation of Adam's taxable estate.

Answers (A), (B), and (C) are incorrect. These answers are incorrect for the reasons given.

19. Since a proceeding to settle a decedent's estate is an *in rem* action, the "situs" state has territorial jurisdiction over property, both real and personal, located in that state. The "domiciliary" state also has jurisdiction over the decedent's personal property wherever located. Accordingly, formal administration could be opened in each of the states, X, Y and Z. *See* UPC § 3-815. Administration proceedings in Y and Z are referred to as "ancillary" administrations; the probate proceeding in X is referred to as the "principal," "primary" or "domiciliary" administration. *See* McGovern § 13.4.

20. **Answer (B) is correct.** While a lawyer may owe certain duties to the beneficiaries of a trust in certain jurisdictions, the general rule is that the trustee is the lawyer's client. *See* ACTEC Commentary 1.13.

21. **Answers (A), (C), and (D) are incorrect.** These answers are incorrect for the reasons given.

Index

SUBJECT	QUESTION
Attorneys (see "Professional Responsibility")	
Augmented Estate	5–15, 8–2, 8–5, 8–6, 8–8, 9–7, 12–8, 12–9
Bank Accounts (see also "Nonprobate/ Nontestamentary Dispositions")	2–1, 2–2, 2–3, 2–4, 2–5, 2–6, 2–12, 2–13, 2–14, 2–15, 2–16, 2–17, 2–18, 2–19, 2–20, 8–16, 13–12, 14–2
Beneficiaries (see "Trust Beneficiaries")	
Capacity to Create	3–1, 3–2, 3–3, 3–4, 3–5, 3–12, 3–13, 3–14, 3–15, 7–1, 9–19, 14–8
Charitable Deduction	13–4, 13–18, PFE 17
Class Gifts	6–24, 6–25, 6–27, 6–28, 6–29
Codicil	4–25
Community Property	1–8, 5–15, 5–16, 7–19, 8–1, 8–2, 8–5, 8–6, 8–7, 8–8, 8–9, 8–10, 8–11, 9–7, 13–9
Conflict of Laws	14–1, 14–2, 14–3, 14–4, 14–5
Constructive Trusts	1–39, 4–22, 5–11, 6–33, 6–34, 6–36, 6–38, 6–39, 6–40, 6–42, 7–6, 7–9, 10–3, 10–4, 10–5, 10–7, 10–10, 10–17, 10–18, 10–19, 10–20, PFE 11
Contracts to Make a Will	7–5, 7–6, 7–7, 7–8, 7–9, 7–10, 7–11, 7–12 7–13, 7–14, PFE 4, PFE 10, PFE 11
Creditors	6–2, 6–4, 6–9, 6–14, 6–30, 9–1, 9–10, 9–11, 9–12, 10–9, 11–1, 11–2, 11–3, 11–4, 11–5, 11–6, 11–7, 11–8, 11–12, 11–14, 12–12, 12–13, 12–14, 13–2, PFE 2
Declaration of Trust	9–3, 9–9, 9–17, 9–18, 9–19, 9–22
Dependent Relative Revocation (see "Will Revocation")	5–2, 5–3, 12–6